THE ROUGH GUIDE TO

Travel Online

There are more than 150 Rough Guide travel,
phrasebook, and music titles, covering
destinations from Amsterdam to Zimbabwe,
languages from Czech to Vietnamese, and musics from World to
Opera and Jazz.

To find out more about Rough Guides,
and to check out our coverage of more than
10,000 destinations, get connected to the Internet with this guide
and find us on the Web at:

www.roughguides.com

Rough Guide Credits

Text editor: Peter Buckley
Series editor: Mark Ellingham
Production: Julia Bovis
Design and typesetting: Peter Buckley
Proofreading: Amanda Jones

Publishing Information

This second edition published June 2004 by
Rough Guides Ltd, 62–70 Shorts Gardens, London WC2H 9AH, 375 Hudson
Street, New York 10014
Email: *mail@roughguides.co.uk*

Distributed by the Penguin Group

Penguin Books Ltd, 80 The Strand, London WC2R ORL
Penguin Putnam USA Inc., 375 Hudson Street, New York 10014, Penguin
Books Canada Ltd, 10 Alcorn Avenue, Toronto, Ontario MV4 1E4, Penguin
Books Australia Ltd,
PO Box 257, Ringwood, Victoria 3134,
Penguin Books (NZ) Ltd, 182–190 Wairau Road, Auckland 10

Printed in Italy by Lego Print.

© Samantha Cook and Greg Ward 2004
368 pages; includes index

A catalogue record for this book is available
from the British Library
ISBN 1-84353-328-6

THE ROUGH GUIDE TO

Travel Online

by
Samantha Cook and Greg Ward

ROUGH GUIDES

Contents

part one: basics

part two: themes and activities

activities

special requirements

specialist holidays

Contents

part three: destinations

Introduction

The Internet has swiftly become an indispensable tool for travellers, with the travel sector established as one of the mainstays of e-commerce. Much like an unfamiliar city, however, the Web can be a daunting place to explore on your own. Even if you have some idea of where you're heading, you can stumble into many a blind alley along the way.

This book is a simple guide on how to plan and buy any trip online. As well as general advice – telling you what's out there and how to find it – it will also point you to hundreds of individual Websites, representing the cream of those devoted to specific destinations or activities. All you need to know is how to go online in the first place; if you don't know that, buy our excellent companion volume, the *Rough Guide to the Internet*.

The most obvious appeal of using the Net for travel arrangements is that if you know exactly what you want – a flight or ferry from A to B, the cheapest possible rental car, a cut-price all-inclusive package – there are great deals to be found. That's just one small part of the process, however. The Net can help you to choose a destination in the first place, using sites that cover the whole world as well as those focusing on particular countries or cities, and to decide where you want to stay and how you're going to spend your time. We'll also show you how to look up the latest news or weather reports before you leave, and even how to stay in touch with home once you arrive.

Throughout the book, we've mentioned whether sites offer online booking, meaning that you can make your choice, and pay for it, without any contact with another human being. While that can be very convenient, it can also tempt you to rush into something you don't know enough about. On top of that, Websites can be very obtuse, and don't always tell you something unless you ask for it – such as the fact that there's another train an hour earlier that costs half as much or takes half as long. So, don't get too carried away. As a general rule, try to combine your Web research with phone or face-to-face conversations; you'll find in any case that many specialist operators insist on talking to all clients to be sure they know what they're doing.

Although security is an understandable concern for all Net users, online fraud is in fact very rare. Common-sense precautions to follow include never sending your credit card details via email, and making sure that all payments are carried out through a secure server. Your browser should advise you whether the connection you're using is secure; a useful indication is when the URL of the site you're on changes to start with "https://" instead of the usual "http://". On a broader level, don't trust sites that fail to carry full street addresses and phone numbers; that are hosted by free servers such as Geocities rather than having their own domain names; and that can't put you in touch with satisfied customers on request.

In addition, as with any business transaction, online or otherwise, it's up to the buyer to beware. Just because a site claims to offer cheap flights (and is found by search engines looking for "cheap flights", or has paid for a link from some "cheap flights" portal) doesn't mean its flights really are cheaper than any others. And the mere fact that a site looks pretty, or expensive, doesn't mean the product it's selling is any good (or even that the site does what it says it will). That's where this book comes in. We've trawled through thousands of sites to find those that are genuinely useful, whether they're beautiful, quirky, or downright ugly. We hope we're going to save you time and money, both at home and on the road, and point you towards some wonderful travel experiences.

ACKNOWLEDGMENTS

The authors would like to thank our editor, Peter Buckley – who made the book look great and was a pleasure to work with – our families, and each other.

part one

basics

Finding what you need

The most essential skill for anyone making serious use of the Net is to know how to look for what you need. Although searching for specific information online might seem like trying to find the very smallest of needles in a haystack as large as China, various research tools can help cut the job down to size. Useful Websites, detailed both in the lists below and throughout this book, include **search engines**, **search agents**, **portals** and **directories**, though the distinctions between these categories are not as clear cut as the names might suggest.

Search engines

The obvious way to start looking for something on the Net is to use a general purpose **search engine**. A search engine is a Website that invites users to specify any combination of words, and then trawls through billions of other Websites to find those that contain the closest match to those words. Contrary to appearances, however, search engines do not literally search the Web in real time. They work by reading a database of Web pages downloaded at some earlier juncture by whoever runs the engine.

You will get different results depending on which search engine you use. Some contain all or most of the contents of the sites they include, which makes successful matching more likely, while others just contain excerpts from the home page of each site. To remain accurate, any search engine should be constantly updating its database, as there's always a delay between the time the information was gathered, and the moment you actually access it. The fact that a search engine finds a particular site is no guarantee that the site still exists.

The ideal search engine should be as clear and straightforward as possible – and that's why **Google** is regarded by general consensus as the best of the major search engines:

Google www.google.com

Too many of its rivals open up with cluttered, advert-filled home pages, and spend too much energy trying to direct visitors towards money-spinning sidelines. Google, by contrast, presents a clean, white screen, and gives the quickest results, with a simple choice between the standard "Google Search", which returns a list of relevant sites, and the "I'm Feeling Lucky" button, which has a remarkable knack of taking you straight to the most appropriate page. It also provides "**caches**" of pages that have disappeared or altered since its latest crawl, or which are for whatever reason unavailable. This is extremely useful when you can't get a link to load. Simply click on "cached" under a search result. If you're only interested in finding **British Websites** in your search, Google also offers a separate UK-only search facility, at **www.google.co.uk**.

If you're unlucky with Google, you should head for **All the Web** or **AltaVista**:

All The Web www.alltheweb.com
AltaVista www.av.com

And finally, you could try **Teoma,** which has a smaller database than the others, but tends to come up with good, relevant results:

Teoma www.teoma.com

You can also find longer lists of search engines, together with very detailed reviews, at both **www.searchengineshowdown.com** and **www.searchenginewatch.com.**

Whichever search engine you use, be sure to familiarize yourself with the techniques for **refining your search**. You'll need to come up with a term that's specific enough to omit redundant results, but broad enough not to miss anything that might be useful. Different engines employ slightly different grammars, but as a rule entering the words **Diving Malaysia** will find pages that contain both the word **Diving** *and* the word **Malaysia**, though not necessarily together, while putting quotation marks in bold around a group of words, in this example, **"Diving Malaysia"**, will find only those pages on which that exact phrase appears. It's also possible to search for pages that mention diving but omit any mention of Malaysia, usually by entering either a **minus sign** (without a space) as in **Diving –Malaysia**. If you want to see pages that contain either of the terms, you can enter an upper-case "OR" between the words. As a rule, engines tend to **ignore** common words (known as "stop words") such as *the* or *it*. If you need to include a stop word in a non-phrase search, place a plus sign in front of it. Finally, most engines take no notice of whether you use upper or lower case.

If you want to refine your search further – for example, you may prefer to see only those pages that include your search term in their **titles**; pages written in a **certain language**; files with a particular **format**; or pages **updated** within, say, the last year – look for an "**advanced search**" link. Google's advanced search page holds several pull-down menus that make the whole process abundantly clear.

If you are using Google or AltaVista, and your search results include pages in a foreign language, the engines offer a **translation service**. Just click "translate" where your result is listed. Be warned, however, that this can produce some hilarious results.

Whichever engine you use, it's worth scanning its "FAQ", "Search Tips" or "Help" sections in order to familiarize yourself with its individual rules and quirks.

For finding travel products, whether flights, accommodation, all-inclusive packages or simply destination guides, there's no advantage in using a so-called "**travel search engine**" rather than Google or one of the other general search engines. In fact, sites that claim to be travel search engines are on the whole indistinguishable from travel-related directories or portals, depending, in exactly the same way, on their own databases of operators and general information.

Search agents and searchbots

In order to throw up as many differing results as possible for a particular search, you may well find yourself running the same query through several different search engines. If so, it's quicker and easier to get an automated "**search agent**" or "**searchbot**" to do your searching for you, by comparing and combining the results from several search engines at once.

The most effective of these, **Copernic**, is a free, stand-alone program, which you have to download, once only, from its Website. You can then instruct it to hunt its way through hundreds of search engines, directories and newsgroups (see p.18): **Copernic www.copernic.com**

Hotbot will search four engines – Google, FAST, Teoma and Inktomi – from one interface:

Hotbot **www.hotbot.com**

Travel-related portals and directories

Both **portals** and **directories** consist of hand-built lists of Websites arranged according to subject matter. Rather than entering a unique personal query, users are more likely to be invited to choose one or more categories from pull-down menus on the home page. Whether you key **Malaysia Diving** into a search engine, however, or choose first **Malaysia** and then **Diving** on a directory site, the results may well be the same. There's a smaller chance of completely irrelevant listings, since travel directories will only include travel-related sites, but there's probably a smaller pool of possibilities to draw on. Be warned that many directories only list sites with which they have some commercial relationship, or that pay for inclusion; it's usually easy to tell if that's the case by the entreaties on the home page to "list your site". In addition, directories are more likely to be out of date than search engines, so it's always worth trying to find out when the directory was last updated.

The precise difference between a portal and a directory is largely in the eye of the beholder, but broadly speaking a portal holds more original content, such as its own database of destination information or travel advice, and perhaps detailed appraisals of the sites it lists, than a directory.

The list below includes several excellent all-round portals and directories, while you'll find listings throughout this book of more specialized directory sites devoted to specific destinations or activities. In particular, be sure to check out the sites reviewed under "General adventure holidays" on p.101. One of the best all-round travel directories is **www.about.com/travel**, listed under "Online-only destination guides" on p.12, and in various relevant sections throughout the guide.

Remember too that most of the larger **ISPs**, such as **AOL** and **Yahoo**, offer their own travel-related content as well as links to other sites and operators, and so do the massive travel-agent sites, such as **Expedia** and **Travelocity**, reviewed under "Online travel agents", which starts on p.29.

Away.com

http://away.com

Providing destination information is just a sideline for this massive, wide-ranging and heavily funded activity travel portal, which is more concerned with selling flights, car rental, and thousands of adventure-holiday packages. Nonetheless, although working your way through its pull-down menus is a slow and cumbersome business, in the end it usually comes up with a meaty practical guide to your chosen destination as well as travelogues and message boards.

Backpack Europe on a Budget

www.backpackeurope.com

The brainchild of American student and veteran backpacker Kaaryn Hendrickson, this site is a gem for any young person about to embark on his or her Grand Tour of Europe. Hundreds of reviewed links are organized into subject areas such as hostels, travel gear, working or volunteering abroad and tour agencies. The huge "Travel Tips" section includes advice on packing, budgeting, staying healthy and keeping in touch; each segment comes with a set of links if you want to find out more. You can research countries individually, and there's a full index of general travel information sites, special sections for women and students, and plenty on how to get to Europe in the first place. It's a huge venture; if in doubt, scan the site index to fast track to where you want to be.

BootsnAll

www.bootsnall.com

Lively information site packed with original content – articles, advice and travellers' tales for independent travellers – all generated by Bootsnall members. You can also ask questions of "local experts" (or become one yourself), buy flights, book hostels around the world, and pay for Eurail passes, car rental and travel insurance. Sign up for a fortnightly ezine and select from a long list of newsletters – *Hawaii Travel Deals* or *Round the World Ticket Watch*, for example. Members (it's free to join, but you will be vetted) can contact other members by accessing a secure database. The forums are busy (see p.26), and the community atmosphere is compounded by the invitation to members to stay, for free, with the BootsnAll founders at their HQ in Oregon.

7

Budget Travel

www.budgettravel.com

Hideous to look at and agonizing to read, this colossal budget travellers' directory is included here simply by virtue of its links. It's got thousands of them, from all around the world. Whether you're after a cheap travel agent in Riga or a ski operator in Kazakhstan, scroll down the home page to the full, scatterbrained list – then click for destination information, travel agents, maps, travelogues and bulletin boards; for accommodation, cycling, hiking, adventure travel, camping, shopping, and transportation sites; and for pretty much anything at all related, however distantly, to budget travel.

Bugbog

www.bugbog.com

An endearing British-produced portal to the world for independent (and predominantly low-budget) tourists. It's far from detailed or comprehensive, and occasionally lapses into traveller-speak – of Bali, for example, it says "the local people can be mercenary" – but it does provide lively overviews of potential global holiday destinations, and holds some great images (including spectacular photos of alien spaceships bombarding Bournemouth).

GKsoft

www.gksoft.com/govt

An extraordinary online resource for travellers, serving as a gateway to almost twenty thousand official and/or governmental Websites in more than 220 countries. The list is endless, including parliaments, ministries, broadcasting corporations and courts as well as tourist boards and embassies. Naturally, most of what you'll find is dry as dust, but if you need the official line on any world issue, you should be able to reach it from here.

Johnny Jet

www.johnnyjet.com

Astonishing portal that has become something of a cult among online travel junkies. The home page lists a vast selection of categories – among them "Airline info", "Bored in hotel", "Religious travels", "Winter", "Weather", "Unhappy traveller" – from where you can link within a couple of clicks to thousands of sites. There are  also useful travel articles, Q&A sessions with dozens of travel experts (it's pushing it a bit to call them "celebrities", as Johnny does) and eccentric extras like the "Sky Girls" and "Sky Guys" feature, where you can ask questions of real-life air stewards, reading their answers while feasting your eyes on their glamorous photos. Signing up for an email newsletter gets you weekly articles, readers' tips, headlines from US travel pages online and in print, and travel deals.

The Paperboy

www.thepaperboy.com

The Paperboy site is a searchable directory of newspapers from all over the world, listed by state in the US (with 118 papers in New York and 94 in Ohio alone), and by country elsewhere (including 64 titles in Switzerland and 22 in Venezuela). Bookmark the site and you'll always be able to keep up with the latest news and weather wherever you're heading; it can even translate it for you (with variable results) if you've yet to master the local lingo. Paying a membership fee of US$2.95 a month or US$25 a year will get you, among other things, a customizable home page and advanced headline search.

Tourism Offices Worldwide Directory

www.towd.com

The addresses, with active Web links wherever available, of every official government tourist office in the world, and also many regional and local tourism organizations, including those of all US states and Canadian provinces.

TripAdvisor

www.tripadvisor.com

TripAdvisor covers destinations in Europe, North America, the Caribbean, Mexico, and the South Pacific. The gimmick is that for any chosen location it not only lists links to several destination guides (mostly drawn from guidebook sites), but also to an extensive archive of relevant newspaper and magazine articles, as well as reports from TripAdvisor users. The same applies to reviews of hotels, packages and attractions. Links at the top of the page direct you to vacation packages and deals offered by the megasites such as Travelocity, Expedia and Orbitz. You can sign up for email updates, indicating which destinations you'd like to hear more about.

TripSpot

www.tripspot.com

For almost any world destination, this portal can point you towards a dozen or more online travel guides. As ever, you're likely to find the guidebook publishers to be the best on offer, but at least TripSpot suggests a few alternatives. They also provide links to sites covering such things as speciality travel, transportation and road trips, all manner of accommodation and most activities you can think of.

Guidebook sites

If you'd like to be able to turn to a single online source for consistently detailed advice on any **destination** in the world, you'd do best to book-mark the Website of one of the major **guidebook** publishers. Only the established book publishers have large enough databases to do the job properly, so most other travel sites that offer global destination guides use information drawn from guidebooks in any case. Currently the pick of the crop for country guides are Frommer's and Rough Guides, followed by Fodor's, while Time Out provides strong guides to individual cities. Lonely Planet's decision not to make its practical listings available over the Internet leaves it trailing well behind, despite its excellent users' forum. The drawback in all instances is that the online version tends to lag behind the print version, so that the information on the Web may be based on research that's already two or three years old.

Fodor's

www.fodors.com

Like the guidebooks it showcases, the Fodor's Website is a rather staid, middlebrow affair, with lots of gentle reassurance for nervous novice travellers. While it seldom strays far off the beaten track, it does provide detailed practical guides to major world destinations, coupled with a cross-section of "Rants and Raves" submitted by its readers. The busy message board is filled with tips about tipping, travel insurance, cruises, online travel booking and travelling with kids. Links to online booksellers make it possible to buy any Fodors book that takes your fancy.

Frommer's

www.frommers.com

Very useful Website, run by the major US guidebook series. The destination information is not all that comprehensive, but for those areas – mainly big-name cities – that are covered, it comes neatly structured in digestible chunks, with thorough reviews and listings. Links allow you to book reviewed accommodation online. There are also plenty of general-interest articles, deals drawn from a variety of online providers and lots of good forums (especially strong on US destinations; see p.26). You can buy all the books online, often at a discount.

Lonely Planet

www.lonelyplanet.com

Although the Website of the best-selling Australian guidebook series offers thorough overviews of destinations throughout the world, the fact that it withholds detailed hotel and restaurant listings prevents it from being much use for day-by-day trip planning. However, its most popular feature is the searchable "Thorn Tree" group of message boards (see p.27), packed with queries, advice and appeals from fellow travellers; many contributors are out on the road as they write, so it's great for up-to-the-minute tips. The Subwwway section holds extensive links to other destination sites, as well as general travel information sites and reservation services, and, of course, you can buy all manner of LP products online.

Rick Steves' Europe Through the Back Door

http://ricksteves.com

North American travel guru Rick Steves made his name as an expert on European travel through his guidebook and TV series *Europe Through the Back Door*. His Website offers excerpts of the books (under "Country Information") and online updates; you'll find few useful listings, but for destination overviews it's not at all bad. Plus feature articles, and the

"Graffiti Wall" message board, which includes reader reviews of the guides themselves. If you want to buy the books – or indeed, maps, phrase books, travel gear, tours or rail passes (with a few extras thrown) – there's a secure online shop.

Rough Guides

www.travel.roughguides.com

Rough Guides haven't actually posted the entire text of all their travel guidebooks on the Web, but they still provide a more comprehensive online world guide than anyone else. Full accommodation and restaurant listings make the site particularly useful, although as they're

taken from the printed versions, like any guidebook, they do eventually drift out of date. There's also a community area, co-hosted with igougo, where you can read and post travel journals and photos, and links to online booksellers so you can buy the books themselves.

Time Out

www.timeout.com

So long as you're travelling to one of the forty or so most popular cities in the world – roughly twenty in Europe, ten in North America and a handful in the rest of the world – Time Out can give you a detailed practical grounding in what to expect. The online text is basically drawn from their published guides, but it's leavened with links relevant to each destination. Would-be purchasers are re-directed to Amazon.

Online-only destination guides

About.com

www.about.com/travel

Like most of about.com's colossal online empire, its travel section is a wonderful information resource, and provides some of the best overall destination guides on the Web. In the first instance, it connects travellers with more than forty subsidiary about.com sites, variously devoted to countries, continents and interests. Each area has a named host (complete with photo, for that human touch), and is packed with articles and additional links. At a glance, it's not easy to tell where About ends and the rest of the Internet begins, but the deeper you dig, the more likely you are to pass beyond its boundaries, perhaps to a specific operator

who can sell you a trip to the destination in question, or to some learned academic journal. The one caveat is that every screen is cluttered with endless menus, adverts and messages from sponsors, making it tiresome to read the text at its core.

Passplanet

www.passplanet.com

General resource for budget travellers in Asia and Central America, put together as a labour of love by a French backpacker. It provides only minimal destination information for countries as a whole, and maddeningly there's no search facility, but it comes into its own with its rapidly expanding database of personal recommendations and practical listings – including a painstaking translation of the Chinese rail timetable.

Travel Intelligence

www.travelintelligence.net

A compendium of articles by seventy or so top-flight international travel writers. Searchable by destination, theme or author, it's designed more to inspire than to provide step-by-step practical advice, but cumulatively it forms a database of information on most countries in the world. The sheer quality of the writing here, and the elegant, user-friendly interface, make this site something special.

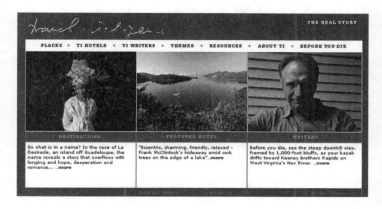

Maps and route planners

Online-only route planners

The Automobile Association

www.theaa.com/travelwatch/planner_main.jsp

Speedy, accurate and admirably detailed route finder, covering even the smallest destination in Britain, Ireland and Europe only. You can choose to avoid motorways, toll roads, and congestion charges; you can also calculate the cost of your journey, taking into account a number of factors. Make this your first choice when planning a route in the UK.

Expedia

www.expedia.com and www.expedia.co.uk

The North American and UK versions of the massive Expedia site share a mapping facility that can produce a not very attractive but reasonable definition zoomable map of almost any world location, keying in hotels if required, and offering on-site links to make travel arrangements of all kinds. The route-finding option is excellent for driving routes within the US, providing fully illustrated driving itineraries between any two US addresses, but is far less valuable when it comes to European routes.

MSN Maps and Directions

www.mapblast.com

Although the actual maps displayed by Microsoft's mapping facility are far from attractive, it can nonetheless show you pretty much any location in Europe or North America, specified by town name, street address, or zip or postal code. Where the site comes into its own is with its route finder, which for any road trip in either continent produces simple, accurate and carefully timed driving directions, beautifully schematized in a hierarchy of maps.

Mapquest

www.mapquest.com and **www.mapquest.co.uk**
Invited to search for any location on the planet, Mapquest will swiftly deliver a reasonably useful online city plan or regional road map, which you can print, email, or download to a handheld device. Both the North American and European Websites also offer good Road Trip Planners for their respective continents; the initial response is just a thick purple line across a continental map, but you can zoom in for as much detail as you require, and if you prefer, choose to read a table of driving directions.

Multimap

www.multimap.com

Excellent mapping site, which, although it has city maps of the UK, Europe and the US (and road maps of the world), is of most use by far for the UK. You can zoom from regional maps down to local street level; Multimap even knows which streets are one way. Each new screen brings up an extensive list of links, including sights and attractions, accommodation, restaurant and train-ticket booking services, weather alerts, retailers selling historic and aerial photograph prints, and even star-marked properties for sale. There's also an adequate route finder, plus an interactive map of London's tube system.

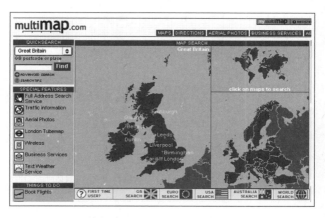

University of Texas Library Online

www.lib.utexas.edu/maps/

The University of Texas has put together a compelling Website that centres on the map collection of its Perry-Castañeda Library, which includes more than 250,000 maps covering all areas of the world. Around five thousand public-domain maps are available online for free downloads, and there's also a phenomenal set of links to "other map-related sites", which range from the very earliest attempts at cartography, dating from 6000 BC, up to the latest images of Mars.

Via Michelin

www.viamichelin.co.uk

The Website of French tyre-and-guide company Michelin suffers slightly in English translation, but for travel in continental Europe, especially, it's a tremendous resource. Its extensive range of road maps and city plans are interlinked with its database of hotels, attractions and general information, so when asked to plot a driving route it can suggest accommodation and pit-stops along the way. In Britain itself it's slightly less comprehensive.

Yahoo

http://uk.maps.yahoo.com

Excellent city map facility, allowing you to pinpoint exactly any address in North America and eleven European countries, including the UK. The maps themselves are attractive, extremely clear, and zoomable down to the finest detail.

Buying maps

Elstead Maps

www.elstead.co.uk

Top-quality independent British mail-order map retailer, which uses its Website to sell around fifty thousand maps, globes, atlases, and CD-Roms to customers all over the world. If you can't find what you're looking for with a straightforward search, they also have a prompt and personal email enquiries service.

Maps Worldwide

www.mapsworldwide.co.uk

British online retailer that sells maps on paper and CD-Rom, including road maps, historical maps, specialist maps showing waterways and cycle paths, and full atlases. Though they specialize in maps of the UK, the scope extends to the whole world. Many prices are reduced; check the Special Offers box on the home page.

Stanfords

www.stanfords.co.uk

Online arm of the venerable British map retailer. Search by destination (drop-down lists include continents, countries, cities and regions) and then choose from the results; whether you're after a sheet map, CD-Rom, globe or climbing book, click and you'll be able to get straight to it. You can also search by author or ISBN. Pop-up windows reproduce small sections from each map, and if you're choosing from a series of maps – trekking maps of Nepal, say – clicking on "View Map Coverage" will get you to a grid showing the span of each map in the series. Subscribe to receive information on new products, Stanfords events, and general travel articles.

US Maps.com

www.maps.com

Well-designed site selling high-quality downloadable digital maps, along with printed conventional maps, atlases, globes, wall maps, travel guides, antique maps, books and travel gear. It also offers a reasonable route-finding facility, as well as entertaining sidelines such as interactive historic maps, showing, for example, the progress of the US Civil War, and even online jigsaws.

Newsgroups, forums, email lists and ezines

For many people, **online discussion groups** are every bit as useful, if not more so, than Web pages. Discussion groups epitomize the original concept of the Internet: a global community based on freedom of speech. The first such groups were established through a network called Usenet, set up in 1979 as a collection of academic bulletin boards or **newsgroups**. Today there are tens of thousands of newsgroups, each devoted to a topic or theme – eating disorders, camper vans, baked beans, Satan – subscribed to by users from all walks of life. Don't be misled by the name; these groups don't exist to send out news as such, but act as forums where anyone can swap information, queries and opinions. They're useful tools for travellers, who can post questions about anything from airline safety to how to find a cheap hotel in Borneo, and who often find the honest responses a welcome relief among the minefield of advertorial, fly-by-night dotcoms and sheer bad travel writing on the Web. How seriously you choose to take the opinions of someone you have never met, however, and whose tastes may be completely unlike your own, is down to you.

Finding newsgroups

First you'll need access to a **newsreader program**. Most browsers, including Internet Explorer and Netscape, come with such programs built in; to get them rolling, consult your ISP's technical help pages, or look at the **Rough Guide to the Internet**, which devotes fourteen pages to the subject of newsgroups. Alternatively, you could choose a specialist news provider, such as **Agent** (for PCs; **www.forteinc.com**) or **MT Newswatcher** (for Macs; **www.smfr.org/mtnw**), many of which have extras over and above the inbuilt programs, and which are usually free to download. Take a look also at **www.newsreaders.com** for more about newsreaders and Usenet.

You can also use the Web to access newsgroups, by going through superfast search engine **Google** (see p.22), but while this is great for searching old posts, it doesn't offer as many options as the specialist providers. With most newsreaders, you can mark messages you've read, and save messages to read later. You can choose to see only messages you haven't read, sort messages by date or subject, select all messages by a certain author or keyword, or skip unwanted subjects or authors. Google offers fewer features.

Ideally (though not always), newsgroup **names**, which are laid out in chunks separated by full stops, should make it clear what the group is about. Most crucial are the three- or four-letter abbreviations at the start of the name. Known as **hierarchies**, many of these are undecipherable, but the best-known are clear enough, telling you the general concerns and tone of the group. Of these, **alt.** ("alternative" topics), **misc.** (miscellaneous), **rec.** (recreational) and **soc.** (society and culture) all hold groups useful to travellers. Thus **rec.travel.australia+nz** will concentrate on travel to and around Australasia, while **alt.travel.greece** is the group to join if you're off island-hopping around the Dodecanese. Don't assume, however, that the alt. group will be full of counter-cultural drop-outs, or that the rec. group is the domain of carefree folk out to play. Newsgroup naming isn't an exact science; there is a lot of crossover between groups, and within each group messages cover a broad range of topics. Most people subscribe to a few groups relating to similar interests.

Using newsgroups

Within each group, individual messages are known as **posts**; an ongoing string of posts is a **thread**. Whether you're using a newsreader or Google, posts and threads are listed by their subject title, in date order, with the newest at the top. Clicking on the subject title opens that message, followed directly in a thread by its **follow-ups** (responses posted for the group, as opposed to **replies**, which are emailed direct to the original poster). While the longer threads may be the meatiest, they are also the most difficult to

Travel newsgroups

These groups are unmoderated unless stated otherwise.

alt: Any topic at all
alt.rec.camping
alt.rec.hiking
alt.travel
alt.travel.canada
alt.travel.eurail.youth-hostels
alt.travel.greece
alt.travel.marketplace
alt.travel.new-orleans
alt.travel.road-trip
alt.travel.scotland.edinburgh
alt.travel.uk.air Buying tickets, jet lag, DVT, delays ...
alt.travel.uk.marketplace Cruises, home exchanges, online street maps ...
alt.travel.usa-canada

misc: Miscellaneous topics
misc.kids.vacation

rec: Recreational topics

Destinations
rec.travel.africa
rec.travel.asia
rec.travel.australia+nz
rec.travel.caribbean
rec.travel.europe
rec.travel.latin-america
rec.travel.usa-canada

Travel topics
rec.backcountry Bear attacks, tent debates, mountain biking — mostly, but not exclusively, in the US outdoors ...
rec.bicycles.off-road (moderated)

rec.bicycles.rides
rec.boats.cruising
rec.boats.marketplace (moderated) Boats, boat engines, books about boats ...
rec.boats.paddle
rec.climbing
rec.food.restaurants
rec.outdoors.camping
rec.outdoors.national-parks
rec.outdoors.rv-travel
rec.parks.theme Safety warnings, theme park queries, rollercoaster reviews ...
rec.scuba
rec.skiing
rec.skiing.alpine
rec.skiing.backcountry
rec.skiing.marketplace
rec.skiing.nordic
rec.skiing.resorts.europe
rec.skiing.resorts.misc
rec.skiing.resorts.north-america
rec.skiing.snowboard
rec.travel.air Booking flights, airline food, good fares, disastrous airlines ...
rec.travel.bed+breakfast (moderated)
rec.travel.budget.backpack
rec.travel.cruises
rec.travel.marketplace Tour guides, ticket agents, B&B owners, home exchangers ...
rec.travel.misc (moderated) Travel tips, courier flights, luggage reviews ...
rec.travel.resorts.all-inclusive (moderated)
rec.travel.world Recommendations, travellers' tales, general queries ...

soc: Social and cultural issues

Most messages posted to the groups in the (selective) list below are written in English. There are many more groups where debates are conducted in the language of the home country, and others, not listed here, concerned with specific regions and peoples – Basque, Breton, Hmong and so on.

soc.culture.african
soc.culture.asean [sic]
soc.culture.australian
soc.culture.baltics
soc.culture.british
soc.culture.burma
soc.culture.cambodia
soc.culture.canada
soc.culture.caribbean
soc.culture.china
soc.culture.costa-rica
soc.culture.cuba
soc.culture.egyptian
soc.culture.europe
soc.culture.french
soc.culture.greek
soc.culture.haiti
soc.culture.hawaii (moderated)
soc.culture.hongkong
soc.culture.indian
soc.culture.irish
soc.culture.israel
soc.culture.japan (moderated and unmoderated groups)

soc.culture.jordan
soc.culture.kenya
soc.culture.laos
soc.culture.latin-america
soc.culture.malaysia
soc.culture.mongolian
soc.culture.nepal
soc.culture.new-zealand
soc.culture.pacific-island
soc.culture.palestine
soc.culture.portuguese
soc.culture.russia
soc.culture.singapore
(moderated and unmoderated groups)
soc.culture.south-africa
soc.culture.soviet
soc.culture.sri-lanka
soc.culture.syria
soc.culture.thai
soc.culture.ukrainian
soc.culture.vietnamese
soc.culture.zimbabwe

trawl through. As follow-up follows follow-up, each message becomes more unwieldy, with text copied from earlier postings and overlong email signatures appended with quotes and annoying ASCII graphics. Regular users soon **learn how to decipher these postings**, scanreading to find the final point, and skipping messages from anyone they've learned to avoid. There tend to be hundreds of **questions** and rather fewer answers in each group; even if you post a question of your own there is no guarantee that anyone will reply, or if they do, that the answer will be of any use. It can be more productive to **browse** debates that have already taken place. This is known as **lurking**, and is perfectly acceptable.

To "delurk", and post your own messages, you need to **subscribe**. This is usually simple enough, but varies according to your ISP. (Posting to a group via Google is slightly different; see below.) Once you've subscribed, your personal choice of newsgroups will appear automatically every time you open the program. It's as simple again to unsubscribe.

Spam

Freedom of speech has its downsides. Many of the most popular groups are inundated with **spam** (junk mail), and **MMFs**, illegal "Make Money Fast" schemes. Some groups are filtered or **moderated** to reject unwanted messages before they are posted, but many more are not. When you do post, note too that your email address is made available so that newsgroup members can **contact you direct**. To avoid being inundated with spam, many people type in invalid addresses – **nojunksam@nospamaol.com**, for example. Other users recognize the dummy phrases (in this case, no junk and no spam) and disregard them when replying (to **sam@aol.com**), while the spammers, who tend to do blind mailshots, will be foiled. This ruse, which entails a bit of untangling on the part of a potential respondent, is frowned upon by some groups. If that bothers you, you could set up a **separate email account** for newsgroups alone. You might prefer to do this anyway, if you're secretive about your email address.

Google

With **Google**, the queen bee of the search engines (see p.4), it's possible to search the entire Usenet archive – that's thousands of newsgroups – dating back to 1995, and to post your own messages. The service is as user-friendly and convenient as you'd expect from Google, and great if you're looking for something specific. Anyone who wants sophisticated preferences, however, will do better with a newsreader (see p.18).

Post and read comments in Usenet discussion forums.

Typing in **groups.google.com** brings up a list of the major categories (**alt.**, **misc.**, **rec.**, and **soc.**). Click each to see a full list of groups in that hierarchy, along with an indicator to show how active they are, and keep clicking to get more specific until you find the group you want. Outside these major hierarchies the thousands of other groups are organized alphabetically via drop-down menus. It would take days to browse them all, which is where Google's search facility comes into its own. You can **search** for a group by typing in keywords – skiing, Graceland, whatever – and quick as a flash the engine will pull up all the messages, in a variety of groups, that include those words. You then click to read the full message – and all its follow-ups, if there are any – and from there you can get to that particular newsgroup's main index. Keying "lesbian guesthouse", for example, links you to messages on **alt.travel.marketplace**, **uk.gay-lesbian-bi** and **soc.women**, among many others, while from "Paris restaurants" you could visit dozens of groups including **rec.travel.europe**, **alt.cities.paris** and **rec.food.restaurants**.

To **post a follow-up**, or to start a new thread using Google, you have to log in, giving an email address and password. Messages turn up on screen within a few hours. To fast track back to your chosen groups, simply **bookmark** them.

Netiquette

In virtual communities, as in real ones, you should think twice about barging in willy-nilly with your opinions. Each group is self-regulating, but there are a few rules defining general newsgroup **netiquette**, and while members will cut a bit of slack when it comes to "**newbies**", they tend not to suffer fools gladly. As well as heading straight for the **FAQs**, or Frequently Asked Questions (regular postings, clearly marked, which cover the group's codes of conduct), you should ideally spend some time **lurking** before subscribing. Not only does this allow you to get to know the group, it may prevent you from making a fool of yourself – your question may well have come up before, and you will be expected to have done some work in finding the answer. You'll also win no friends by blithely turning up with queries that can be easily solved by a quick surf on the Web ("Where can I find the address of the Japanese tourist board?", for example).

Though it's by no means obligatory to buy into Net speak, with its copious use of abbreviations and **emoticons** – such as **:-)** or **:-0**, which translate as smiling, or shock – you should know that to post a message in

Just for newbies: newsgroups about newsgroups

The hierarchy **news.** denotes a group devoted to Usenet newsgroups. Though we've given each a broad review below, as ever there is a lot of crossover.

news.announce.newusers (moderated)
Basic information, news and updates.

news.answers (moderated)
FAQs from a number of different newsgroups.

news.groups
General issues relating to newsgroup use; lots of debate about moderation and freedom of speech.

news.groups.questions
From how to reply to how to start a group of your own.

news.groups.reviews
Reviews from users about their favourite groups.

news.newusers.questions (moderated)
All sorts of questions, some of them technical.

capital letters is counted as shouting, and is generally frowned upon. To emphasize a word or phrase, it's best to tag it with asterisks. Capitals tend to be used by **trolls**, members who are known for their **flames** (offensive messages) – if you get flamed, rather than starting a **flame war**, simply ignore the message and move on. **Cross-posting** – when you copy a message to more than one newsgroup – should be done very sparingly, and only if it is truly relevant to each group. And, of course, you should *never* send spam, use members' email addresses for your own mailing lists, or post a personal email sent from someone else without their consent.

For the wittiest, sharpest and most sarcastic take on Netiquette, log on to **www.psg.com/emily.html**.

Online forums

There are many other discussion groups – known as **forums**, communities, bulletin boards, egroups, communities or **message boards** – across the Web. The biggest and best come on guidebook sites, including **Rough Guides**, **Frommer's** and **Lonely Planet**, but many of the sites we've reviewed for travel agents and specialist operators have their own. **AOL** and the major search engines also have travel forums; as with the newsgroups, however, you have to be prepared to trawl through a certain amount of drivel to glean useful information. To post your own message you usually need to **register**: a simple case of supplying email address, a "user name" (nickname), and password.

AOL travel boards

Type in keywords "Travel Talk" to access discussions on destinations and interests (beach travel, road trips, restaurants etc). Though many of the topics on discussion are US-dominated, and postings can be rather general, AOL does have some unusual destination forums, including Antarctica and Micronesia, where messages tend to be detailed and articulate. Members can simply tap in a reply, and after a first visit choose to see only new messages.

Better Bidding

www.betterbidding.com

Based upon the premise that to bid online you need to have done your research, this moderated forum is devoted to getting the best deals when bidding with **www.priceline.com** (see p.44 and p.64) or when using its main competitor

www.hotwire.com (p.43 and p.64). The site is of most use when booking a room; user reviews build up a database of which hotels Hotwire and Priceline offer in particular cities, along with their amenities – a great help if you want to guess which hotel you may be bidding for or agreeing to. New users with basic questions should check the "Tips and Tricks" folders.

Biddingfortravel

www.biddingfortravel.com

Similar to Better Bidding, but concentrating on **www.priceline.com.** It's geared mainly towards users of the American site, though there is a section for non-US bidders too; it also has so much general information on finding bargains online that it's an indispensable tool. FAQ sections (one each for airline tickets, hotels and rental cars) lay out the fundamentals of Priceline bidding. Elsewhere you can read about successful and unsuccessful bids, user reviews of various discount airline and hotel-booking sites, and a section on Priceline's competitor, Hotwire (though this is not a bidding site in the same way; see p.43). Links take you to airline and hotel chain Websites where you can check published rates. They'll even offer personalized bidding strategies; you need, however, to be ready to bid immediately, to have all your info available, and to respond with a follow up.

Bootsnall

http://boards.bootsnall.com

Interesting range of forums from Bootsnall, the lively portal in which content is drawn from an enthusiastic community of independent travellers (see p.7). While there are forums for individual destinations – Asia and Europe are particularly busy – there is also lots of traffic on more offbeat subjects including travel writing, RTW travel, and travel buddies.

Frommer's

www.frommers.com

Frommer's site (see p.10) has a good range of forums, with hundreds of discussions. Click "Community" to see the full list, and then again to get to the individual folders. You can also do a keyword search, which brings up relevant threads. Forums are well organized by region (of all the guidebook sites this is the only one to divide the US into states) and topic. Highlights include "Ask the Expert", where you can post a query direct to someone in the know – usually a Frommers author – or browse through archived discussions. The "Hot Issue of the Month" is another archive of debates on subjects such as air miles, national parks, booking holidays over the Net and so on, finishing in October 2002. Plus forums on road trips, winter sports, cruises, family holidays, student travel and travel partners, among others, many with a US-bent.

igougo

www.igougo.com

This innovative travel journal site, packed full of personal accounts and photos, works in a similar way to a forum, providing first-hand information on places around the world from various correspondents. You can search by destination and contact community members who have been there before you. The

site also offers a range of incentives for "travel club members" and is partnered with our very own **http://travel.roughguides.com.**

Rough Guides

http://travel.roughguides.com

Click "Travel Talk" to be involved in discussions about world destinations – organized by region – and special forums devoted to finding travel partners, women travellers, gay and lesbian travellers, health and safety and round-the-world trips. Registration is required if you want to post.

Thorn Tree

www.lonelyplanet.com

Lonely Planet's forum, Thorn Tree, includes discussion groups on 21 regions, plus more than twenty other topics including gay travellers, long-haul trips, diving and snorkelling, politics, food, the arts, and travelling with kids. Though the information can be useful, especially when it comes to Asia, there seem to be more flamers on these forums than on those linked to the other major guidebooks.

Email lists

Email lists, though similar in intent to forums, are groups or communities that use email to exchange information: once you've joined a group, every email you send is received by every member, and vice versa.

There are hundreds of email lists devoted to travel topics, and several **directories** where you can find them. The best of these, **www.topica.com**, uses handy icons to show which lists are most informative or intriguing, which are available to read via the site, which insist upon approval for new

The Leader in Email Discussions & Publishing Solutions   Welcome Guest!

sign up now   login

subscribers, and so on. Topica's many travel-related lists are divided into categories from adventure travel to trains, with a good few devoted to particular destinations. Click on the name to find out about the list's content, who runs it, how many members it has and how many messages per day you can expect. Sometimes messages are available to browse before subscribing. You can subscribe right here on the site (after submitting all your personal details); store the immediate email confirmation somewhere safe, as it will tell you how to unsubscribe. Then select whether to receive all messages as they come, digested weekly or monthly, or, in some cases, not by email at all but solely through the site (where they are listed as though on a message board).

If you don't find what you're looking for on topica, check **http://groups.yahoo.com** (travel is filed under "Recreation and Sports"), which has lists organized into more than thirty categories from dude ranches to whale watching – for most of these, however, you have to join blind, as the archives aren't viewable by non-members.

You might want to set up a **separate email account** to deal with the sheer volume of mail that many groups attract, or at least establish a special folder in your current email program.

Email newsletters and ezines

You can also sign up to receive free **email newsletters** (also known as one-way lists, or **ezines**) from a variety of companies. An increasing number of Websites, and many of those reviewed in this book – including the guidebook sites (see p.10), which also have their own forums, and the major airlines, who will email you their latest deals – offer their own email newsletters. We've mentioned the most useful in our individual reviews. For an alphabetical directory of big-name email newsletters, a handful of them travel-related, check Netscape's "In-Box Direct" at **http://wp.netscape.com/ibd**, which links you direct to the individual Websites.

Online travel agents

In addition to the sites listed below, young people and students in search of travel bargains should check out the operators reviewed on p.150. We've also listed specialist operators for most of the destinations covered in Part Three of this book.

a2btravel

www.a2btravel.com

This large British online agent provides information, advice, and easy bookings for anyone travelling from, to, or within the UK. As well as flights, hotels, ferries and car rentals, it offers a database of last-minute holiday bargains, a brochure-ordering service for all major operators, and links to associated sites such as the cut-price **www.bargainholidays.com** and the self-explanatory **www.ferrybooker.com** and **www.1ski.com.**

Advantage Travel Centres

www.advantage4travel.com

Website that pools the resources of Europe's biggest network of independent travel agents. You can search for package holidays of all kinds, as well as flights, cruises and city breaks, or look for last-minute deals by selecting from a long list of popular resorts. Most, but not all, of the participants offer online booking.

American Express

http://travel.americanexpress.com

The travel section of the massive American Express site doles out destination advice culled from Fodors and *Travel & Leisure* magazine, and has some mouthwatering 360° panoramas of major world destinations. For travel shoppers, it's probably best as a source of individual components of your trip, such as flights, car rentals or accommodation, but in association with various big-name partners it also offers all-inclusive packages and last-minute special deals, all available online. And, of course, you can also buy your traveller's cheques ...

ebookers

www.ebookers.co.uk

Having started life as the online arm of the discount air specialists Flightbookers, British all-round agency ebookers bought out its parent company to become the tail that wags the dog. Its vast database of all-inclusive packages ranges across all the continents, taking in beach holidays, adventure trips, luxury holidays etc; the site also sells flights (see p.42), cars, hotels, insurance, and cruises.

Eurovacations

www.eurovacations.com

Impressive site devoted exclusively to selling European tour packages to North American customers. If you don't know where you want to go, its Destination Guide will lead you step by step in choosing a vacation. Once you do know, the site is effortlessly interactive, enabling you to custom-design every detail of your trip, from flights and transport arrangements to specific hotels. Prices are very reasonable, and rail travel is a speciality. You can complete the whole booking process online, though human operators are available to answer phone enquiries.

Expedia

www.expedia.com (North America) and **www.expedia.co.uk (UK)**

Expedia is one of the titans of Web travel sites. In addition to selling flights, lodgings, car rental, packages, and cruises, it offers any number of fancy extras, including detailed destination information, plus online maps, airport guides, and currency and weather information. Certain services on each site (such as car rental) are available to international customers, but to be sure that you'll actually be able to buy what you see on screen it's safest to use the site targetted at your home country. US users looking to buy all-inclusive packages can choose from 600 destinations, worldwide, from India to Morocco, as well as domestic. In many cases, optional extras such as excursions or shows can be booked in addition to basic flight, room and car packages. UK customers using the "Holiday Search" are offered a truncated selection from the same list.

Go-today.com

www.go-today.com

Internet-only travel agency based in Seattle, specializing in cut-rate packages from the US to Europe, Central and South America or Asia. The primary focus is on last-minute travel, but many deals are available up to three or even six months in advance. Trips range from guided tours, city breaks and fly-drives (for which automatic cars cost only slightly extra), to cruises and barge rentals. The site itself is exceptionally easy to use, with pull-down menus making it clear which departure cities are available for each itinerary, explicit itemized on-screen prices, and full online booking.

Lastminute.com

www.lastminute.com

Legendary, in its home territory of Britain at least, as the definitive over-hyped and over-valued dotcom-boom Website, Lastminute has nonetheless survived and, within reason, prospered. More a source of stimulating ideas than of rock-bottom deals, it also holds an impressive selection of off-the-wall "experiences", including coasteering and survival weekends, as well as city breaks to Paris or Brussels by Eurostar or by air. Not everything is last minute; conventional holidays bookable a month or more in advance include plenty in long-haul destinations like Barbados or Egypt. The database is easily searchable, at any stage of your process, by date, destination, and/or type of accommodation; you can also click to see the list of results appear in price order. If you don't fancy going anywhere at all, the site also provides a foodfinder so you can order a takeaway online.

Luxury Link

www.luxurylink.com

US-based site centring on a database of expensive and opulent vacation possibilities offered all over the world by assorted up-market operators. Click on "Travel Search" to specify your interests or desired destination, and its simple search engine returns a long list of alternatives, complete with links to the relevant Websites. Luxury Link also sells some of its featured package deals via a special offers page or by auction. Results of past auctions are available to provide a sense of what might constitute a winning bid, and make very interesting reading. You can get some good deals here.

Opodo

www.opodo.co.uk

Pan-European travel agent (the name refers to the "opportunity to do" and reads the same upside down) owned by nine airlines – British Airways, KLM, Air France, Alitalia, Aer Lingus, Austrian Airlines, Finnair, Iberia and

Lufthansa. With a modern, clean interface, it works in much the same way as Expedia and Travelocity, and is certainly in the same league, offering flights, hotels and car rental at competitive prices. You can also search by interest – skiing, beach holidays, romantic breaks, and so on.

Orbitz

www.orbitz.com

As it's owned by five major US airlines, it's only natural that the Orbitz Website is most useful as a source of air fares, as described on p.44. It does, however, also offer its North American-only customers a reasonable assortment of discounted package vacations, not only within North America, but also to the Caribbean, Central America, Europe and the South Pacific (although not Asia and Africa). The best bargains are in the Last-minute Getaways section (easiest to access via the Site Map), in which you search according to your departure city; at present these are only available for North America and Central America.

Site59

www.site59.com

Fast, efficient North American site, open to travellers of any nationality, and devoted exclusively to "last-minute weekend getaways" – the name refers to the 59th minute – from more than seventy North American cities. Specify where you're travelling from, and whether you want to go "this weekend", "next weekend" or on any date in the next two weeks, and it comes up with literally hundreds of well-priced city breaks, with pull-down menus to choose exact flight schedules and extras such as car rental. Naturally, most breaks are in North America, but if you're leaving from a hub airport you'll be offered a good number in Central and South America and Europe, too. Complete the whole process online, if you like what you see, otherwise sign up for an email newsletter of future offers.

Travelocity

www.travelocity.com (North America) and www. travelocity.co.uk (UK)

The Travelocity megasite, owned by Sabre and available in separate versions in North America and Europe, is Expedia's largest rival as an all-round online travel agency. Much like Expedia, it sells flights, accommodation and car rental singly or together, and offers comprehensive destination guides (courtesy of Frommer's in North America and Lonely Planet in the UK). For all-inclusive packages, the North American site draws on deals from half a dozen big-name tour operators and major airlines, while the UK version restricts itself largely to conventional package-holiday destinations but uses a larger database of operators through it and offers a separate, useful "Late Deals" section. Succinct comparison charts make it easier to weigh up your options, but for most packages you can only complete bookings by phone.

European city breaks

Also visit **www.inntravel.com** (see p.104) for more excellent short breaks.

City Breaks 4 Less

www.citybreaks4less.co.uk

Part of the **lastminute.com** empire, this UK online tour operator and consolidator offers holidays and flights to Europe and worldwide. The site is quick and easy to use, with a pull-down destinations menu and the best deals highlighted on the home page, but unfortunately there is no online booking. To make a reservation simply fill in the email request form and one of their operators will email or call you back.

Inghams Eurobreak

www.eurobreak.com

This British tour company provides very much what you'd hope for from a city break site; the home page opens with a large map of Europe, on which several dozen cities are highlighted. Click on one and you're offered a brief description, with another menu of hotels, and a button to find the price, flight details and such like. What you see is simply a JPEG of the relevant brochure page, but so long as it's more than a week before you plan to travel, you can nonetheless go on to check availability and complete your booking online.

Webweekends

www.webweekends.co.uk

UK-based site that acts as an "online distributor". While you can get details on some 2000 enticing, well-priced short city-break and activity packages, searchable by destination, price, timing and other criteria, actually booking them requires you to contact the individual suppliers direct – whose name you only get once you register – with no guarantee as to availability. Most trips are within Europe, though other destinations, including the US, feature here and there, depending on what's available. There are separate searches for budget breaks. luxury options and late deals, as well as an accommodation finder.

Major BAM operators

In addition to the specialist Internet travel agents listed in this section, many of the large BAM operators – BAM stands for "Bricks and Mortar", to denote companies that have a physical presence outside the virtual world – also maintain useful Websites. Where appropriate to specific destinations or activities, you'll find those sites reviewed throughout this book.

UK

Club 18–30 www.club18-30.co.uk
Club Med www.clubmed.co.uk
Erna Low www.ernalow.co.uk
JMC www.jmc.com
Kuoni www.kuoni.co.uk
Lunn Poly www.lunn-poly.co.uk
Magic of the Orient www.magic-of-the-orient.com
Saga Holidays www.saga.co.uk
Thomas Cook www.thomascook.co.uk
Thomson Holidays www.thomson-holidays.com
Titan Travel www.titantravel.co.uk
Trailfinders www.trailfinders.com
Virgin Holidays www.virginholidays.co.uk
Voyages Jules Verne www.vjv.com

US

Abercrombie & Kent www.abercrombiekent.com
Contiki www.contiki.com
Cosmos Tours www.globusandcosmos.com
Globus www.globusandcosmos.com
Maupintour www.maupintour.com
Saga Holidays www.sagaholidays.com

Buying flights

Budget airlines

A number of **budget airlines**, competing via their Websites to sell cut-price scheduled flights from Britain to popular European holiday spots, have effectively created a market in spur-of-the-moment and weekend breaks, carrying passengers as likely to have been tempted by the price as by the destination. When the Internet boom started, **Ryanair** was already in business, offering bargain-basement shuttles between Ireland and England; **easyJet** and Buzz were subsequently set up by entrepreneurs keen to exploit the new potential of the Web; and Go was spawned as British Airways' hasty response to their brash new rivals. EasyJet (who bought out Go) and Ryanair (who swallowed up Buzz) now dominate the market, hotly pursued by a rash of budget competitors with lower profiles and, occasionally, even lower prices. In response, many **charter** and **scheduled** airlines, which traditionally charged prohibitive prices, are now **undercutting** each other – and the budget airlines – by offering low fares, great promotions and previously unknown flexibility. Nowadays, more than ever, it pays to shop around.

Purchasing flights

Buying a flight with any of the airlines reviewed below will result in a broadly similar experience. All offer straightforward sites, bedecked with eye-catching offers and detailing their routes and schedules. Only when you enquire about flying on a specific date are you quoted exact fares, usually with each leg of a return trip priced separately. What's more, that fare tends only to apply if you book immediately; call up the self-same journey tomorrow, and it may cost double. The airlines make their money by charging exactly what the market will bear at any moment, and the first few seats are often sold at ridiculously low promotional rates. As each plane fills up, the prices rise, and will only fall again if too many seats remain unsold. Thus you're more likely to get a better deal by booking **early** rather than late. In addition, you should keep on trying different permutations of days and times – even the slightest change can make a vast difference – and remember that travelling mid-week rather than at weekends normally pays dividends. Be sure also to check whether taxes and extra charges are included. And finally, check whether your destination airport really is close to the city you're trying to reach: budget airlines are notorious for offering flights to "Frankfurt", for example, that actually land as much as fifty miles away.

Though many airlines nowadays don't bother sending you a paper "ticket" – **eticketing** means that you're given a confirmation number which you use at check-in to claim your seat – it is always a good idea to print out any receipt and take it with you to the airport, along with your credit card as ID.

Flight planning

About Flights

www.aboutflights.co.uk

No fuss and no nonsense. Key in your departure airport (Britain only), your destination and your dates, and up comes a table of the options, listed in ascending order of price, tax included. Usefully, you can sometimes see at a glance if there are seats available, though when it says "unchecked" you have to do a little more clicking to find out.

Airlines of the Web

www.flyaow.com

Huge US-based directory with links to hundreds of airline sites worldwide. If you're looking for Web-only deals, last minute specials, RTW fares, or any number of vacation and accommodation promotions, there'll be a link from this site.

Flybudget.com

www.flybudget.com

Useful flight-planning site, linking you to most of the European budget airlines. Click onto the name of your departure point and your destination, and then compare your options – different routings, sometimes involving a change of airline are offered, and it may take a few clicks before you come up with routes that aren't completely bizarre. You can also scan a chart detailing which destinations are served by which airlines, with short airline reviews, or click onto an airport name (South American cities have yet to be added) to be sent straight to the airport site.

Whichbudget.com

www.whichbudget.com

This useful directory features more than a dozen budget airlines that fly from Europe (and in the case of flybe, from New York). It's very useful if you want to know what's available from your hub airport, or to check all the airlines that fly to your favourite destination. Simply click on the name of the place you want to get from or to, and up pops a list of all the airlines, plus links, that serve your destination.

Budget airlines in Europe

bmibaby

www.bmibaby.com

Budget arm of bmi – British Midland as was – which is the second largest full-service airline in the UK after BA. It's a good option if you don't want to travel to the major hubs to fly; their main hub is Birmingham East, with (fewer) departures from Cardiff and Manchester. As a rule, it's the domestic flights (currently to Belfast, Edinburgh, Glasgow and Jersey) that present the real bargains, though it's worth checking for European destinations too, especially if you can book well in advance. There's a £5 discount if you book online, but note that airport taxes aren't included in the original price quoted. As with most of the budget airlines, no on-board meals are served. The site itself is clean and easy; quite apart from the simple booking facility, good features include a live flight arrivals board and nicely designed timetables. Signing up for the ezine keeps you up to date with the latest deals, but you have to choose two departure airports only.

easyJet

www.easyjet.com

Calling itself "the Web's favourite airline", easyJet uses pull-down menus to list its no-frills flights between 24 European and twelve British cities. To keep costs down, there are no on-board meals, just the opportunity to buy snacks from the in-flight "easyKiosk". Use the menus to specify your destination and departure points, and whether you want a single or return fare, and you'll be presented with options for your day of choice, a day earlier and a day later. Many flights are scheduled for antisocial hours. Taxes and airport fees are not included, and tend to add £5–10 to a typical return price. No online check-in, so no seat selection available.

Flybe

www.flybe.com

Previously known as British European, flybe is notable for its wide choice of destinations. Flights leave from more than twenty UK airports to other British cities plus France, Belgium, the Channel Islands, Italy and Spain. You'll find their cheapest fares on the Website; and though it's best to book in advance, last-minute offers are detailed on the home page.

MyTravelLite

www.mytravellite.com

One of the newer budget airlines, with flights from Belfast, Knock and Birmingham to a decent range of European destinations. Booking online gets you a discount of £2.50 each way.

Now

www.now-airlines.com

Launched in autumn 2003, this independent airline now flies from London Luton to major European centres, including Manchester, Jersey, Dusseldorf, Hamburg, Ibiza, Rome, Valencia, Lisbon and Tenerife. All destinations are priced according to a simple zone system. This means prices may not always be the lowest, especially if you have time to book well in advance elsewhere, but it provides a reassuring consistency, and at least you know the guy in the seat next to you didn't get his ticket for a quarter of the price of yours.

Ryanair

www.ryanair.com

Still the first choice for many budget travellers for its astonishing special deals to a wide range of European destinations, Ryanair does not seem to be suffering from reports of passengers, stranded by cancellations, being left to fend for themselves. Ryanair's core business remains between Ireland and Britain, with connections between a total of six airports in Ireland and fifteen in the UK, and up to thirteen flights daily between Dublin and London Stansted alone. They also fly from Stansted to more than sixty European cities. Quoted fares can drop as low as £2 for a return flight to Brittany, or just £25 to Venice; by the time you've factored in taxes and extras a £40 return fare can work out at around £60, but it's still not something to be sniffed at.

SkyEurope

www.skyeurope.com

A new-concept budget airline in Central Europe, with routes to Prague, Berlin, Munich, Stuttgart, Zurich, Milan, Dubrovnik, Split and Zadar. They also offer flights from London and Paris to Bratislava with bus links to Vienna and Brno.

More budget airlines

Quite apart from those reviewed on the previous pages, the following budget airlines are worth checking, especially if you're flying from regional airports.

Aer Arann Express
www.aerarann.ie
Serves a range of Irish airports plus Birmingham, Bristol, the Isle of Man and Prestwick.

Air Europa
www.aireuropa.co.uk
Flights from twenty airports in Spain to other Spanish destinations, plus London, Milan, Paris and Rome, New York, Cuba and Caracas.

Air Scotland
www.air-scotland.com
From Glasgow and Edinburgh to Barcelona and a number of Spanish resorts including Mallorca and the Canaries.

Air Wales
www.airwales.co.uk
Swansea and Cardiff to Cork, Dublin, Jersey and London; from Cardiff you can also fly to Belfast and Plymouth. A number of combinations are possible, including flights from London to Cork, and from Dublin to Cork and Plymouth.

FlyGlobespan.com
www.flyglobespan.com
Glasgow and Edinburgh to Nice, Palma, Barcelona, Rome and Malaga.

Jet2 Airways
www.jet2.com
From Leeds Bradford to Spanish resorts plus Barcelona, Faro, Amsterdam, Prague, Geneva, Milan and Nice.

Planet Air
www.planetair.co.uk
Leeds Bradford to Alicante, Malaga, Tenerife and Faro.

Budget airlines in the USA

Airtran

www.airtran.com

Destinations include Las Vegas, New Orleans, Orlando, LA and the Bahamas. The site is clear and user-friendly, allowing you to search for a flight date with two days leeway on either side. Online check-in available.

American Trans Air

www.ata.com

Founded in 1973, Airtran is a reliable cheapie, with fewer frills than some of the others. One big plus is its variety of destinations, including Honolulu, Lihue and Maui in Hawaii, Guadalajara, Puerto Vallarta and Cancun in Mexico, Aruba, Grand Cayman and Montego Bay. Online specials and last-minute deals are highlighted on the home page, or you can sign up for a newsletter. Online check-in available.

Jetblue

www.jetblue.com

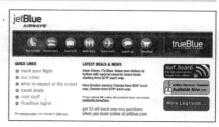

Based in New York (with its own terminal at JFK), this budget airline consistently wins awards for good value and service, and the Website sings the praises of new planes, comfy leather chairs, seat-back satellite TVs and Hugo Boss-clad stewards. Good range of destinations including Fort Lauderdale, Fort Myers, Tampa and West Palm Beach; New Orleans; Las Vegas; Long Beach, Oakland and San Diego; Ontario, and San Juan, Puerto Rico. You get $5 off each way when you book online.

Midwest Express

www.midwestexpress.com

Lots of destinations, especially in the West, and including New York, Boston, Atlanta, Las Vegas, Orlando and LA. Midwest is a cut above its competitors when it comes to in-cabin food; also, unusually for the budget airlines, it offers a frequent-flier programme. The site, rather a staid-looking, old-fashioned affair, offers lots of clear information, and you can even find the weather forecast for your destination city. Online check-in available.

Online flight agents

Airhitch

www.airhitch.org

The "Airhitch" concept is not for everybody; judging by the Website's insistence on clichés about "tourists" and "travelers", it's largely designed for those who like to feel they're beating the "system". Restricted to US-based users only, the idea is that you specify roughly where you're travelling from, where you're going (Europe, Hawaii or the Caribbean), and when (within a five-day range). A few days before you set off, you're finally told when and where you're going – and you have to accept it, even if it's Amsterdam rather than Paris. So long as you're comfortable with the uncertainty, you'll end up benefiting from such flat-rate one-way fares, available even in high season, as just under $200 to Europe from the East Coast, or $280 from the West Coast. "Usually", though, you do get the exact destination you asked for.

Airtreks

www.airtreks.com

Although it can quote you (unexceptional) prices for standard round-trip flights anywhere in the world, San Francisco-based Airtreks outperforms its competitors when it comes to putting together multi-stop globetrotting trips. Constructing your own routing online couldn't be simpler; it's beautifully designed, user friendly and very fast. Wherever in the world you want to start from, travel to, and end up, they'll present you with a number of fare options, including lowest cost, most for your money and fewest stops. You'll then need to fill in a form, and they will call or email you back.

Cheap Flights

www.cheapflights.co.uk and www.cheapflights.com

The concept on both these sites is simple and effective: you just key in a destination and the airport you want to leave from and up come the range of options available over the coming months – all of them, as this is not an agent, but an impartial source. Scan the list to see which dates apply to you, and click through to the relevant online operators to find out more.

ebookers

www.ebookers.com

The online arm of the Flightbookers travel agency (see p.30) quotes competitive fares to and between destinations worldwide. You can compare fares and departure times on a chart, picking the combination that suits you best. Long-haul trips tend to be the best value.

Expedia

www.expedia.com (North America) and **www.expedia.co.uk (UK)**

Expedia sites provide users with the easiest interface of all the online air ticket merchants, and they're sufficiently wide-ranging that they're always worth trying as you scout around for a deal. Bear in mind, however, that the flight search doesn't check airlines' Internet only fares, so as ever you should make sure to shop around. Be warned also that it might suggest truly bizarre routings; scan down the list of recommendations and you may well find a much more convenient schedule for a mere $5 extra.

Hotwire

www.hotwire.com

Hotwire offers good last-minute fares on scheduled flights. However, their "Hot-Fares" come with their own unique restrictions – most obviously, you only find out the exact times of your flights, and even which carrier you're using, once you've bought your ticket, with no possibility of alterations. In addition, all flights must originate within the United States. You can specify a maximum number of stopovers, or where applicable that you won't accept a red-eye or overnight flight, but otherwise you have to decide on the basis of price alone and forgo frequent-flyer and other such benefits. In the current climate, with the proliferation of budget airlines and price wars across the industry, it may be better to use Hotwire for hotel bookings (see p.64), and turn to other sources for bargain flights. Before buying, take a look at **www.betterbidding.com**, Hotwire's companion information site (see p.25).

1click4flights.com

www.1stnetflights.com

UK travel agency site that offers an easily searchable database of scheduled flights, arranged by destination and bookable online. Fares are Internet only; you may be quoted a different price if you call. They cover both European and long-haul destinations, but all trips must originate within Britain and Ireland. Separate sections sell one-way flights and a large array of charter flights, to Canada all year round, and to major European destinations in summer only.

Opodo

www.opodo.co.uk

Opodo, the Johnny-Come-Lately of online travel agents (see p.31) is particularly recommended for its airfares; you don't have to register to search, and the engine is fast and efficient, coming up with good deals not exclusively from the participating airlines. (It doesn't, however, search the budget airlines.) In addition to allowing you to pre-book your seat and claim frequent-flyer miles, it even lets you request special meals.

Orbitz

www.orbitz.com

Jointly owned by five airlines – American, Continental, Delta, Northwest, and United – and subscribed to by several dozen more. The fares thrown up by its slightly slow-witted search engine aren't bad, but they're not conspicuously better than what you'd find elsewhere. It can also take too long before you find out your choice is unavailable. Flights must originate in North America.

Priceline

www.priceline.com (North America) and **www.priceline.co.uk (UK)**

Priceline has come a long way since William Shatner announced its arrival in the US in 1998. The premise remains the same as ever; you tell them how much you're prepared to pay for a particular round-trip flight (or hotel room, or rental car), and they'll get back to you if an airline accepts your offer. Much like Hotwire (whose fares it often, but not always, beats), the catch is that you're buying "opaque inventory"; you're not told which carrier you're using, or the exact times of your flight, until after you've made the purchase. And much like Hotwire, it's currently wiser to depend upon Priceline for the cheapest hotels rather than the cheapest flights; there's simply too much competition out there. If you do want to bid, be sure to check **www.betterbidding.com** (see p.25) and **www.biddingfortravel.com** (p.26) beforehand.

QIXO

www.qixo.com

The "Quest for Impossibly eXcellent Offers" trawls through some thirty other ticket-purchase sites, including both airlines and agencies, so you don't have to; it displays interim results as it searches, so you get an exciting couple of minutes of screen-watching. Once you've found a fare that appeals, register to buy your ticket.

Note that you have to list a departure airport, so if you're flying from somewhere with more than one you might have to run a couple of searches; also, flights have to be longer than a fortnight away. You pay a $20 premium per ticket, but if you're in a hurry it's not a bad deal. Although the flights can be anywhere in the world, you must have a credit card with a US address to buy.

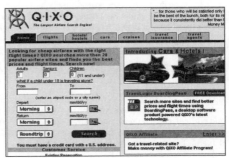

STA

www.statravel.co.uk and **www.statravel.com**

Airfares here are available only if you are a student or under 26. Assuming you fall within that remit, are planning a journey that originates within your home country, then there's a good chance you'll find an acceptable deal.

Thomas Cook

www.thomascook.com

A pleasant surprise, this – a mainstream UK travel agent whose flight search engine frequently comes up with fares as good as or cheaper than the big online operators. Departures from Britain and Ireland only.

Travelocity

www.travelocity.com and **www. travelocity.co.uk**

Travelocity rank among the very biggest names in online travel, with a straightforward search engine for flight deals that set the standard for the rest of the pack. The fares thrown up by the Sabre system continue to match what's available on more overtly budget-oriented sites – not surprisingly, as many also use Sabre – and they also provide a range of other travel services, such as accommodation deals and all-inclusive packages.

Car rental

The process of **renting a car** is ideally suited to the Internet. Most renters know exactly what they want, and so long as they get the cheapest rate they don't care who supplies it. The range of prices you're offered on the Web is quite extraordinary, so there are huge savings to be made. Searching for a week's rental from London's Heathrow airport, for example, the highest rate quoted to us was eight times the lowest.

All the **major international rental chains** run similar Websites, offering online availability checks and booking. Unless you have a very strong reason to choose a particular one, however – such as a corporate discount or frequent-flyer deal – there's no point in using the chain's own sites. Most are frustratingly slow, with ponderous and pedantic interfaces that require you to state the exact minute you'll pick up the vehicle, or to tick "check all rates" as well as "check rates" before they'll give you a quote. None provides any useful extra content that isn't available elsewhere, and the rates they offer never seem to be better than those you'll find, even for the same company, on more **general comparison sites**. Surprisingly few allow customers travelling in Europe to request a vehicle with automatic rather than manual transmission – something it's much easier to ensure on a general site. Note also that most offer different rates for exactly the same

The major chains

	US site	UK site
Alamo	www.alamo.com	www.alamo.co.uk
Avis	www.avis.com	www.avis.co.uk
Budget	www.budget.com	www.budget.co.uk
Dollar	www.dollar.com	www.dollar.co.uk
Hertz	www.hertz.com	www.hertz.co.uk
National	www.nationalcar.com	www.nationalcar.co.uk
Thrifty	www.thrifty.com	www.thrifty.co.uk

vehicle to customers from different parts of the world. It consistently tends to be cheaper to rent a car in your own home country than overseas; thus Avis and Dollar are the worst offenders for charging British citizens more than Americans for rentals in the US.

Cruise America

www.cruiseamerica.com

The largest North American rental company that specializes in RVs (Recreational Vehicles) – those thirty-foot behemoths designed for family touring vacations and crammed with bedrooms, bathrooms, kitchens and even garages. Simple menus facilitate bookings for round-trip and one-way rentals from locations throughout the US and Canada. Rates are not cheap, however, and there's a surcharge if you drive more than a thousand miles per week. Only residents of North America can book online, though international agents are listed who handle reservations for foreign visitors. In addition, Cruise America rent motorcycles, though only Hondas, with no online booking facility.

easyRentacar

www.easycar.com

Proclaiming itself "the world's first Internet-only car rental company", easyRentacar was created as an offshoot of budget airline easyJet, and provides inexpensive car rental at most – but not yet all – of the European destinations that airline serves. That currently amounts to eight European cities and five British ones, though its 23 London locations do not include the major airports. On the whole, the overall rates are significantly lower than the standard rates offered by its larger competitors, but not necessarily the very lowest to be found, and there are drawbacks. Prices are quoted for each specific day you rent; thus you might pay as little as £2.15 for a Monday, but more than ten times as much for a Saturday. In addition, you can't request a specific type of car or transmission – a basic small Renault Clio may be the only option – and the quoted rates only cover 75 miles per day, which for most holidaymakers is nothing like enough.

Expedia

www.expedia.com (North America) and www.expedia.co.uk (UK)

Wherever you access it from, Expedia returns much the same rate for any specific rental, and as a rule it'll be a good rate too, in whichever part of the world you're looking to rent a car. On top of that, for car rentals Expedia customers don't have to buy from their "own" home-based site – you can shop from either. While the rate won't always be the cheapest you could find, if you let Expedia set a benchmark you'll know you're doing well if you manage to beat it.

Holiday Autos

www.holidayautos.co.uk (UK) and **www.kemwel.com (North America)**

British-based Holiday Autos call themselves "the largest vacation car rental broker in the world", and the UK version of its Website offers probably the simplest online car rental around. Operating from the common-sense premise – oddly rare elsewhere – that you want to rent a car, its straightforward pull-down menus set out exactly which locations they serve and how much a car will cost. Their great strength is the sheer quantity of obscure European destinations they serve, which tie in nicely with many cut-price flights; the prices are for the most part reasonable, though seldom cheaper, where comparison is possible, than those offered by their major competitors. Only the British site offers rentals in the US; Kemwel only deals with overseas destinations.

Sidestep

www.sidestep.com

The much-vaunted Sidestep system, which only works with Windows, amounts to no more than the sum of its parts. Sidestep is a program which you have to download and install before you can use it; it then pops up as a sidebar on your screen and invites you to search for airlines and hotels (both of which tend to come out expensive, which is why Sidestep is not reviewed in those sections of this book) or rental cars, in North America only. Searching through all the big-name rental operators' sites, it comes up with the same list of prices you'd get if you trawled through them individually. So it saves time, and it finds you the best conventional deal; it just won't find any bargains. Mac users can access the same search procedure by visiting **www.globetrek.com**

Travelnow

www.travelnow.com

Although the rental-car section of this North American site seems at first glance to cover only a handful of US cities, those are simply its most popular destinations; a full search facility enables you to find almost any domestic or international location. Similarly, while Travelnow checks rates and availability across a wider range of companies than other comparison sites, the results it throws up point you first in the direction of its "preferred partners", such as Alamo and Thrifty. Scroll down beyond the most prominent results, however, and you may well find some excellent deals.

Travelocity

www.travelocity.com (North America) and **www. travelocity.co.uk (UK)**

As with airline tickets (see p.45), the Travelocity search engine can be relied on to work quickly and efficiently in finding great-value car rental offers, both in North America and Europe.

Woods

www.woods.co.uk

British rental agency Woods offers a reasonable though not outstanding flat rate for rentals in the UK only, serving London (offering all the airports plus delivery to any central address) plus 56 other UK cities. The site itself is easy to use and aimed largely at American travellers, who are most likely to appreciate the tips on driving in Britain, and the fact that there's no drop-off fee if you return the car to a point other than where you picked it up.

Trains

If you're planning a rail journey in Europe, you should also see
http://ricksteves.com (see p.11) which sells a variety of train passes online.

Accent on Travel

www.accentontravelusa.com

No-nonsense site from a highly rated Oregon-based US travel agency. Train enthusiasts Ted
and Sylvia Blishak can custom design rail trips and tours throughout North America for
most budgets, arranging accommodation along the way and suggesting itineraries. They
also handle overseas rail tours on trains such as the Orient Express, The Royal Scot and The
Al Andalus Express. No online ordering – email them to request a booking – but the site is
useful for rail travel tips, links and detailed rail travel reports from the Blishaks.

Die Bahn

www.bahn.de

Using a mind-blowing database of rail stations – 150,000 in Germany alone – German rail
network Die Bahn provides online schedules for rail (and many road and sea) connections
all over Europe. You can book online, but not if your trip is less than two months away.
Click on "International Guests" for an English-language version.

Europrail International

www.europrail.net

Well-designed and user-friendly US site selling the major European rail passes, with links
to Die Bahn (see above) for schedules, and an easy facility for checking ticket prices
between any two points. You can order passes online and download printable maps of
European rail routes.

Euro Railways

www.eurorailways.com

Marvellous US-based site bringing together information on rail travel throughout Europe.
It's an astonishing venture, enabling you to plan your route and buy thousands of tickets

and single and multi-country passes, including youth passes, online. There are pull-down menus everywhere you turn, and, if you're really lost, a "personal travel assistant"; simply type in the countries you want to visit and the type of accommodation you require, and they'll email you a suggested itinerary.

Eurostar

www.eurostar.com

Slick, visual and vibrant, Eurostar's site offers timetables and fare charts for their high-speed rides between London, Paris and Brussels, with online booking up to ninety days in advance. They also provide all the gen on trips to Disneyland Paris and the French Alps, details of special Eurostar packages, and a "Euroguide" to shopping, eating and drinking in the cities they serve. Register to receive latest offers and save time booking.

Eurotunnel

www.eurotunnel.co.uk

Eurotunnel's official Website does a good job with timetables (for up to three months in advance) for their Folkestone–Calais service, a fares calendar, and online booking. The site also provides details on local events and sights (market days and gardens in Normandy and so on), with links under "Shopping and Services" for online route planning and travel insurance. Booking online can save you up to £6 on standard fares.

Great Rail Journeys

www.greatrail.co.uk

UK operator Great Rail Journeys organizes luxury escorted group holidays throughout Europe, North America, South Africa, Japan and Morocco. Choose from a pull-down menu of train operators or click on thumbnail photos of destinations to read details of a good range of journeys, from a tour of northern Spain to a nineteen-day coast-to-coast USA trip. You can check availability on the site and make provisional reservations, but to book you need to fill in a hard copy form (downloadable in PDF format).

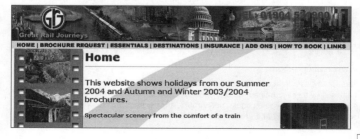

The Man in Seat 61

www.seat61.com

Railway fansite *par excellence*, put together by British obsessive (and former British Rail station manager) Mark Smith, and named after his favourite seat on Eurostar. The main focus is on catching trains from London to anywhere and everywhere, within the UK as well as beyond, with fares, timetables, and detailed practical recommendations. On top of that Smith's remit also extends to advice on rail (and, to a lesser extent, sea) travel the world over, making his site an invaluable resource at the planning stage of almost any expedition. Though it's entirely noncommercial, so you can't buy or book anything here, all the necessary contact numbers and Web links are provided.

Orient Express

www.orient-express.com

A surprisingly static site for such a silver-service venture, with details of the various Orient Express tours through the UK, Europe, Australia, and Southeast Asia. Prices are high, as you might expect – a three-day/two-night Singapore to Bangkok journey costs from £920 per person, hotel accommodation included – but there are some Internet-only offers. Secure online booking.

Rail Serve

www.railserve.com

This speedy, comprehensive, and easy to use directory of rail sites is a vast labour of love managed by teenage train enthusiast Christopher Muller. Scroll down the list of departments – antiques and collectibles, books, newsgroups, and sound effects, among others – to the sections on passenger and urban transit (subdivided into Africa, Asia, Australasia, Europe,

North and South America), where you can click onto literally hundreds of links. Europe brings up more than 315 sites, from the tram network of Charleroi to trainspotting sites in Wales; almost as many links come up for North America, including local train network sites from Alaska to Wisconsin.

TrainWeb.org

www.trainweb.org

Searchable US portal for a vast range of railroad sites including model railroading, forums, photos and rail cams. The travel section includes links to Amtrak and VIA services along with rail hotels, travelogues, railtour agencies, tourist railways, dinner trains and the like.

USA by Rail

www.usa-by-rail.com

This site, the online arm of Bradt's useful guidebook *USA by Rail* (which you can buy here), offers a comprehensive guide to train travel throughout not only the USA but also Canada, with details of the national networks, steam railroads and railway museums. There are good links to North American railway travel sites, with reviews of all the major Amtrak routes, including The California Zephyr, one of the world's great trains. See p.344 for more on train travel in the USA; p.208 for the same in Canada.

Note that Websites devoted to rail travel in any one country can be found in the relevant section within our Destinations chapter. These include:

Alaska Railroad www.akrr.com	see p.344
Amtrak (US) www.amtrak.com	see p.344
Indian Railways www.indianrail.gov.in	see p.251
John Steel Rail Tours (Canada) www.johnsteel.com	see p.209
Public Transport Information (UK) www.pti.org.uk	see p.322
SD Enterprises (India)	
www.dandpani.dircon.co.uk	see p.253
SNCF (France) www.sncf.com	see p.237
Train Hoppers Space (US) http://catalog.com/hop	see p.345
The Trainline (UK) www.thetrainline.com	see p.322
UK Railways on the Net www.rail.co.uk	see p.322
Via Rail Canada www.viarail.ca	see p.211

Ferries

All Greek Ferries

www.ferries.gr

If you need to find and/or book a ferry trip to or within Greece, don't trawl through the many individual ferry companies that operate in Greek waters; head instead for this site, run by a travel agency on Crete. It holds up-to-date timetables for international connections with Italy, Cyprus, Albania, Israel, Egypt and Turkey as well as most but not quite all the myriad inter-island routes, and provides instant online booking.

Brittany Ferries

www.brittanyferries.co.uk

Brittany Ferries operate cross-Channel services from Portsmouth, Poole and Plymouth in southern England to Brittany and Normandy in France, and to northern Spain, and also connect Ireland with France. On their excellent Website, you can easily check schedules and make online reservations, search through a huge number of all-inclusive packages and accommodation deals, or simply order their printed brochures.

DFDS Seaways

www.scansea.com

Information and online reservations for ferry routes across the North Sea from England to Scandinavia and beyond. Sailings operate between Newcastle and Norway or Holland, and between Harwich and Denmark or Germany. The site itself is surprisingly easy to use, though you may have to guess a little Danish along the way.

Ferrysavers

www.ferrysavers.com

Of the many British Websites that claim to offer discount deals on all ferry crossings, Ferrysavers comes the closest to delivering the goods. As well as the standard routes to France, it covers sailings to Ireland, Spain, Belgium, Holland, the Channel Islands and Scandinavia; slightly irritatingly, however, you have to check each individual region, and sometimes each company, in turn. In the end, however, search by time and date, and you'll be given a range of alternative fares, including any special offers that may apply, with a price guarantee that they'll undercut any cheaper rate you're offered for the same itinerary elsewhere. Strictly speaking, your booking is not quite interactive; you have to await email confirmation.

Hoverspeed

www.hoverspeed.co.uk

Hoverspeed's Website provides schedules, prices and online booking for their trips between England, France and Belgium (none of which are by hovercraft, despite the name). They also sell good-value short breaks to nearby Continental cities such as Antwerp, Honfleur, and Rouen.

Irish Ferries

www.irishferries.com

Timetables, prices and easy online reservations, with instant confirmation of availability, for sailings between Ireland and both Britain and France. You can also take 360° virtual tours of all their fleet, including *Ulysses*, the world's largest car ferry, which plies the Holyhead–Dublin route.

Loglink

www.loglink.net/ferries.htm

You may not be interested in the multitude of academic treatises and technical specifications that are accessible from the Loglink ferry site, but it's invaluable in providing links that make it possible to plan trips with almost any ferry company in Europe or North America.

P&O European Ferries

www.poferries.com

The main home page for P&O European Ferries carries links to the five separate subsidiary sites that handle sailings from Portsmouth to Le Havre and Cherbourg in northern France, and Bilbao in Spain; on the Dover–Calais route between England and France, in conjunction with Stena Line; across the Irish Sea between Larne and Cairnryan; to Orkney & Shetland from the Scottish mainland (**www.poscottishferries.co.uk**); and over the North Sea to Zeebrugge and Rotterdam (**www.ponsf.com**). In each case, the step-by-step online booking service is easy to use, though it doesn't go out of its way to guide you towards any special offers or bargain rates that might be available if you adjust your travel dates. And if you're curious about the "Just For Fun" section, don't be.

Sea Containers

www.steam-packet.com

Schedules, fares and reservations for the Steam Packet line between the Isle of Man and northern England, as well as Irish Sea Ferries routes such as Belfast to Troon in Scotland, and the Superseacat service between Liverpool and Dublin. The online booking procedure is reasonably efficient, with a two-percent discount for Net reservations.

SeaFrance

www.seafrance.com

French operator SeaFrance run this straightforward Website to promote the Dover–Calais ferries they run in competition with their British counterparts. It offers a simple online booking procedure from its opening page, plus special offers and short city breaks in Paris in particular.

Stena Line

www.stenaline.co.uk

Though maddening to use, with its tiny print and endless pull-down menus, this Website does enable you, in the end, to make confirmed online reservations for Stena's ferry routes from England, Scotland and Wales to both Ireland and Holland.

Trasmediterranea Ferries

www.trasmediterranea.es/homei.htm

The English-language version of the Website of Trasmediterranea Ferries, who operate several Spanish ferry routes. English speakers can easily make online bookings for all their services, from Barcelona and Valencia to the Balearic islands, from Algeciras, Almeria or Malaga in the south across to the North African coast, and from Cadiz out to the Canaries.

Youra.com

www.youra.com/ferry

Dan Youra, an American ferry obsessive, has equipped his "Ferry Guide" with links to ferries and ferry systems all over the world, including China and Japan as well as most of Europe. His listings are especially strong close to his home base of Washington state, with the various Puget Sound operators well represented, and he also covers a selection of cruise lines and shipping companies. He doesn't sell tickets himself, but users can buy the printed version of his newsletter.

Note that Websites devoted to ferry crossings in any one country can be found in the relevant section within our Destinations chapter. These include:

British Columbia Ferry Services www.bcferries.com   see p.208
Caledonian MacBrayne (Scotland) www.calmac.co.uk   see p.332
Public Transport Information (UK) www.pti.org.uk   see p.322
TT-Line (Australia) www.tt-line.com.au   see p.199

Buses

For overlanding bus trips, see p.124.

Budget Travel

www.budgettravel.com/eurobus.htm

The sprawling budget travellers' informaton site has a useful directory of European bus links. Though it needs tidying up, to say the least, scrolling down the page brings you to a variety of links to even the most obscure sites, many of them with short reviews. Whether you want to check the local schedules in Belarus or plan a coach tour around Wales, you'll find a site to help you here.

Busabout

www.busabout.com

A great idea for independent travellers – hop-on-hop-off coach trips to fifty destinations in sixteen European countries, with optional door-to-door service to a range of Busabout-recommended hostels, campsites and hotels. There are eleven passes: six of which give unlimited consecutive travel over fixed periods, and five "flexipasses", which allow you to choose how many days you travel in a given time span. You're looking at spending

anything from £219 for a two-week consecutive pass to £739 for a season pass; the flexipasses range from £219 for seven days in one month to £579 for 24 days travel across five months. You can also buy add-on tickets to Budapest, Croatia, Corsica, Sicily, Turkey, the Greek islands and Morocco. The site has secure online booking, and as soon as you've bought your pass you can, if you wish, book all legs of your journey online. If you want to reserve Busabout accommodation, check the site's city and hostel guides, then browse the message boards for reviews and feedback.

Eurolines

www.eurolines.com

Eurolines is the umbrella organization for 35 companies running scheduled buses between 500 destinations throughout Europe. As well as individual fares, they offer the money-saving Europass, which gives unlimited travel between 31 cities for up to 15, 30 or 60 days (from £113 for a low-season youth pass lasting 15 days, to £299 for an adult 60-day pass in high season). The site (go for the non-Flash version, unless you've got time to kill) has a table of fares and timetables for all the major destinations, and you can buy passes online (as long as you've got at least seven days before you set off).

Wallace Arnold Holidays

www.wallacearnold.co.uk

The UK coach holiday specialists, best-known for their tours of the UK and Europe, actually offer hundreds of holidays including trips to North America, New Zealand and the Far East. These are a good bet for anyone who wants an easy life: with more than 1600 pick-up points in the UK, it shouldn't be a hassle to get to one, and once you have, all your bags are carried for you right up to your hotel room. Hotels are upmarket and most of them offer full-board plans. You can browse the range by using the "Holiday Finder", but it can take a while to trawl through the choices, and even then the site features just a selection; for more, you'll need to order hard copy brochures. It is, however, possible to check availability and book online.

Note that Websites devoted to bus travel in any one country can be found in the relevant section within our Destinations chapter. These include:

Green Tortoise Adventure Travel (US) www.greentortoise.com   see p.344
Greyhound (US) www.greyhound.com   see p.345
Greyhound Canada www.greyhound.ca   see p.208
National Express (UK) www.nationalexpress.com   see p.322
Public Transport Information (UK) www.pti.org.uk   see p.322

Accommodation

W hen it comes to booking a room, many people are seduced into believing that they're going to find the cheapest rates online. As with so much received wisdom about the Internet, this is often not the case. However, on the Web, as in the real world, research is the key to getting good prices, and for that the Net is invaluable. The obvious first ports of call include **multipurpose megasites** such as Expedia and Travelocity; these are efficient and fast, and offer competitive rates, although they tend to concentrate on major chains and up-market accommodation. **Directories** usually offer a wider range of options, often with online reservations. Sites that specialize in **discounted rooms** and **last-minute offers**, including **travel auction sites** (which work in the same way for hotel rooms as they do for flights or packages), are worth a look, but you may find that their rates are no better than those offered by the bigger sites. More importantly, they may even be higher than those you'd be quoted if you called the hotel direct.

The Web is also flooded with sites specializing in **B&Bs**, along with **villa and condo rental sites**. The vast majority are based in North America, and the condo sites in particular tend to be aimed at senior travellers who will enjoy the nearby golf courses and facilities in the sunshine resorts featured. However, booking villas online is also increasingly popular in the UK, especially for properties in southern Europe. **Home exchange sites** – where property owners swap homes or take turns staying with each other – are undeniably good if you're on a budget and really want to live like a local. However, there's so much fussing to be done before you can get going – reference checking, arranging dates, letting each other know how the hot water works and so on – that some people find the savings are simply not worth the effort.

Researching and booking a hotel online

First and foremost, be sure the site has full contact details for the property, along with a rundown of all facilities. It's always best to see **photos** (while exercising the same caution as if you were looking at a hard copy brochure – they'll obviously portray the property in the best possible light) and it's useful to have a **map**. When booking, check if the **rate** quoted is for single or double occupancy – some places charge supplements for solo travellers in double rooms, while others will charge more for two people – and note any potential extras. If you're after a discount rate, always check the site's cancellation policy. Many companies allow no changes whatsoever to discounted rooms booked online. Then, and this is crucial, once you've done your research, log off and **call the hotel direct** to see if they can better the price. You may well be offered a lower rate than those quoted on the Net.

If you do find the best rates online, or simply decide to book on the Net for convenience, bear in mind the differences between dealing with the property direct and going through a booking site. Though it's usually more time-consuming to deal with an **individual hotel** – and you'll need to do more research than if you were simply booking a flight or even a package holiday – it does have its good points. Emailing hotels direct allows you to ask questions, make requests, and perhaps even do some bargaining – and at least you know your reservation is secure. Using **booking services or consolidators**, though fast and simple, can be nerve-wracking. Always call the hotel direct to check the reservation has been made. And however you choose to book, always make sure to get an email **confirmation**, detailing the full cost charged to your card.

Though we've reviewed the best general sites below, many of the biggest sites concentrate heavily on properties in the US. For **country-specific accommodation** – chains, individual properties, hotel groups – turn to the destinations section of this book (where we've devoted an entire section to **UK accommodation**, by the way). Often the official **tourist board sites** (most of which we've reviewed, if they're any good at all) have sections devoted to accommodation, concentrating on the types of places special to that particular country or region.

For family **camping vacations** and family-friendly hotel chains, see p.141. And for details of sites that specify **gay-friendly properties**, see p.147.

Portals and information

About.com

http://hotels.about.com

The about.com concept – which combines links and original content on a huge variety of subjects, each masterminded by a human "guide" – works well when it comes to hotels. The emphasis veers towards the US, but there is plenty of stuff from around the world with links to online hotel directories and discount sites, plus sections on unique hotels and the like.

Cheapaccommodation.com

www.cheapaccommodation.com

Well-composed information site. Key in the first letter of the place you're visiting, from Aachen to Zurich, to see a page of links to booking sites, home exchanges, B&Bs, local chains and so on for that destination, each with a brief site review. The "Hot Deals" section, which fast tracks you to the deals on offer from various accommodation sites, is useful, as are the links to international chain hotels.

Discount sites

All-hotels

www.all-hotels.com

Searchable directory of some 100,000 hotels worldwide. While there are listings for smaller places, you'll do best if you're looking to stay in a sizeable town or resort, especially if it's in the US. Hotels are sorted via district, in folders labelled luxury, standard, budget and discount. Within each folder hotels come with overview, price range and photos. You have to click the "Book" button to check availability and rates on your preferred nights; you can then choose a room and book online through the site's secure server. A separate section links you direct to various discounted hotels.

NEWSGROUPS AND USER REVIEWS

Don't forget the various **newsgroups** (see p.18) and forums on the Net – as well as the popular newsgroup **rec.travel.bed+breakfast**, many region- and country-specific groups feature discussions on accommodation, while a number of the sites listed below have their own forums.

There are also a number of **Websites** where users post impartial advice about tried and tested accommodation; try **www.igougo.com** (see p.27) and **www.tripadvisor.com**. Though primarily directed towards users of the bidding sites **www.hotwire.com**, **www.priceline.com**, **www.betterbidding.com** (see p.25) and **www.biddingfortravel.com** (see p.26) are indispensable for anyone looking to research and book a room online.

Expedia

www.expedia.com (North America) and www.expedia.co.uk (UK)

With its database of more than 40,000 hotels in all the top US destinations and major European cities, Expedia leads the way in online accommodation booking. Searches result in a dizzying choice; those with the logo "Special Rate" are listed first, and can be booked immediately. Although Expedia guarantees those rates to be the lowest online price available, and promises to refund the difference if you prove them wrong within 24 hours, it's worth doing a little double-checking – don't just assume that you won't be offered a better price on the hotel's own site. That caveat applies especially to smaller destinations, where there's usually a good choice, but prices are not always that low. Unlike for flights, customers in the US and UK can book accommodation through whichever site offers the best price, though they're likely to be very similar.

Hotel Reservations Network

www.hoteldiscounts.com

This searchable consolidator site offers discounts of up to 65 percent on more than 3000 hotels in major cities and resorts around the world, with the highest concentration in North America. Search results, laid out in a horizontal line, give you the hotel's star rating, its general location and the lowest prices for your chosen nights (in US dollars, with a currency converter link); click for full address, facility list, reviews and photos. In many instances you're not told how much, if any, of a discount these prices represent, so once you know a place is available, it's worth calling direct to see if you can get a lower rate. Online booking is simple and secure.

Hotwire

www.hotwire.com

Nowadays, given the airline price wars, Hotwire is better for finding accommodation than airfares (see p.43), though the element of mystery remains as to what you are actually agreeing to. And though they promise to cut up to 75 percent off published rates, prices are by no means always the lowest you'll find. It's a generally reliable source of budget accommodation, however, and although you don't know the name of your hotel until you've agreed to pay, the risk isn't that high. User reviews and hints on the **www.betterbidding.com** message boards (see p.25) can give a good idea as to what's on offer, and the site itself presents a map, carved into geographical areas – with some information about each – so you can choose where you'd like to stay. Specify your required dates to get a list of rates for a selection of nameless hotels, along with a run-down of their amenities and customer reviews where applicable. Then, if you're ready, simply go ahead and book online.

Laterooms

www.laterooms.com

UK-produced database of discounted late availabilities on a wide range of accommodation, with sections for hotels (including guesthouses and B&Bs) and holiday rentals (gîtes, apartments, condos and villas). Most properties are in the UK, but the US, Italy, France, Germany, New Zealand, India and Spain are well represented too, and there are a few hotels each in a longer list of countries. Search by town or region and refine your choice by opting to see only big savers, budget beds, best deals, four/five-stars or hotels with disabled access – unlike many of these sites, the results aren't limited to chains. Rates are conveniently quoted for each night of your stay rather than as a total amount. For hotels you can search from the same day to three weeks in advance of your stay; rental listings, on the other hand, can be viewed up to a year ahead. Most places offer online booking.

Lodgingdiscounts.com

www.lodgingdiscounts.com

Good discounts and lots of choices on this bare bones US-based discount reservations site. Search results – for North American destinations, at least – are user friendly and up to date, quoting full address and nightly rates even before linking you to more details. Other countries covered have less detail, though the discounts can be good. You can also search for printable discount coupons from individual hotels at your destination.

Priceline

www.priceline.com (North America) and **www.priceline.co.uk (UK)**

Major travel auction site, dealing in flights, rental cars and hotels. Tell them where and when you want to go, in which area of town you want to stay, select a star rating, state how much you're willing to pay for a room, plug in your credit card details and they'll get back to you within an hour. There are major catches: you have to buy if they come up with a match; you're not told which hotel you'll be staying in until after you've bought it (they deal mostly with chains); and all deals are non-negotiable and non-refundable. But if price is your priority and you're a gambler at heart, then it's a good option. Both sites allow you to search in Europe, North America, Mexico, the Caribbean and Asia (which includes Australasia!) and to request more than one room. Local hotel taxes are added to the price, along with a small booking fee (always £5 on the British site). If you are using the North American site, same day bookings are generally available at American hotels until 6pm on the day. The UK site usually takes bookings up to a day in advance.

Quikbook

www.quikbook.com

Good-looking, user-friendly site offering low rates at hotels throughout North America, Mexico and the Caribbean. Rates are quoted per day for multi-night stays and same-day bookings are possible. Usefully, you can also reserve more than one room at once – even if dates and types of room need to be different. Best of all, usually no prepayment is required and where it is, cancellations or changes incur a fee of just $10. If you find a lower rate on the same room within 48 hours, they'll refund the difference. Before keying in your dates you can also see a map showing all the Quikbook hotels in each city, with full information on each. Depending on your destination the choice may not always be that wide, but this excellent site is always worth a first look.

Travelocity

www.travelocity.com (North America) and www.travelocity.co.uk (UK)

Both Travelocity sites work beautifully if you're looking to stay in North America, less so if you're heading off elsewhere. For the US and Canada the fast and efficient search engine has the edge over its competitors, and the "GoodBuy" rates – which will refund the difference if you find the same room cheaper anywhere else, but require full prepayment, and carry a $25 penalty for changes or cancellations – prove to be among the lowest you'll find. (Even so, it's still worth checking the deals offered on other sites to see if it's possible to shave off a few dollars.) Travelocity also carries a growing database of travellers' reviews of specific properties. When it comes to booking hotels outside North America, the choice tends to be more limited, with search results listed in apparently random order and the big US-based chains over-represented even when their nearest hotel is fifty miles or more from your chosen destination.

Travelweb

www.travelweb.com

Discounted rates at more than 10,000 (mostly upscale chain) hotels in hundreds of cities, predominantly in the US. Enter your destination, dates (they accept same-day bookings in the US) and number of guests (only one room per booking). Refined searches allow you to specify the area of town, star rating, hotel name and so on. Results come up in a random list, so it's important to scan the full range; i-DEAL rates offer up to 50 percent off published prices, but can often still seem quite high. However, if, within 24 hours, you find a pre-tax rate lower than the lowest i-DEAL rate for the same room, then Travelweb will refund the difference.

Directories and booking sites

Accommodation Search Engine Network

www.ase.net

With links to around 150,000 hotels, this admirable site, fuelled by a highly efficient search engine, comes up with matches in some pretty obscure locations. It also boasts some handy extras, including a fast track from the home page to hotels in major destinations such as London, New York and Paris, Disney World and Yellowstone National Park. After selecting a destination and choosing a currency (click the "Languages" tab), you can set a sophisticated range of preferences, depending on how important it is to have a certain budget, a central location, or such like, to pull up a customized list of possibilities. Reviews, as well as featuring photos, maps and a rundown of amenities, provide links to as many Websites as are relevant (often hosted by other accommodation sites, or local tourist boards) so you can compare rates and descriptions. Log in (you'll need a user name and password) to store your favourites and jot down notes. All this and swift, secure online booking.

Hotelguide.com

www.hotelguide.com

Though the directory itself – with more than 85,000 properties in 200 countries, from golf resorts to guesthouses – isn't the best out there, neither is it the worst, and is certainly worth including for its informative email newsletter, Hotel Talk, which features articles, readers' questions and recommendations, along with news of special deals around the world. The site allows you to search by destination or in more detail by budget and facilities, business services and so on; results come as a no-frills list that you click for more details.

QIXO

www.qixo.com

The "Quest for Impossibly eXcellent Offers", though best known for its airfare searches (see p.44), is also useful when it comes to booking a hotel; plug in your dates and destination (with more options on the advanced search) to retrieve a list of options, with full details and nightly rates. You have to have an American credit card to book.

Chains

For **links** to hotel chains around the world, go to **www.cheapnights.com/general/hotel_chains.html**.

Accor

www.accorhotel.com

With more than 38,000 hotels in more than ninety countries, the Accor group includes Europe's Etap and Formule 1 chains and slightly more luxurious Ibis hotels, along with the more upmarket Sofitel, Novotel, Mercure and Thalassa hotels and US cheapies Motel 6 and Red Roof. You can search by country or town, or for hotels along a driving route from one country to another (complete with door-to-door directions), or by keying in a place of interest or postal address near which you'd like to stay. Reviews come with $360°$ tours, but you need to have started the booking process before you discover how much they want you to pay.

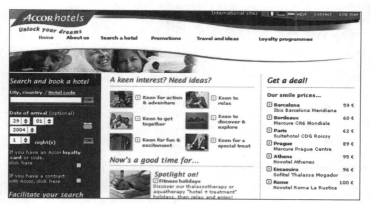

Major US chains and hotel groups

Baymont Inns

www.baymontinns.com

The reliable US cheapie Budgetel has moved slightly up-market to become the Baymont, with rooms starting at around $60.

Best Western

www.bestwestern.com

Best Western is the largest hotel chain in the world; the site has a worldwide directory of its reliably clean, affordable hotels.

Choice Hotels

www.hotelchoice.com

Major group of mid-priced US lodgings, including **Comfort Inn**, **Econolodge**, **Quality Inn**, **Clarion**, **Sleep Inn** and **Rodeway Inn**.

Days Inn

www.daysinn.com

Inexpensive US hotels that pop up around the world.

Hilton Worldwide

www.hilton.com

The swanky Hilton is now a worldwide group, including the less expensive chains **Doubletree**, **Embassy Suites** and **Hampton Inn**.

Howard Johnson

www.hojo.com

Established, low- to mid-price chain with more than 500 franchises in twenty countries.

Intercontinental Hotels

www.ichotelsgroup.com

Worldwide group that includes **Crowne Plaza**, **Holiday Inn** and **Staybridge Suites**.

La Quinta

www.lq.com

Around 300 vaguely Hispanic-themed motels and suite hotels throughout the US, many of them in Texas and the West.

Marriott Hotels

www.marriott.com

Mid-market to up-market US chain whose "family" includes **Renaissance Hotels**, **Courtyard**, **Residence Inn** and **Fairfield Inn**.

Motel 6

www.motel6.com

Part of the Accor group (see p.67), this classic roadside chain, where they "leave the light on for you", has more than 800 reliable, low-priced motels in the continental US.

Radisson

www.radisson.com

Posh hotels around the world.

Ramada

www.ramada.com

With Inns and Plazas throughout North America, Ramada runs the gamut of cheapies to business-class towers.

Red Carpet Inns/Scottish Inns

www.reservahost.com

No-fuss cheapies concentrated in the central and eastern US.

Red Roof Inns

www.redroof.com

More than 360 motels in 49 US states. So you can indeed "always stop at red". Part of the Accor group (see p.67).

Select Inn

www.selectinn.com

Few frills but good prices in Minnesota, North Dakota and Wisconsin.

Starwood Hotels

www.starwoodhotels.com

Includes **Westin**, **Sheraton** and the newer, hipper (some say pretentious) **W hotels**.

Bed and breakfast

See also the newsgroup **rec.travel.bed+breakfast.**

Bedandbreakfast.com

www.bedandbreakfast.com

Comprehensive directory of more than 27,000 B&Bs around the world (20,000 of them in the US). An intelligent and speedy search facility pulls up scores of possibles, whether you key in a city name or click on a map of the US. Member B&Bs are covered most extensively, but you can also find out a lot about non-members. Though it's possible to make a reservation request or book through the site, in most cases you can contact the owner direct. Check the message boards for honest opinions of some of the B&Bs featured on the site.

InnSite

www.innsite.com

Big directory of B&Bs that lets you search by country, city, keyword or from a huge number of offbeat options (cats on site, canopy beds, espresso bars nearby ...). Reviews come with contact details, rates and so on (some offer discounts to InnSite users), and some have ratings calculated from visitor reports. You can make reservation requests through the site, or contact properties direct – in most cases there are links to the B&B's site, which is where you are most likely to find photos. Innsite's own forum is usually full of questions and fewer answers; best to follow the hotlink to the newsgroup **rec.travel.bed+breakfast.**

Lanier Travel Guides

www.lanierbb.com

Published by hotel guidebook writer Pamela Lanier, this is a searchable database of more than 44,000 characterful accommodation listings – many of them B&Bs, inns and guesthouses – mostly in the US. You can't book through the site, but it does provide details of themed packages and special offers.

Distinctive accommodation

Design hotels

www.designhotels.com

Ice-cool site for people who believe that hotels are the new black, with a bookable database of hip urban hotels around the world. There's not that much hard information,

just thumbnail pictures and PR reviews, but you can find out more by clicking the "Book It" link – and besides, if all you're after is somewhere to see and be seen at one of the world's coolest destinations, who wants to bother with details?

EcoRes

www.eco-res.com

Reservations at eco-lodges – a broad term, including wildlife and kayak camps, hilltribe lodges, mountain retreats and yurts, among others – around the world. You can search by destination or category to read information on each lodge, including details of current package deals (quoted in US dollars). Bookings are made by emailing the site.

1st Travelers Choice

www.virtualcities.com

The strength of this rather old-fashioned looking directory is in the kind of place it lists – no chain hotels here, just B&Bs, country inns, boutique hotels, dude ranches and vacation rentals in North America and Mexico (with a scattering in the Caribbean, Africa, Australia and Europe). Search by state or region or by theme – the site suggests pet-friendly inns, ski resorts, good places for romantic breaks, and so on. Lodging details are available, but you need to contact the owners direct to book.

GoNOMAD

www.gonomad.com/lodgings/lodgings.html

Excellent directory of unique and alternative lodgings around the world – from eco-lodges and igloos to paradores, caves and monasteries. Top picks are organized by region, with detailed reviews and contact details. You can also use pull-down menus to search by lodging type and country. Prices range from budget (a raft on the River Kwai) to expense account (a 115-foot cypress tower on Kenya's Lake Naivasha). Plus guides to farmstays, retreats, follies and home exchanges, with relevant contact information.

Organic Holidays

www.organicplacestostay.com

Bare-bones but efficient site listing a good selection of organic hotels, B&Bs and farmstays around the world. Clicking on the map or the list of countries pulls up reviews with photos, contact details, and tempting accounts of the delicious food served or grown. Though the majority of listings are in the UK and Europe, you'll find fabulous lodgings in destinations as exotic as Morocco, Sri Lanka, Hawaii and Peru.

Organic Places to Stay

Accommodation on
organic farms and
organic smallholdings
(includes self-catering and catered) ...

Hostels

To ask advice from other hostellers, check the forums on **www.hostels.com** below. You can also visit a number of newsgroups (see p.18) including **uk.rec.youth-hostel**, **rec.travel.europe**, **rec.travel.usa-canada** and **rec.travel.budget.backpack**.

Hostelling International (HI)

www.iyhf.org

Official HI site offering online booking at 500 of the association's main hostels. Though you don't need to be a member to book a bed, you do need to join before sleeping in it. The site allows you to search for hostels worldwide and tells you how to join (membership gives you discounts on, among other things, travel passes, guidebooks and visitor attractions), either in advance or at individual hostels. All YHA hostels are part of the HI organization; you can check them out in more detail at **www.yha.org.uk**, **www.syha.org.uk**, **www.irelandyha.org**, **www.yha.org.nz** and **www.yha.com.au**, among others.

Hostels.com

www.hostels.com

Superb one-stop resource for anyone interested in travelling on a budget, including older travellers and families. Independently run (which means it doesn't necessarily endorse the hostels on the site), this is primarily useful for its searchable database of thousands of hostels worldwide, with links to sites where available. Some you can reserve directly from here, but there are no reviews, so make sure to do a little more research – perhaps by asking around on the bulletin board, or simply by emailing the place direct – before booking.

Hostels of Europe

www.hostelseurope.com

Searchable directory of more than 450 independent hostels and budget hotels around Europe, with information on rates and facilities and links to individual sites. You can book online, and order a Hostels of Europe discount card; this gives 5–15 percent discounts at most of the hostels, as well as reductions on tours, activities, transport, Internet access and museum fees.

Hostel World

www.hostelworld.com

Online bookings for a selection of hostels, budget accommodation and package tours around the world. The list is ever expanding, but at present you'll do best if you're looking to stay in a city. They also offer brief city and country guides ("Infozone" and "Things2do").

House swapping and hospitality

House swapping is one area where the Net comes into its own. Joining an agency offline you have to pay for a directory, send letters and make calls overseas, and sit around waiting for responses that might never come. **Internet-only services**, on the other hand, are usually cheaper, and as listings can be altered immediately online, their lists are often more up to date. They tend to lean heavily towards North American destinations, however, so anyone who wants to venture further afield may prefer to plump for established companies, such as Homelink, which use print directories as well as online services – their reputations also mean that they tend to attract the most experienced and reliable home owners.

Global Freeloaders

www.globalfreeloaders.com

Produced by an eager young Australian to harness the hospitable streak in the "travelling community", this site matches travellers in need of a bed with others willing to put them up. Enter your destination and dates to pull up a list of potential hosts, with information about who they are and what they have to offer. Once you've chosen, you fill out a form, which is forwarded by the site, and wait for the hosts to email you back. The catch, of course, is that you have to return the hospitality to other global freeloaders. The registration period is six months, during which you can block out any time you don't feel like welcoming visitors, and the service is entirely free. While members range in age from 18 to 70, apparently the average freeloader is in their mid-30s. You can specify any age preferences upon registering.

Holi-Swaps

www.holi-swaps.com

This site's amateurish appearance and spelling mistakes belie its efficient house swapping service; it's widely used, and responses tend to be fast. If you're looking for a place, browse the list of worldwide property owners offering swaps or rentals, and email them direct (via the site). You'll do better, however, making a swap if you list your own property. This costs £25/$37 for a year, and you write your own entry, which can be as long as it needs, with none of the abbreviations used in print directories. You can also update it whenever you like, adding photos or links if you want. Once you've posted, your details are emailed to a list of active current members so you can get going quickly. You can also ask to be sent new offers as they arise.

HomeExchange.com

www.homeexchange.com

Internet-only site offering some 6000 home exchanges, hospitality schemes or holiday rentals in more than seventy countries (around half of the swaps are based in the US). Though anyone can access the directory and email owners without having to post their own information, users who pay to list details of their property and their requirements receive benefits including access to the most up-to-date lists and email updates on upcoming swaps. The search mechanism on this site is one of the best – you can opt to find exchangers who want to stay in your area, homes in places you want to go, swappers who are looking for certain dates, or all of these. If you don't succeed in exchanging during your first year, your second is free.

HomeLink International

www.homelink.org

HomeLink's slick site reflects its clout as the world's largest and longest established home exchange organization, with thousands of properties in more than fifty countries. The home page takes you to your country's own site, each of which has a searchable database of properties. Though you can't fast track to particular destinations within a country or region, you can search for places on or near the sea, and click a checklist of facilities. You can also opt to see only properties added in the last week or 48 hours. Entries themselves read like truncated lists of amenities (a hangover from HomeLink's roots as a huge, hard-copy directory), but they're accessible enough, and most have colour photos. To access contact details you'll need to join; members receive three printed directories, and their listings are kept online for at least a year. American travellers can join online, but if you're looking at the UK site you'll need to email or call.

Servas

http://servas.org

International voluntary organization promoting world peace with a homestay programme involving 14,000 hosts in more than 130 countries. As a host, you'll provide a bed for two nights or longer, and share an evening meal with your guest. When the trip is over guests have to write a report of their stay. The site has contact details for coordinators in your area.

Vacation rentals

See also the discount sites reviewed on pp.62–66, most of which have sections devoted to self-catering accommodation, and the home-swap sites listed above, which often have separate sections for rentals.

Cyberrentals.com

www.cyberrentals.com

Chunky database of privately owned vacation rentals, the vast majority of which are in the US. Click on the name of a state or a country, or enter a town name, and you'll pull up a list of matches with thumbnail descriptions including number of bedrooms and the nightly or weekly rate. Then click for more details, including links to Websites, and book direct with the owner. You can also search for award-winning properties and pet-friendly homes by clicking the links on the home page.

Holiday-rentals.com

www. holiday-rentals.com

Well-established directory of some 6000 private rental properties (from barns to ski chalets) in more than 50 countries – there are almost 2000 in Spain alone, 1400 in France, and hundreds more in the UK, Italy and Florida. You can search by destination, facilities or keywords, using the advanced search to specify price, property type and suitability for kids. Under "Holiday Ideas" they've grouped properties into themes such as city centre, villas with pools and mountain properties. Matches come with full details and at least four photos. To return to a particular entry you'll need to note the property number, as there's no suitcase facility. Booking is done direct with owners, or, occasionally, through the site. They also detail special offers, and link to car rental companies and flights.

Vacation Rentals By Owner

www.vrbo.com

Nearly 19,000 private villas and apartments around the world. Click on the name of the US state or the country you're interested in to pull up a list, then click for more details (not always including photographs). You then email the owner direct to book. Many of the properties are special, and prices aren't always that low, but the broad selection makes this site a good place to start.

Embassies and visas

Bureau of Consular Affairs

http://travel.state.gov

This government site, run by the US Department of State, provides the definitive official lists of visa and/or entry requirements both for US citizens travelling to any country in the world, and for foreign travellers coming to the United States. As well as contact details for the relevant foreign embassies and consulates in the US, it also offers links to US representatives abroad, and carries the latest travel warnings and advisories.

Embassyworld

www.embassyworld.com

Elaborate directory-cum-search-engine that enables users to find any embassy or consulate, either by the government it represents or by the country in which it is located. If you need to find the Brazilian embassy in Japan, for example, this is the place to look. However, there's no guarantee that the embassy you require will have its own Website; you may have to settle for a phone number or address.

Express Visa Service

www.expressvisa.com

Express Visa Service, which has offices in seven US cities, handles passport and visa applications for US citizens in need of urgent travel documentation, and can also deal with visa requests on behalf of non-US nationals.

Passport Express

www.passportexpress.com

Commercial US agency that guarantees to obtain or renew passports for eligible US citizens as quickly as you need them; their Website holds all the necessary forms. UK citizens can also use the service, though it will usually take five days, or sometimes longer.

United Kingdom Passport Service

www.ukpa.gov.uk

This official UK site enables British residents to apply online to renew, change or obtain their UK passports. If you have at least two weeks before you travel it's possible to request an application pack via the site, and with four weeks you can apply online. Anyone who needs an urgent response is advised to head straight for their nearest passport office. The site also explains the requirements for obtaining British citizenship, details visa requirements for overseas travel, and lists all their offices, as well as offering an express service if required.

Visa Connection

www.visaconnection.com

Canadian visa expediter, with offices in Vancouver, Calgary, Ottawa and Toronto, whose Website sets out visa requirements for Canadian travellers all over the globe, and provides printable forms to help speed up your application.

The Visaservice

www.visaservice.co.uk

The London-based Visaservice company processes visa and passport applications for UK residents travelling abroad, and can also help visitors to the UK both with UK immigration and visa requirements.

Visiting Australia – Visas

www.immi.gov.au

The official Australian government guide to entry and visa regulations for prospective foreign visitors to Australia, which includes details of, and the ability to apply online for, the "Electronic Travel Authority" (**www.eta.immi.gov.au**), which precludes the need for a traditional printed visa.

Health and safety

Blood Care Foundation

www.bloodcare.org.uk

If you're travelling in places where
health care isn't what it might be,
you'll want to check the site of the
Blood Care Foundation, a fine charity
that sends screened blood and sterile
transfusion equipment to members
wherever they are in the world, and
offers special consultancy services for
on-site medical staff. Annual membership costs £36, plus a registration fee
of £30 (payable once only), or you
can get short-term memberships
from £8.50 for a month. You can't
join online, but they provide all
contact details.

Centers for Disease Control and Prevention

www.cdc.gov/travel

Excellent US-based site run by the federal CDC. Though it's most useful for checking
inoculation requirements, other good features include health and safety ratings for all the
major US cruise ships – marks are given out of 100, with details of every dirty plate and rusty
pipe. You can also get the scoop on outbreaks and trouble spots around the globe, download
or order a range of CDC books and reports. Good links, too, for various health organizations.

Foreign and Commonwealth Office

www.fco.gov.uk/travel

The FCO provides up-to-the-minute news of trouble spots and safety issues for British
travellers. The country-specific advice notes – detailing political unrest, lawlessness, violence,
natural disasters, epidemics, anti-British demonstrations, and aircraft safety – are up to

date and useful. You can search for countries using a drop-down menu, and subscribe to receive news by email. For an equivalent service, travellers from the US should check **http://travel.state.gov/travel_warnings.html.**

Flyana.com

www.flyana.com

The Website of Diana Fairechild, US author and champion of air travellers' rights. She knows all there is to know about the causes and cures of jet lag, phobias, air rage (lack of oxygen, apparently), DVT, skypoxia (yes, really), ear agony, etc. Though you might balk at stuffing your nostrils with vegetable oil and chanting affirmations, most of it makes a lot of sense, and is lively reading in a gruesome sort of way.

International Association of Medical Assistance for Travelers

www.iamat.org

IAMAT advises of health risks, diseases, immunization requirements and sanitary, environmental and climatic conditions around the world. You can join online, for free (though they welcome donations) to get various useful bits and bobs, including an immunization chart which covers 200 countries, climate charts and risk charts for malaria and other diseases.

Medical Advisory Service for Travellers Abroad

www.masta.org

Run by MASTA, based at London's School of Hygiene and Tropical Medicine, this authorative site has all the information and advice you need on potential health hazards in far-flung corners of the world, and a rundown of recommended and required immunizations. You can buy health products online, including repellents, water purifiers and medical equipment, with a Web discount of 5 percent. Under "Travel Tools" the jet lag calculator is a handy little gizmo: type in your starting place and destination, the direction you are travelling, the length of stay and your normal sleep times, and they'll advise you on how to minimize jet lag at your destination. The chat room, dominated by tales of swellings, sand flies and small pox, makes compelling reading.

MedicAlert

www.medicalert.org and **www.medicalert.org.uk**

MedicAlert bracelets, which detail health and personal information including medical conditions or drug allergies, are particularly useful when travelling abroad. You pay a one-off fee for the bracelet, plus a smaller annual membership; there's no way to join online, but you can download an application form.

Travel Health Online

www.tripprep.com

This user-friendly US-based site provides detailed health profiles for more than 220 countries, comprising country information, vaccination requirements, malaria risks and the like, with a consular fact sheet for each one. You'll need to register. Everything is covered here, from precautions around insects, food and drink, to how to avoid crime and deal with medical emergencies (the list of recommended travel health providers around the world comes with full contact details). The directory of diseases, which covers some pretty obscure ailments, is a hypochondriac's dream. All this plus maps, foreign entry requirements (for US visitors) and advice for travellers with special needs.

World Health Organization

www.who.int/en

Though it's not specifically geared towards travel health, the impressive, multilingual site of the World Health Organization tells you all you could ever want to know about every communicable disease under the sun, including details on vaccination requirements, up-to-date disease outbreak news, and advice on how to avoid and treat potential health hazards when travelling abroad. Along with news stories and a searchable database of reports and features on travel health, you can also access hundreds of WHO documents.

Insurance

Travel insurance is one area where you can make good savings on the Web. But you need to shop around, as rates and coverage vary widely, as does site usability; some demand reams of personal contact info before they will even hint at a quote.

Financial Information Net Directory

www.find.co.uk/insurance/NT

FIND lists all the travel insurers you can access on the Web. With short reviews of many of them, and hotlinks to them all, this is a good start if you're wanting to do lots of research and obsessively shop around.

GoSure.com

www.gosure.com/quote/quote.asp

Internet-only travel insurers, providing single-trip, backpacker and annual multi-trip policies on a very easy-to-use site. Key in the number of people in your party, where you're going and the duration of your trip. You can also choose extras and reduced cost options; quotes appear almost instantly, and if you want to buy, all details are confirmed before you go ahead. Their rate comparison chart shows that their prices are consistently cheaper than many of the other major providers (but it's always best to check how far the comparison dates back). Policies are emailed to you within fifteen minutes, and there's a cooling-off period of fourteen days.

Insuremytrip.com

http://insuremytrip.com

North American travel insurance comparison site offering around 50 different plans from a variety of companies. To compare policies head straight for the quotes page; real-time ordering means that you are emailed a confirmation almost immediately, then the policy is mailed to you.

Leading Edge

www.leadedge.co.uk

Here the speciality is backpacker (up to age 40), multi- or single-trip cover (up to 45) or snowcover (up to 55), and you'll find some good prices. Online policies are emailed instantly, and can be bought right up to the moment of travel. Cooling off period is seven days.

Rough Guides Travel Insurance

www.roughguidesinsurance.com

Rough Guides' own travel insurance is available for anyone, of any nationality and any age, travelling anywhere in the world. Unlike many policies, the Rough Guides schemes are calculated by the day, so if you're traveling for 27 days rather than a month, that's all you pay for. If you intend to be away for the whole year, the Adventurer policy will cover you for 365 days. The elegant onscreen premium calculator will work out exactly what you have to buy (and it's normally a very competitive rate), but online ordering is only available to UK citizens, and even for them online applications are dealt with during normal office hours.

The Travel Insurance Agency

www.travelinsurers.com

Though it looks a bit rough, this fast and efficient site offers a nice variety of policies, including one for people already on the road and another for budget travellers. Quotes are given instantly, without you having to key in any personal information, and online ordering isn't too time consuming. Guaranteed 48-hour delivery, and a fourteen-day money-back option.

Travel Insurance Online

www.travel-insurance-online.com

Competitively priced policies for single-trips, long-stays, and a "young traveller" for the under-45s. There's no shenanigans here; type in the number of people travelling, your destination and dates (it's possible to buy on the day of travel), and you'll get an instant quote. Policies are sent online and, if there's time, by mail, and if you change your mind within fourteen days they'll give you a refund. Links from the home page direct you to sister company **www.annual-insurance.com**, which specializes in annual multi-trip policies available to UK residents.

Travel Insurance Services

www.travelinsure.com

North American travel insurance that is available to nationals, green-card holders, temporary residents and international visitors. Online ordering, and if you don't want to wait for the policy certificate you can print it from the site.

Currency and money

American Express

www.americanexpress.com/travel

US travellers can order up to $1000 in traveller's cheques online (plus $15 handling fee and a shipping fee); UK travellers hoping to buy cheques should log on to **http://home3.americanexpress.com/uk/homepage.asp** for details of Amex services in Britain. For local ATMs, check the locator under **http://maps.americanexpress.com/expresscash/mqinterconnect?link=home** and key in your location; you'll pull up maps and detailed directions to the nearest ATM. To locate your nearest Amex office, with address, phone number and opening hours (plus mapping features for North American cities) go to **http://travel.americanexpress.com/travel/personal/resources/tso**.

Mastercard

www.mastercard.com

The ATM locator finds Mastercard/Cirrus cash machines around the globe – though only those in the USA come with small maps and full directions. To find them anywhere else in the world entails a lot of clicking, and results in a list of addresses in random order. You can also access numbers to call in case of emergency, but again this involves a lot of clicking.

Oanda.com

www.oanda.com/channels/traveler

This huge venture quotes daily exchange rates for 164 currencies. Useful features include printable "cheat sheets" – converters for any combination of currencies you like – and customizable expense reports, great for business travellers, that automatically calculate how much you've spent in your own currency. US travellers can buy cash and traveller's cheques online, with free shipping for two-day delivery. There's a message board, a before-you-go checklist, and a fast link to a VISA ATM locator. And if you're curious about what currency they use in Bhutan, or in Haiti, they've produced a handy little device that will tell you (it's the ngultrum and the gourde respectively, if you were wondering). Palm Pilot users can download the currency converter and cheat sheet, and the currency converter is also available for mobile phones.

This Is Money

www.thisismoney.com/tourist.htm

General money advice site from the UK, with a list of all the major rates against the pound, updated daily, and sensible advice on taking money abroad, what to look for when buying travel insurance, and how to go about claiming compensation for holiday disasters.

Travlang

www.travlang.com/money

Simple money conversion for travellers: click on any two currencies to draw up the current exchange rates between them, with a graph showing that same exchange rate over the last four, eight or twelve months, and a calculator that allows you to convert arbitrary amounts to and from each currency. They also produce a printable exchange rate converter for the chosen currencies, some information about them, and photos of the major notes and coins. Pity about the glut of adverts.

Universal Currency Converter

www.xe.com/ucc/full.shtml

Updated every minute, this easy-to-use site gives the exchange rates for more than 180 currencies and features a number of useful services including the "Personal Currency Assistant" (**www.xe.com/pca**), a pop-up currency exchange window that floats on screen as long as you need it. Business travellers should check also **www.xe.com/tec**, a travel expenses calculator that takes into account dates of transactions and credit card charges to estimate how much you can claim. At **www.xe.com/ict** you can create cross-rate tables for major currencies in the base currency of your choice, and query rates for dates as far back as 1995. All services are available on your mobile, Palm Pilot or pager.

Weather guides

Accuweather

www.accuweather.com

This US site usually takes a while to load – hardly surprising when you take into account its huge visual content. With satellite maps of the world and animatable radar maps of all the US regions, it also boasts golf maps (showing wind and lightning) and ski maps (snow, ice and rain, plus five-day forecasts for the major US resorts). The "travel" section, which covers the US only, has maps for travelling by land (storms and snow, six-day interstate forecasts), by air (flight delays) and sea (wind, hurricanes). One area that doesn't use maps to best advantage, however, is the world weather forecasting facility. Searching by destination either pulls a result or it doesn't; a map, showing all places covered, would allow you to make a second choice if you didn't get a match for your first. Forecasts themselves span fifteen days and include "realfeel" maximum and minimum temperatures. Creating a local page allows you to access weather information for your home town – or wherever you choose – but climate charts (which you can use to predict conditions when planning a holiday) are only accessible to "premium users", who pay a small subscription fee.

BBC Weather

www.bbc.co.uk/weather

Very good, user-friendly site with a number of handy tools, including interactive maps, detailed world forecasts, satellite and radar images. Under "Travel Weather", you can read general climate information for hundreds of cities. They're arranged alphabetically rather than shown on a map, so if you're checking the weather in a small resort, look at a map first and come prepared with a few back-up destinations in case your first choice isn't covered. Under "Sports Weather" you can check weather forecasts for major upcoming sports events and skiing conditions around the world.

CNN

www.cnn.com/weather

Five-day forecasts for more than 10,000 cities, with a good range of destinations. Each forecast includes minimum and maximum temperatures, humidity, wind, and sunrise/sunset. Plus numerous radar (US only) and satellite maps (worldwide).

Intellicast

www.intellicast.com

Concerning itself with "weather for active lives", this colossal US-based site is a great tool for anyone planning on spending time outdoors in the States. Groaning with radar and satellite maps, it offers information on everything from kite-flying conditions to national park forecasts. The home page gathers seasonal features from throughout the site – allergy reports, storm warnings, beach conditions and travel delays in summer; snow and flood warnings and wind-chill reports in winter. US ten-day forecasts – click on the nationwide weather map – bring up nicely designed and detailed charts; you can then use the menus at the top of the page to pull up separate maps detailing particular conditions.

Snow-forecast

www.snow-forecast.com

Three-day snow forecast maps cover more than thirty countries, including Japan, Bolivia and Iceland, while detailed three-day world ski resort forecasts show snow depths, rain, freezing levels and wind, and, usefully, real temperatures on the slopes themselves. You can also find information on the nearest resort to your chosen destination (where snow is forecast; where it will be mostly sunny; where it will be below freezing). There are hundreds of resorts detailed, and the list is growing all the time. There's also a world snow overview, which pinpoints where snow and rain will fall in the next three days, and you can sign up for snow alerts by email (free for one resort), or WAP forecasts on your mobile.

Wunderground

www.wunderground.com

Real-time weather around the world, with detailed three- and seven-day forecasts for most places you can think of. If the destination you're after doesn't show on another site, there's a good chance you'll find it here. Local US forecasts (use the Fast Forecast search to get straight to your destination) are even more detailed, with radar and satellite maps, marine forecasts and allergy information. To look up what weather you can expect when on holiday, search for the city you're interested in, choose a date in history, and read daily weather readings for every day since 1994.

Kit and gear

See also the online shops listed at **http://ricksteves.com** (reviewed on p.11) for bags and accessories.

The Brasher Boot Company

www.brasher.co.uk

Athlete Christopher Brasher, designer of the "boots that bring happiness to your feet" spends as much time on how to get the best fit and how to care for his remarkably comfortable footwear as on insisting you buy. Half catalogue, half mission statement, the site includes details of the Chris Brasher Trust, whereby a fee from the sale of every shoe – or sock, or pole, or whatever – goes towards preserving the wild places of Britain. No online ordering, but every product is detailed with clear photos, and you can search to find your nearest retailer. Customers from outside the UK can buy by mail order.

Christine Columbus

www.christinecolumbus.com

Rather wonderful site selling an amazing range of gewgaws for female travellers, ranging from the genteel – a feminine urinary director – to the downright indispensable – wrinkle remover spray (for clothes, sadly), lightweight luggage and specialist guidebooks. Though in truth many of these products are suited to either gender, and there's even a "For Him" section (retractable extension cords, weather alert radios and the like), the site is permeated with a feel-good, all-gals-together ambience right down to the travellers' tales and packing tips. There's an emphasis on security, with products that you don't see elsewhere; check out the half-slip with zippered pockets concealed under the lacy hem, for example. Based in the US, they accept international orders, but you'll need to email them to find out the shipping charges.

Craghoppers

www.craghoppers.com

Glossy online catalogue for Craghoppers' innovative range of extra-lightweight and crease-resistant gear. The site features everything from skirts to fleeces, waterproof rucksacks and a selection of walking poles. No online ordering, but British travellers can enter their postcode to pull up a list of local stockists. Don't miss the links to outdoorsy Websites in the UK (National Trust, Ramblers Association, etc).

Eagle Creek

www.eaglecreek.com

This San Diego-based outfit produces a wide range of really useful, well-designed travel products including various handy travel packs. There's no online buying, but once you've browsed the range (including some nifty animated product rotations) you can click on a link to be sent to an online dealer. Buying Eagle Creek gear you have the added satisfaction of knowing that some of the profits go to good causes, including Eagle Creek's Children of Nepal fund, an orphanage in Mexico, and an American Food Bank. There's a special section for travel stories, checklists and packing tips.

Independent Travel Stores Association (ITSA)

www.travelstores.com

Online members' directory of a group of North American travel stores. Between them, they should be able to provide any guidebook, map or travel-related product you may require.

Leatherman Tools Online

www.shop-for-leatherman-tools.com

Leatherman knives have come to overtake the trusty Swiss Army Knife as the multi-function tool of choice for intrepid campers. Each of the twelve is versatile and ergonomic, from the Micra (nine tools including scissors, tweezers, nailfile and three screwdrivers) to the phenomenal 17-tool Wave, which has everything from pliers to screwdrivers to wire cutters, and they all come with a 25-year warranty. You can have a good look at them all, with full details and user reviews, and buy them via **Amazon.com.**

Magellan's Travel Supplies

www.magellans.com

Magellan's Santa Barbara store has got a reputation as one of the best places in the US to get state-of-the-art travel products. The user-friendly site offers their full range of high-quality, low-priced luggage and travel clothing – with a wider than usual choice for women – but where they really excel is in accessories. This is the place to buy superb surgical rubber braid clotheslines, lightweight drawstring shoe bags, leakproof folding cups, modem and phone accessories, adapters and converters and much more. Check the regular clearance sales for bargains. Online ordering is secure, your goods are shipped within 24 hours within the US (or within 48 hours for international orders), and all products are backed by an unrestricted guarantee. If you have queries, log on to their Live Help facility, and have an online chat with a member of staff (remember the time difference if you're calling from outside the US).

One Bag

www.onebag.com

This "Compendium of Opinions and Ideas on the Art of Travel" from Canadian Doug Dyment is one of the best travellers' sites out there, a must for businesspeople and budget backpackers alike. You'll find everything you ever needed to know on what to pack, what to pack it in (guess what: just one bag), and how to pack it (the fine art of "bundle wrapping"), along with genuinely useful travel tips and dozens of reviewed links. The packing list is bible-sized; a bookmark menu allows you to get to the sections you need, and a downloadable one-page checklist version is provided. Recommended products, from knives to crumple-free little black dresses and guidebooks (hotlinked to Amazon), are reviewed in detail, with supplier contact information.

Recreational Equipment Inc

www.rei.com

Enormous Internet store from the US chain that specializes in sturdy gear for camping, climbing, cycling, snow sports and so on, along with clothes and boots, including several under their own brand. REI has been a co-op for more than sixty years, and though you don't need to be a member to shop here, membership (a one-off fee of $15) gets you an annual dividend of up to 10 percent of what you spent with them the previous year, plus savings on repairs and rentals at REI stores, discounts on REI Adventures trips and more. Head to **www.rei-outlet.com**, separate from the main site, if you're after bargain prices on discontinued products. Online ordering is secure, and they detail shipping charges for international orders.

Rock+Run

www.rockrun.com

Produced by Rock+Run, the British mountaineering stores, this site features a searchable database of top-quality camping and climbing gear, footwear, clothing, rucksacks, sleeping bags, wrist computers, navigation tools and the like. Prices are quoted in sterling, with a currency converter for buyers from elsewhere. A separate menu offers the latest deals. Online ordering is secure, and international shipping rates are reasonable. Even if you're not buying, this is a good site for information on climbing and safety, with travel features, weather forecasts, forums and links.

SimplyScuba

www.simplyscuba.co.uk

The biggest online dive store in the UK. Thumbs up to the user reviews, and to the loyalty scheme whereby you save "bubbles" redeemable against all non-sale gear in the range. Online ordering is secure – UK customers will usually get their stuff within 24 hours, and they ship to most places worldwide.

Tilley Endurables

www.tilley.com

This classy adventure clothing specialist, best known for floatable, unshrinkable hats, offers a selection of high-quality travel wear, which stands up to the toughest treatment, on a user-friendly site. Prices (from £44 for a hat) reflect the quality, and everything comes with a lifetime guarantee. The site has separate entrances for US, UK, Canadian and international visitors, making online ordering easy and efficient as well as secure.

On the road

D ay by day, the Internet is making it easier to stay in touch with your family, friends, or workplace, from wherever you may be on the planet.

Travellers have two principal options. Either you can carry your own **laptop** around with you, or you can pay to use publicly accessible computers on the road. Each alternative has its advantages and drawbacks, but broadly speaking, most people travelling for pleasure find it more convenient to use **cybercafes** and the like. There's no need to take your own machine just to communicate with home; it's only worth it if you're trying to keep up a more complicated working and/or social life.

For several years, it's been claimed that the imminent arrival of improved global-ranging cellular phones, enabled by WAP technology (Wireless Application Protocol), is on the point of providing an equally convenient third approach. For the moment, however, they're not quite good enough to compete.

Web-based email and storage

Whether or not they already have email back home, most travellers now prefer to use free **Web-based email** accounts (also known as "freemail") instead. Unlike an account with an ISP – for which users pay to access the Internet and thus to be able to send and receive email – with Web-based email you need only visit the appropriate Website to read your email. There's no charge, partly because the sites carry a lot of advertising, and partly because they attract potential customers themselves.

With a conventional ISP account, your own computer saves copies of all incoming and outgoing email, and you can read it whenever you choose. Web-based email, on the other hand, is stored by whoever provides the service, and you can only access it online. What's more, they'll only allow you a certain amount of memory, and they'll only keep it for a certain period; both vary according to the provider. That effectively means you can only store a limited number of messages, and that number will be further limited if you're trying to keep downloaded material as well.

By far the best known provider of Web-based email, readily accessible from any computer on the planet, is **Hotmail** (www.hotmail.com), owned by Microsoft. However, Microsoft now "freezes" any account that hasn't been used for thirty days, so if you don't check your email for more than a month, not only will you have to register again, but all your existing messages will have been deleted. In addition, Hotmail is a notorious target for spammers (senders of unwanted mass-circulation emails). Alternative options include MyRealBox (www.myrealbox.com) and FastMail (www.fastmail.fm), while both www.fepg.net and www.emailaddresses.com list countless other sources of free Web-based email accounts, ranging from Postman Pat to Manchester United. In each instance, including Hotmail, the procedure to set up an account is straightforward. Just follow the simple instructions on their Websites; all you need is a unique name and password.

A further refinement of the concept is to sign up for **free Web-based storage** as well, in order to be able to access any personal files you choose to store whenever and wherever you log on. Providers do tend to come and go, or to start charging for services that were previously free, so it's worth storing copies of your files in more than one place. Forty or so suppliers are listed on the Storage Search site (www.storagesearch.com/edrives.html). You may even have some free Web space available as part of your regular ISP account – why not use that?

Accessing your traditional email account

Depending on your ISP, once you're online at a cybercafe it will almost certainly be possible to check your usual email account. There are two types of ISP mail account, **Webmail**, which is collected by Web browsers, and **POP3**, which stands for Post Office Protocol, and is collected by email programs such as Outlook Express. If you don't know which kind you have, ask your provider.

To collect Webmail, simply go to your ISP's Website, and enter your usual details. You can obtain POP3 mail by running Outlook Express or whatever email program is available, but it's likely to involve re-configuring the program with such details as the name of your POP3 server, which you'll have obtain in advance from your ISP. Instead, it's much simpler to receive and send POP3 mail via either Yahoo or Hotmail, both of which provide straightforward instructions for users to access their usual email. Even if you have no intention of ever using a freemail account with Yahoo or Hotmail, it's worth opening one for this reason alone. Finally, the **www.thatweb.com** site promises to enable any user who tells it their email address and password to pick up their mail.

Travelling with a laptop

Most of the pros and cons of taking a **laptop** on your travels are self-evident. A computer is heavy, vulnerable to damage, and a constant security risk (be warned that airport X-ray machines are notorious locations for opportunistic laptop thefts). On the other hand, you have all your files and programs with you, and you can access them, or the Web, whenever you like.

From a communications point of view, the most obvious reason to carry your laptop is in order to access your own ISP, and thus your usual **email account**. How easy that is depends on your ISP; in fact, it's an important factor in choosing an ISP in the first place.

The central issue is whether your ISP has an **access number** – preferably toll-free, but at least local – that can be dialled from the location in which you're travelling. Otherwise, you'll have to make an expensive international phone call to your home country every time you go online. The easiest way to get round that problem is by choosing an international ISP such as AOL (**www.aol.com**), UUNET (**www.uu.net**), or AT&T Business (**www.attbusiness.net**), all of which offer worldwide coverage.

However, many smaller ISPs have banded together to form "**global roaming**" groups, which enable their members to use shared access numbers in different world destinations. Typical groups include the I-Pass Alliance (**www.ipass.com**) and GRIC (**www.gric.com**). Check with your own ISP to see whether it belongs to such a network; if it does not, it should be able to suggest some alternative. Finally, whatever kind of ISP you're using, be warned that there will almost certainly be a significant

Enterprise Connectivity Services

Linking remote and mobile workers to their business-critical information—via wired and wireless connections around the globe

surcharge for accessing your account from abroad.

Unless you're fortunate enough both to have a laptop equipped with **Wi-Fi** technology, and to be travelling in a region where you can expect to find **hotspots** (see box), the biggest question facing you will be **hardware** – how you physically connect your computer to a telephone line. Ideally, you want to be able to plug your modem directly into a phone socket. Most modems these days are equipped with an **RJ-11 phone jack**, which is the standard plug used in North America, the Far East, and other countries such as Greece, Spain, and Ireland. Machines sold elsewhere, including in the UK, tend to come with a removable clip-on adapter to suit local sockets.

Wi-Fi hotspots

The time is fast approaching, especially for travellers in the US and UK, when you'll no longer need any of the cables and adapters described above, or any technical knowhow whatsoever, to connect your laptop to the Internet. A high proportion of new laptops these days come ready equipped with some form of **Wi-Fi technology**, which enables them to make wireless connections to public networks, and in turn, the Internet. If your machine doesn't already have Wi-Fi capability (the Mac version is known as **AirPort**), then you can obtain it by buying a PC card (which slots into the side of your laptop) from major retailers for around $50/£35.

Armed with Wi-Fi, your laptop can access the Internet using so-called **hotspots**, which are dedicated transceivers placed in public locations. Most major airports in the US now have them, and they're also rapidly appearing in cafes and British motorway service stations, as well as being installed by hotels. The snag is that you can expect to pay, and often quite heavily, to use a hotspot (either by-the-hour, or via a subscription service from a company such as T-Mobile, whose hotspots can be found in many branches of Starbucks and elsewhere). That said, many independent cafes are now setting up **free Wi-Fi hotspots**, and you may even stumble across one of the growing number of non-commercial hotspots set up by enthusiasts. For a list of known hotspots, try one of the online directories:

Boingo www.boingo.com
Wifinder www.wifinder.com
Hotspot Locations www.hotspot-locations.com

Travellers in the US and Canada should therefore have no problem hooking up to hotel-room or payphone sockets; travelling anywhere else, you'll need the relevant RJ-11 adapter. The trouble is, there are dozens of different jack designs. Several of the Websites reviewed below can tell you which jack is required for which location; some can sell it to you too. You should also be able to buy adapters in local hardware or computer stores when you arrive.

If you can't get hold of the appropriate jack; or if your hotel phone not only lacks a data port, but it's wired directly into the wall; or if you simply don't know which country you're going to end up in, it's possible to strip your modem lead down to the bare wires, and hard-wire them either to a telephone or straight into a wall socket. An easier solution is to buy an **acoustic coupler**, a device costing around £80/$130 that slots into your modem at one end and clips around a telephone handset at the other, and thus avoids the need for any wires to connect at all. Advice on both methods can be found on **www.laptoptravel.com** and **www.roadnews.com**

Even once you've made a physical connection, the process of dialling the ISP number is surrounded by yet more pitfalls. First of all, some hotel and business exchanges use **digital** technology, as opposed to the analog technology used by computer modems; to put it simply, trying to dial on a digital system could well destroy your modem. A dedicated data port will always be analog, but with ordinary phones you can't spot the difference. Either check with the management each time; invest in a line tester, costing around £20/$30; or, once again, use an acoustic coupler. Secondly, phone systems may be either pulse or tone, and your modem has to be set to match. Depending on what computer and/or ISP you're using, that's done either by checking a box in the software, or by flipping a switch on the machine itself.

Further potential complications include having to dial an initial number to get an outside line, and the possible inability of your machine to recognize an unfamiliar dialling tone. Both should be solvable by finding the appropriate option in the modem or ISP software.

If you're worried by the sheer cost of making long phone calls from a hotel room, you may find it possible to use a **prepaid calling card**. The trick is to program your modem with the full phonecard number and codes as well as the ISP access number, but to separate the two components with strings of one or more commas.

Finally, if you're having real difficulties, you could always try taking your laptop to a **cybercafe**. It might sound a little counter-intuitive, but many cybercafes allow customers to plug their own laptops into the Web, and in an unfamiliar country the staff can be an invaluable source of help and information.

Help For World Travelers

www.kropla.com

Although it conatins no information as yet on wireless technology, Steve Kropla's handy site otherwise remains the best source for clear, concise advice on how to connect your laptop to the Internet. Its World Wide Phone Guide features illustrated country-by-country charts of the myriad plugs and adapters used for both telephones and electrical appliances all over the world, and there's also a guide to using mobile phones to pick up email. The site holds links to online retailers who sell the relevant products.

Laptop Travel

www.laptoptravel.com

The Laptop Travel site, run by a Minneapolis company, can sell you any adaptor or piece of connectivity equipment that it's possible to imagine, but sadly now offers precious little advice to steer you through the maze.

RoadNews

WARNING: Don't take your computer anywhere without us!

Tips & Tricks for Laptop Computer Equipped Travelers

Welcome to RoadNews!

This site contains all the information you need to know if you are traveling with a computer. Whether you are going on a cruise, looking for tips for your PDA, looking for a new wine experience along the road or seeking help with your exchage rate (currency exchange). Even if you are seeking help in going wireless we are your first choice. For your internet computer use in your RV on the local back roads or international travel, IBM has chosen our site as best of breed for on the road support for portable computers. Think of us as your visa to assistance in staying connected with your laptop computer. If there is a way to stay connected with your notebook computer, we can help with the connection - worldwide. Take us along on your journey and happy travels!

Roadnews

www.roadnews.com

Roadnews provides detailed advice on all aspects of travelling with computers, including reviews of the latest gadgets and gizmos, and step-by-step troubleshooting instructions for anyone trying to go online via a hotel phone. The trouble is, of course, that you have to get online in order to read it.

Teleadapt

www.teleadapt.com

Visit the sites listed above to find out which "laptop connectivity products" you need, then buy them from Teleadapt, who operate two separate online stores, one for customers in the US and one for all the rest. Both are accessed through the same Website, which contains very little advice or information apart from technical specifications.

part two

themes
& activities

Activities

General adventure holidays

Adventure Directory

www.adventuredirectory.com

The Adventure Directory, a London-based adventure portal, offers users a staggering list of activities, from canyoning and cave diving to wake boarding and round-the-world sailing, plus a hierarchy of interactive maps. Most searches produce a long list of operators in any chosen destination, the majority of whom have their own Websites.

Away.com

http://away.com

As described on p.7, the huge US-based away.com site is an all-round online travel agency and information resource, but it also comes up trumps if you're simply looking for an adventure-tour package anywhere in the world. Activities on its intricate hierarchy of menus range from grizzly-spotting in Alaska or sea kayaking off the Komodo islands to horseback riding in Chile; simply email to request a reservation.

Backroads

www.backroads.com

From its origins as an exclusively cycle-tour operator (see p.108), San Francisco's Backroads company now arranges upmarket adventure vacations of all kinds, in every continent. Besides hiking, golf and watersports, it even offers "Active Gourmet" trips in Europe, walking between luxury inns in Tuscany and Provence. All trips are fully described onscreen, as well as being easy to find via pull-down menus, and can be reserved online.

Exodus

www.exodus.co.uk

British adventure-tour operator Exodus arranges expeditions in more than eighty countries, from Japan to Morocco; the travelling is definitely part of the experience, with different trips focusing on hiking, biking, overland safaris and even camel trekking. Though the Website is structured to correspond to the company's various brochures, its actual content is very detailed and often interactive, and it features full online booking. Prices are quoted according to your country of origin, and trips are sold with or without airfares.

Explore Worldwide

www.exploreworldwide.com

The UK-based Explore Worldwide company offers a tantalizing programme of small-group tours worldwide, ranging from sailing tall ships in the South Pacific, via trekking through the rainforests of Borneo and Madagascar, to hiking in the deserts of Namibia. Whether you fancy rafting, trekking and even "ethnic or tribal encounters", you'll find it described onscreen, with up-to-the-minute availability; once you've made your mind up, email to reserve a place.

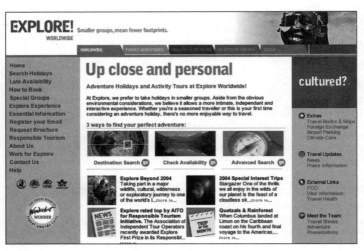

Footprint Adventures

www.footprint-adventures.co.uk

Extensive, exciting list of wildlife, bird-watching (see p.188), cultural and trekking holidays run by UK-based operator Footprint Adventures. It leads small groups of eco-travellers in around thirty countries; click on the destination menu to find a trip that suits you. It takes a little time to get all the information you need (prices are listed separately from the holidays they refer to, for example) but at least you can fill in a booking form and make all payments online.

Gecko Travel

www.geckotravel.co.uk

Specializing in Southeast Asia, this UK operator offers a variety of reasonably priced small-group adventures, whether you want to visit the hill tribes of Vietnam, trek through Laos, or help build a house in Cambodia. All tours are detailed fully on the site; to book, fill in the form and wait for an agent to contact you.

Geographic Expeditions

www.geoex.com

San Francisco-based tour company Geographic Expeditions aim to reveal "Inner Asia", "Inner Europe", "Inner Africa" or the "Inner Americas" – along with the (not, for some reason, "Inner") Pacific and Arctic/Antarctica – to adventurous travellers prepared to join its creative (and expensive) programme of tours. Specific trips might include mountain trekking, yachting or sea kayaking, with tours and treks from "easy" to "rigorous"; for the latter, the site takes pains to point out the standards of mental and physical fitness expected. Book by email or phone.

GoNOMAD

www.gonomad.com

This US-based resource centre sets out to inspire and inform "alternative travellers" – defined here as those prepared to participate and engage in the culture of whatever place they're visiting. Use its feature articles, destination guides and mini-guides to such topics as "Volunteer Vacations" or "Teaching English Overseas" to focus your interests, then search its database for companies and organizations that provide relevant trips.

GORP

www.gorp.com

The US-based GORP (Great Outdoors Recreation Pages) Website is probably the single best online resource for adventurous travellers. As well as running its own tours worldwide, sorted here according to activity, destination and interest, it provides a vast amount of general information, with feature articles and Top 10 lists to whet even jaded appetites. Dig deep into its US national park coverage and you'll find detailed hiking guides; elsewhere it holds practical advice on biking, climbing (see p.106) and other active sports. Click on "Community" for a number of useful forums, including experts' advice on everything from women's sleeping bags to the joys of igloo-making.

High Places

www.highplaces.co.uk

High Places, a UK company with offices in northern England and New Zealand, offers small-group trekking, climbing, cycling, skiing and all-round activity holidays from Britain to everywhere from the Arctic to the Andes. The Website sets out all the necessary information with little superfluous clutter; download a booking form, email or phone to book whichever trip catches your fancy.

Holiday Bank

www.holidaybank.com/holcosp.asp

British one-stop holiday shop with a section devoted to activity holidays. Here you'll find links to companies offering everything from scuba diving in Turkey to golfing in Hawaii or horse riding in Maine. Searching by activity brings up a list of companies, with reviews; those with Websites are covered in most detail, but there are separate – very long – lists for others that you can contact by phone or email.

iExplore

www.iexplore.com

Run in association with National Geographic, the excellent iExplore database holds more than three thousand adventure-travel opportunities, within the US and around the world, offered by over 130 separate companies. Search by activity, destination, or both; arrange the results by price, date or level of difficulty; and then receive personal advice by email. Prices are guaranteed to be the cheapest available anywhere. There's also plenty of destination advice and tips on specific activities, both from experts and from fellow travellers (via igougo; see p.27), and you can buy books or equipment by linking to the wonderful National Geographic online store.

Inntravel

www.inntravel.com

UK tour operator offering excellent short breaks, walking, skiing, cycling and riding holidays (see p.121) in Europe and New England. You can browse all their options online, searching by activity or destination; make reservations online, or email them to order a hard-copy brochure.

KE Adventure Travel

www.keadventure.com

KE Adventure Travel is unusual in maintaining offices in both the US and the UK, which makes it easy to reserve places on its expeditions to most of the major mountain ranges on earth. Some of the trips involve trekking and biking (see p.109), others are long-distance jeep safaris in search of rare wildlife, and yet more are fully fledged mountaineering expeditions. Separate online booking facilities cover British and North American travellers; look out for last-minute discounts.

Outside Online

http://outsideonline.com

Linked to away.com (see p.101) and GORP (p.103), this online arm of *Outside* magazine, an award-winning US publication, has lively feature articles, advice and news relating to all things strenuous, wild and adventurous.

Sierra Club

www.sierraclub.org/outings

Among its many activities devoted to raising awareness of environmental issues, the US-based Sierra Club runs its own programme of more than 300 outdoors-oriented "outings" for adventurous travellers. As detailed on p.346, most are within the US, but it also has around 60 expeditions in widely scattered countries around the globe. Search according to region and/or activity and/or dates, and you're instantly told how many spaces are left on each relevant trip; sign up online, then phone with your credit card details.

Wild Dog Adventure Directory

www.wild-dog.com

Whenever your cursor hovers over an active link on this appealing British-run directory of worldwide adventure operators, the Wild Dog wags its tail. Search by country or activity – or both – and it returns long lists both of tour companies that can take you to the relevant destination, and local operators who can cater for you if you arrive independently. Technically, the connections are buffered, so you can only order brochures while you remain on the Wild Dog site, or use the "Perfect Lead" facility to request emails from the various operators that meet your specific needs. However, it's easy enough to find your way onto their own sites, and complete your arrangements online.

WILD DOG
adventure

Do you want to go overlanding in Africa? Heli-skiing in British Columbia? Discover remote Peruvian villages by mountain bike? Or Walking in the Tuscan Hills?

Whatever the adventure you are looking for, Wild Dog can tell you how, where and with whom.

Wilderness Travel

www.wildernesstravel.com

Californian adventure-tour company Wilderness Travel offers a huge array of stimulating trips in all continents, from elephant trekking in Thailand to sea kayaking off Baja California. Some are luxurious, as with the "Palace on Wheels" rail excursion in India, others more gruelling. Its Website is quick and instinctive, with a search that can suggest vacations to match whichever destinations or activities you are interested in, or whatever dates you have free. To reserve, either call or download and complete the booking form.

Worldwide Adventures

www.worldwidequest.com

Canada-based operator offering lots of small-group (fifteen people maximum) adventure tours, safaris, hiking trips and cultural jaunts in a wonderful range of destinations such as Borneo, Papua New Guinea, Ethiopia, the Silk Road and Greenland. Prices don't include air fares; email to book. For their biking trips see p.111.

Climbing

About.com

http://climbing.about.com

The climbing section of the huge about.com Website serves as a portal to many of the world's best mountaineering Websites, but also offers plenty of its own content, with articles, book reviews, equipment sales and general advice.

GORP

www.gorp.com/gorp/activity/climb.htm

This comprehensive climbing site, run as part of the US-based GORP site (see p.103), contains an astonishing array of information, ranging from advice for newbies, through technical tips for experts, to accounts of legendary expeditions. For North American users, it can point you to your nearest climbing club or organization, while the interactive E-quipper (click "Gear") helps you choose and buy equipment online. Best of all, however, it sells climbing vacations all over the world. Call up the details on screen, then call or send an email.

Jagged Globe

www.jagged-globe.co.uk

Jagged Globe is a leading British operator of mountaineering courses and holidays. Learn to climb in Scotland or the Alps, then join an expedition – or even put together your own – to the world's highest and most challenging peaks. All trips are available to climbers from anywhere; book the whole thing online, or talk it through on the phone if you prefer.

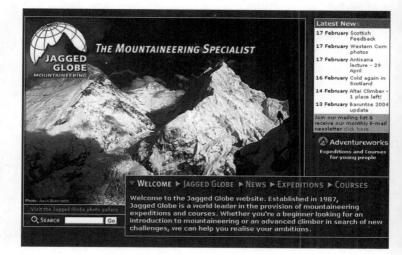

Rocklist

www.rocklist.com

General climbing Website, based in Arizona but offering news, features, photography and even poetry on mountaineering all over the world. Less male-dominated than most such sites, it includes an interactive climbing guide, an online guidebook compiled by site users, a bulletin board and a plethora of climbing-related links. Sign up for a (nearly) monthly email newsletter.

Cycling

If you'd like to combine cycling with fine cuisine, check out **www.bikeridertours.com**, reviewed in our food, drink and cookery section on p.167.

Backroads

www.backroads.com

California-based adventure-travel company Backroads (see p.101) arrange around sixty specialist biking holidays each year. They're scattered all over the world, from Ireland or Italy to Argentina or Alaska. Trips to the North American national parks involve camping, but the vast majority use fancy inns, comfortable hotels or gorgeous lodges, and thus work out pretty expensive. The Website offers copious details of all tours, plus online reservations.

CycleActive

www.cycleactive.co.uk

British operator offering mountain bike tours in all parts of the world, some of which involve other sports into the bargain. As well as plenty of European and North American trips, it features more unusual destinations such as Malawi and Ethiopia. Every trip is graded according to ability, and there are detailed itineraries with photos. Booking is by email or phone.

Cycle Rides

www.cycle-rides.co.uk

This British company offers bike tours throughout Europe, graded to all levels of fitness and experience. You don't have to ride with the group if you prefer not to, but each day your luggage is carried ahead to the next evening's hotel or camp site. The Website enables you to select from all upcoming tours, and make reservations online.

Cycling Links

www.cyclinglinks.com

As the name suggests, this site is solely devoted to providing as many bicycle-related links as possible, covering cycling history as well as up-to-date racing news – and other pages of cycling links. Though originating in North America, it covers the whole world. For travellers, it's most useful for the long list of international tour operators.

Discover Adventure

www.discoveradventure.com

British tour operator specializing in mountain bike and trekking vacations. As well as exotic marathons in Peru, Morocco, Vietnam and Thailand, it offers shorter European jaunts, with a few biking weekends in the UK. The Website features plenty of very enticing photos and some even more enticing prices (flights are included on international tours); email for availability and booking.

Easy Rider Tours

www.easyridertours.com

Easy Rider Tours arranges cycling and hiking vacations not only in its home base of New England and the neighbouring Canadian Maritime Provinces, but also across the Atlantic in Portugal, Spain and Ireland, including across Spain following the ancient pilgrim route to Santiago de Compostela. All tours are van-supported, while the actual cycling is just demanding enough to make you feel entitled to gourmet picnic lunches and comfortable inn-style lodging. Airfares are priced separately. Email the online form to make a reservation, and you'll be called back for your credit card number.

KE Adventure Travel

www.keadventure.com

KE Adventure Travel, who have offices in both the US and the UK, organize trekking and mountain biking expeditions to "some of the most outlandish places on earth". Biking destinations range from Kazakhstan to Costa Rica, trip lengths from two days (weekends in England's Lake District) to four weeks; most are demanding, a few are strenuous, and some are moderate. Once you've checked availability by email, you can make secure reservations online.

Maui Downhill

www.mauidownhill.net

Maui Downhill fulfil the ultimate fantasy in effortless biking; a forty-mile ride down the mighty Hawaiian volcano of Haleakala, in which you barely need to brake, or even pedal, as you enjoy the stupendous views. Decide between the sunrise tour, the half- and the full-day jaunt, and make your reservation online. Rates include all gear including bike rental, and, of course, the van-ride to the summit.

Rim Tours

www.rimtours.com

Thanks to the magnificent red-rock country that surrounds it, Moab in southeast Utah has become a mecca for mountain bikers from all over the world. Local operator Rim Tours specialize in catering for their every need, renting bikes as well as arranging tours. Its stock in trade is in day-trips along Moab's own Slickrock Bike Trail, or into nearby Canyonlands National Park, but it also offers multi-day camping trips, accompanied by guides and chefs, and ventures further afield into Bryce and Zion national parks, Arizona, Oregon and Colorado. Reserve online or by phone.

Rough Tracks

www.rough-tracks.co.uk

UK operator that arranges both road and mountain-biking holidays in various European countries. On the whole, the trips are relatively undemanding; luggage is carried by van, daily distances average under forty miles, and accommodation is in small hotels and B&Bs. As well as weekends in England, destinations include rural and mountainous regions of France, Portugal, Spain and Morocco. Email the online form to check availability and make a reservation.

Saddle Skedaddle

www.skedaddle.co.uk

Another British cycle-tour company, whose holidays extend from the UK and Europe to cover North America, Latin America and New Zealand. If you're pushed for time, you can enjoy a three-day weekend in Mallorca, Greece or Sardinia, or a couple of days in the Brecon Beacons. Online reservations.

Suffolk Cycle Breaks

www.cyclebreaks.co.uk

Despite the name, this small-scale British cycle-touring company ranges slightly further afield than Suffolk – but only as far as neighbouring Norfolk. That means all its tours, which range from three to fourteen days in length, are through the flat-as-a-pancake landscape of East Anglia. Since they average less than thirty miles per day, and include transport for your luggage and comfortable inn accommodation, this makes for a gentle, easy vacation – and the prices are not too demanding either. Email for availability and reservations.

Wild Cat Bike Tours

www.wildcat-bike-tours.co.uk

Scotland's premier adventure bike tour company gained its reputation through running the coast-to-coast Scotland trips that still form the centrepiece of its brochure. These have now been joined by several more itineraries through the Highlands and islands and a wide range of holidays further afield, including off-road jaunts along ancient caravan routes in the Atlas Mountains, trips through France, Spain and Sardinia and the Gobi Desert. Weekend jaunts, tandem holidays and women-only trips are listed separately. Enquire by email for availability, then book by phone or email.

Worldwide Adventures

www.worldwidequest.com

Canadian company (see p.106) that arranges small-group cycle tours, designed to suit all levels of fitness and experience, in far-flung destinations such as Tibet, India and Vietnam, and also coast-to-coast Cuba trips. Its "Best of China by Bike" is an 18-day tour that takes participants through the limestone scenery of Guilin as well as cities such as Xian and Beijing, while its 28-day tour of India is promoted as an "Introduction to Expedition Travel". Trip prices exclude airfare, which can be arranged separately. Email to book.

Diving

Aquatours

www.aquatours.com

Under the slogan "Adventures for thinking divers", this UK-based operator sells tropical dive holidays and live-aboards across most of the world, including the Red Sea, the Indian Ocean, and the Caribbean, but not the Great Barrier Reef. It offers both BSAC and PADI training. The Website includes last-minute deals, but there's no interactive booking.

Barefoot Traveller

www.barefoot-traveller.com

This London-based dive operator specializes in the Bahamas and the Caribbean, but also offers a handful of Indian Ocean and Asian destinations including Thailand, Sri Lanka, Sipadan and the Maldives – and is experienced in catering for disabled divers. Its Website isn't hugely informative on prices – you can put together your own package, depending on the number of dives you want to do – though it does claim to cover all budgets. Complete the online form for more details.

British Sub Aqua Club

www.bsac.co.uk

The Website of the UK's official body for certifying dive schools and instructors can put members in touch with local branches and training facilities, but its most useful feature is the links page at **www.bsac.org/world/links1.htm**, which, as well as dive sites the world over, offers connections to subjects ranging from underwater archeology to marine biology and the elusive giant squid.

DIVEChannel

www.divechannel.co.uk

This general UK dive site sets out to be a one-stop dive travel shop, enabling users to search a database of holidays available from around ten different operators. The "Dive The World" section, open to all, provides general information on diving destinations worldwide, but to get very far with specific holidays (search by date, destination, requirements and price) you have to register with DIVEChannel. As well as making it possible to book last-minute holidays at dramatically discounted prices, this brings you regular email updates on new offers. The site also has feature articles, an online dive equipment shop and information on dive courses.

DiveQuest

www.divequest.co.uk

Online version of this UK dive operator's brochure, detailing diving vacations in the Caribbean, Southeast Asia, Australasia and throughout the Pacific, and including plenty of live-aboards. It also offers tailor-made tours. Along with lengthy rave reports from satisfied customers, the site does at least carry full prices and details; use the email form to book.

Divernet

www.divernet.com

The online version of British monthly magazine *Diver*, this excellent site holds a searchable archive of articles from its print counterpart – invaluable if you're researching a particular destination – plus links to, among other things, equipment suppliers, charter boats, diving organizations and tour operators. The forums, on everything from wrecks to medical issues, are well worth checking for diveboats with last minute spaces and for private sales of secondhand gear.

Explorers Tours

www.explorers.co.uk/dive/dive_home.htm

Leading UK dive operator that arranges scuba vacations in all the major destinations, with a huge list in the Red Sea, but also such exciting Micronesian adventures as descending to the "Ghost Fleet" of Truk Lagoon. The site offers some great last-minute deals and secure online booking.

If You Dive

www.ifyoudive.com

General database of UK dive operators that asks users to select a date and a destination for their next scuba trip, and returns a selection of holidays with relevant companies. Before you commit yourself, be sure to check out the extensive reviews of specific worldwide dive sites.

Jules' Underwater Lodge

www.jul.com

What claims to be the world's only underwater hotel, in Key Largo, Florida. The "Jules" in question is Monsieur Verne, and this futuristic fantasy, perched on stilts at the bottom of a

tropical mangrove lagoon, is straight out of science fiction. To reach it, you have to dive 21 feet down, then swim up from underneath. Rather than passing through an air lock, you emerge from a small swimming pool to find yourself in a cottage-like structure that holds two guest bedrooms, a kitchen and a lounge, but is also a genuine research laboratory. The basic package, including unlimited diving between 5pm and 9am, dinner and breakfast, costs around $295 per person per day; luxury deals, with the services of a gourmet "mer-chef", work out around $100 more. It's also possible to train as a diver for the first time.

Live/Dive Pacific

http://pac-aggressor.com

This American company, based in Kona, Hawaii, sails its "Aggressor Fleet" of luxury live-aboard yachts to dive destinations throughout the Pacific, from Tahiti to the Solomon Islands, and also ventures into the Caribbean and Central America. Its best-known vacation is aboard the Truk Aggressor live-aboard in Micronesia's Chuuk Lagoon, which abounds in World War II wrecks. The Website is packed with enticing photos and video clips, and though this is the top end of the market, the prices are not as high as you might expect. Book by phone or email.

Maui Dive Shop

www.mauidiveshop.com

The leading dive operator on the best of the Hawaiian islands for scuba diving, running daily boat-diving excursions to the tiny volcanic islet of Molokini Crater, and regular trips to prime sites off the south coast of nearby Lanai. As well as making online reservations for all trips, users of the attractive Website can also request a free Maui dive guide.

Professional Association of Diving Instructors

www.padi.com

PADI's international headquarters is located in California, though most national branches of the world's leading authority for certifying schools, instructors and individual divers also maintain their own Websites. As well as providing information on rules and regulations, the main world site is also the place to access the PADI Travel Network, through which it's possible to book dive vacations for all tastes and levels of experience in almost a hundred countries.

Regal Diving

www.regal-diving.co.uk

The straightforward Website of this British scuba specialist caters for beginners and experts alike, and offers dive trips to worldwide destinations, with a special emphasis on the Red Sea. Booking is by phone or email, but there's plenty of stimulating information to work your way through first online and a handful of special offers to give you ideas.

ScubaDuba

www.scubaduba.com

Perhaps the best place to dip your first toe into the mysterious waters of the online scuba world, this general US-centred resource is determined to be "the Ultimate Scuba Diving Site On The Web". Alongside the expected chatrooms, scuba-related news stories, and small ads from divers selling equipment or seeking buddies, it offers such eccentric features as the ScubaDuba Top 5: A Worldwide Attempt At Scuba Humor (eg "The Top 5 Reasons Not To Dive With Your Doctor"). The real reason to drop in, though, is for the copious, carefully categorized pages of links, including operators all over the world. If you're looking for someone who can take you diving in Bulgaria, they're probably here already, looking for you.

Scuba Safaris

www.scuba-safaris.com

Luxury diving holidays are the speciality for this British tour company, whose seventeen dive destinations circle the globe, from the Indian Ocean to Central America. As well as representing the Aggressor fleets of live-aboard yachts (see opposite), it also offers resort and beach-based diving holidays, with side trips to keep non-divers entertained. Reserve by phone or email.

Golf

Classic Golf Tours

www.classicgolftours.com

Based in Colorado, but with additional offices in Scotland and Ireland, Classic Golf Tours arranges self-drive and escorted golfing vacations in the US and around the world. All the legendary Scottish courses are available, with prices depending on the standard of accommodation, and substantial discounts for non-golfing members of your party. Email to make your booking.

Classic **Golf**™ Tours
Golf Travel Masters *Since 1989*

3045 South Parker Road
Aurora, Colorado 80014

Toll Free 800-359-7200
Local 303-751-7200
Fax 303-751-7526

FreeGolfInfo

www.freegolfinfo.com

Calling itself "the world's largest golf community", this comprehensive US-based site combines a worldwide golf course guide, sales of new and secondhand equipment, online instruction, and hundreds of links.

GolfBreaks

www.golfbreaks.com

UK company that specializes in short golfing holidays in Britain and France. Whether you simply want to play a particular course, or to take one of its standard three-day breaks, the user-friendly advanced search mechanism makes it easy to pick your destination online and find a suitably priced trip. Email a request, and they'll contact you.

Golfonline

www.golfonline.com

Produced by *Golf Magazine*, this huge US site carries masses of tournament news, feature articles, technical advice and equipment reviews, but it's also invaluable for golfing travellers, with a useful section devoted to golfing vacations, albeit predominantly within North America. Click on Travel to access a huge range of travel articles. Courses and resorts are ranked and compared, and there's a weighty database of tour operators, with active links to almost everything featured. A separate section, Travel Deals, pulls up a database of courses and resorts with photos and information; click to be sent a brochure.

Golfpac Travel

www.golfpactravel.com

US-based agency offering golfing holidays in North America and around the world. Use the vacation finder to make your choice from more than 250 resorts and 600 courses. Most of the information you need, including cost, is here, and you can book by email or online.

The Golf Travel Company

www.e-golftravel.com

US tour company specializing in golf tours of Europe, with extensive programmes in Scotland and Ireland, and also an annual trip to watch the British Open. The Website sets out full itineraries and course specifications, with an online form to submit if you want to make a reservation.

ifyougolf

www.ifyougolf.com

The leading Website for British-based golfers, centring on a wide-ranging selection of world golfing holidays. Search by destination, or choose a particular course from its database, then look for tour operators or accommodation options in that vicinity. Ifyougolf also holds around 2000 pages of news, reviews and general golfing information, plus a bulletin board and equipment shop, and – appropriately enough – a fine set of links.

Health breaks and spas

For another range of alternative treatments, see p.174.

About.com

http://spas.about.com/travel/spas

Another useful directory from the huge about.com stable. With hundreds of intelligently arranged and reviewed links, the site tells you all you'd ever need to know about a spa holiday. Among other things, you can search for spas around the world, check which ones cater for specific needs – including weight loss, Ayurvedic or maternity – and read reviews and related articles from the world's media. Also spa news and special deals (mostly in the US), and links to relevant books and magazines.

Blue Lagoon Iceland

www.bluelagoon.is

Iceland's Blue Lagoon, around forty minutes' drive from Reykjavik, is a mineral-rich, milky-blue geothermal pool steaming away in the middle of a lava field. At the heart of the up-market spa of the same name, it's particularly invigorating in the middle of winter, when you can languish in the muscle-warming waters, sipping a lurid blue cocktail, while shielding your eyes from snow-blindness. The Website tells you all about the treatments, the geothermal sauna, the various pools (including a cave pool) and the lagoon itself. There's also a restaurant, but no accommodation.

Canyon Ranch Health Resorts

www.canyonranch.com

Set in Arizona's stunning red rock desert, the original Canyon Ranch spa resort is consistently rated as one of the best in the US. With hundreds of therapies, from the spiritual (breathing, Chi Gong, "Oriental vitality", yoga), to the physical (ballet, stride, line dancing, spinning), you're also offered help with problems you may never have realized you had. Who could resist "healing heartache with humour" or "getting past the past"? All-in packages are cheapest in summer (it gets very hot in Arizona); four nights between November and June will set you back from $2400, based on two people sharing.

Chiva Som

www.chivasom.net

Repeatedly voted the best in the world by readers of *Condé Nast Traveler* magazine, Thailand's Chiva Som spa resort is as luxurious as you'd expect, with just 57 rooms in a seven-acre beachfront setting dotted with lagoons and waterfalls. The Website is great, too, though it can take a while to download: not too gushing, with clear accounts of the huge array of treatments (which include Anapanasati Mind Training, chakra balancing and floatation) and even a few recipes thrown in. It costs a bomb, of course, and prices aren't actually quoted on the site; you'll need to submit a form to check availability.

Daintree Eco Lodge

www.daintree-ecolodge.com.au

Fabulous Australian spa in the rainforest of Queensland, where guests sleep in one of fifteen luxurious treehouse villas set high in the canopy. The Website will set your mouth watering, with lots to read about the facilities, the rainforest and the various therapies – the signature "Mala Mayi" includes a warm mud wrap, a scalp massage, and rain therapy, which is an invigorating blast of pure water from Daintree's waterfall. It also organizes trips to the Great Barrier Reef, along with Aboriginal rainforest walks and cultural performances. You can book online, but the server is not secure; email direct if you prefer.

Erna Low

www.bodyandsoulholidays.com

This UK operator is a great start for anyone planning a spa holiday. It can pack you off to luxurious resorts around the world, in places including South Africa, the Maldives and India – and at reasonable prices. Search by treatment or by destination: click on the resort you fancy to read about its therapies, facilities and types of breaks, then send an email form for a quotation. Prices vary, depending on the resort and the treatments you're after; if you want to save time, check the special offers page for a variety of holidays with costs already detailed.

Grand Wailea Resort

www.grandwailea.com

The kind of thing they do so well in Hawaii: an ostentatious spa resort that manages to combine holistic "wellness" with extraordinary luxury. Clichés like tropical paradise don't do this place justice: on a white sand beach on the island of Maui, it's the ultimate in spa heaven, with two swimming pools – one of them a six-level pool made up of nine areas linked by waterslides – hot-tub grottoes, and a "hydrotherapy circuit", in which you wade from one water therapy to another. The site is admirably thorough, giving full details of all the rooms, with floor plans and rates (from around $400 per night to $10,000 for the 5500 square-foot Grand Suite). The therapies will set you back a bit – you're looking at more than $200 for fifty minutes lomilomi or Ayurvedic massage, hydrotherapy included – but day packages are available. Browse and dream, and start saving now.

International Thalassotherapy Federation

www.thalassofederation.com

Clumsily translated site covering the history and benefits of thalassotherapy – the chic French hydrotherapy that uses heated seawater, seaweed and mineral-rich mud to cure all number of ills. The site has a selective list of locations in France, Spain, Tunisia, Mexico and Turkey, but only a few are hotlinked (and, of course, most of the sites are in French).

Rajah Healthy Acres

www.ayurveda-in.com/index.html

Spread across one hundred acres in the lush southern Indian state of Kerala, Healthy Acres offers Ayurvedic treatments for many types of illnesses, nutritional advice and rejuvenation therapy for anyone in need of a rest. Rooms cost from $15 to $82 per night, depending on whether you want to stay in a bamboo hut or a two-bedroom villa panelled with herbal wood; each one has a kitchenette, and there's a dining room on site. You can also book packages, including accommodation, food (as advised by a doctor) and treatments; these range in length from three to 28 days. Check the links for other Ayurvedic health centres, resorts and practitioners throughout Kerala. You'll need to email to make a booking.

Somatheeram

www.somatheeram.com

Fifteen-acre Kerala beach resort offering Ayurveda and yoga, plus cultural programmes of Indian dance and music. Room rates vary widely: a Christmas break in a thatched cottage, built of mud and bricks and with a sea view, will set you back $94 per person per night (based on two sharing), though you could spend as little as $16 and as much as $210 depending upon season and style of accommodation. The many Ayurvedic treatments and courses cost extra (from €3 for a one-off to more than €600 for a fortnight-long programme), as do flights and meals (€6 for breakfast, €11 for lunch and dinner). Use the email form to make reservation.

Sources de Caudalie

www.sources-caudalie.com

Healthy living with a difference: surrounded by vineyards near Bordeaux, Sources de Caudalie is a four-star "vinotherapie spa", which claims to combine grape polyphenols, grape-seed oil, wine yeast extracts and tannin with natural thermal waters to create anti-ageing and slimming treatments. So you can have red-wine baths and Merlot wraps, Sauvignon massages and Cabernet body scrubs while staying in fabulous themed rooms and stuffing yourself on gourmet French food. You're encouraged to enjoy vintage wines at the "Bar du French Paradox" – and talking of paradoxes, it's an odd sort of spa that offers a cigar bar ... Though rates are detailed on the site, much of the treatment information is in the form of downloadable PDF files. Email to book.

Horse riding

British Horse Society

www.bhs.org.uk

Visiting the Website of the British Horse Society is hardly the most thrilling experience you'll ever have online, but it's great if you need to get in touch with riding clubs or schools anywhere in the UK. It also has information on and links to companies that offer riding holidays in Britain and around the world.

Equitour

www.equitour.co.uk

This established UK-operator offers great riding holidays suitable for all levels, including instructional trips specializing in dressage or showjumping and horse riding-cultural holiday combos. Non-riding partners and children can also be catered for. There's a great selection, from trail rides in Spain's Sierra Nevada to ranch holidays in Wyoming, with a nice choice of longer-haul trips to places like Botswana, Namibia, Jordan, Argentina, Chile and Brazil. Accommodation is in rustic inns, ranches or tented camps. Flights are not included in the price. To book, download and mail them the form.

Guest Ranches of North America

www.guestranches.com

Texas-based Website that hosts home pages for guest ranches throughout the US, plus a handful in Canada and one in Mexico. Each individual ranch provides details of its rates and facilities, and can be contacted directly, but apart from the listings being arranged by state there's no overall search engine to help you pinpoint the horse-riding vacation that suits you. A separate section details job opportunities at the various ranches.

Hidden Trails

www.hiddentrails.com

Vancouver operator Hidden Trails offers horseback holidays in 19 US states, 4 Canadian provinces, and more than 45 overseas destinations, with 5-percent discounts on all guest ranches. Highlights of its list include riding through Tanzanian game parks to Mount Kilimanjaro, and a week- or fortnight-long adventure from Valley of the Gods in Utah to Monument Valley; it also has separate Best Rides and Best Deals sections. Availability for each tour is constantly updated, so you can make a reservation simply by emailing the form with such personal details as your height, weight, and, of course, your credit card number.

Holiday On Horseback

www.horseback.com

This plum address belongs to Warner Guiding and Outfitting, based at Banff National Park in Canada, who run horseback trips through breathtaking mountain scenery. Standard inexpensive multi-day excursions (including Adventure Expeditions, which head into isolated areas of the park) involve overnight camping; others, described as "roughing it the civilized way", stay overnight in wilderness lodges. Specific themes include park history or, alarmingly, grizzly bears. Day-trips, cookouts and picnic excursions are also available. Bookings can be made online.

Inntravel

www.inntravel.co.uk

British operator Inntravel (see p.104) specializes (though not exclusively), in horseback holidays in Spain, Portugal, Italy and France as well as in Britain; there's even a couple of options in Botswana and Mexico. Accommodations range from dorms in equestrian centres to inns or comfortable hotels; rates vary accordingly. Reservations can be made by email, but at present you need to call to give credit card details.

In The Saddle

www.inthesaddle.com

This British tour company offers ranch stays, predominantly in North America; riding holidays in Europe, based as a rule in equestrian centres; and riding expeditions in far-flung corners of the globe such as Malawi, Mongolia and Patagonia. It caters for riders of all levels; one trip, in Ireland, allows experts to go on unaccompanied trail rides for as much as two weeks. The site is clear, fast and informative; email for availability and general advice, then make your reservation by phone.

Outlaw Trails

www.outlawtrails.com

British company Outlaw Trails offers exactly what its name suggests; the chance for hardy riders to follow the self-same trails (in North America, Mexico and South America) used by legendary Wild West outlaws such as the Wild Bunch and the Hole-in-the-Wall Gang. Long-distance trips require participants to camp en route; others, such as in the legendary "Robbers' Roost" district of Utah's remote canyonlands, involve stays at working ranches. Rates are reasonable, and are quoted without airfares, so all nationalities are welcome. To pursue your enquiries, send an email.

Ranchweb.com

www.ranchweb.com

The definitive Website for horseback vacations, run by Gene Kilgore, who writes (and sells online) the five-hundred-page *Ranch Vacations in North America*. A cornucopia for wannabe cowboys and city slickers alike, it lists well over a hundred holidays in the USA, Canada, Argentina and Brazil. The search facility is superb, enabling you to pick a ranch according to whatever criteria matter to you – a request for Wyoming ranches available in June that also offer golf and swimming throws up 41 suggestions – or you can simply point to a spot on the interactive global map. Some ranches offer online booking, while others you will have to email.

Ride Worldwide

www.rideworldwide.com

This attractive site opens up to the thunder of approaching hoofbeats; then the words "Ride Worldwide" gallop into view, and skid to a halt. Sadly, though the British tour company runs a very impressive programme of worldwide riding and ranch holidays, from dude ranches in Wyoming to yurting safaris in Kyrgyzstan, the site itself can only whet your appetite. The only thing it actually lets you do is order or download its print brochure.

Unicorn Trails

www.unicorntrails.com

British company Unicorn Trails sells horse-riding holidays in destinations worldwide, catering for novices and experts alike. It has a particular penchant for deserts, with trips to the Pushkar Camel Fair in Rajasthan and across Namibia, but also includes other unusual options such as swimming with horses in Crete. The quoted prices do not include airfares, so independent travellers can link up with chosen tours. Email enquiries rather than actual bookings are invited; onscreen photos and biographies add to the personal touch.

The Wild Horse Sanctuary

www.wildhorsesanctuary.org

The Wild Horse Sanctuary, a non-profit-making organization located near Lassen Volcanic National Park in northern California, invites travellers to join trail rides among the wild mustangs. It offers two- or three-day weekend pack trips, and also four- to six-day cattle drives and round-ups, with accommodation and food provided in cabins beside Vernal Lake. Online booking available. Alternatively, you can stay at home and simply sponsor a wild horse.

Overlanding and long-haul bus trips

For a review of America's own Green Tortoise bus company, see p.344.

Bukima Expeditions

www.bukima.com

This British operator, which also has agents in Canada, Australia and New Zealand, runs trans-continental camping safaris by jeep across Africa, the Middle East, and South America (which works out a little cheaper). You can join a trip for just ten days, or by combining various segments travel for as long as 28 weeks. The site lays out everything you need to know; once you've chosen, print off the form and fax or post it to your nearest office.

Bukima Adventure Travel
you've never seen enough

You've never seen enough

What is adventure travel?
Bukima explores the mysteries, cultures, and diverse regions of far away places. Our routes have been designed to blend fun, excitement and

Contiki

www.contiki.com

More than a hundred overland bus tours, in the US, Canada, Europe, Africa and Australasia, for 18–35 year-olds from all over the world. Each region has its own Contiki site. Find a trip by clicking on a world map or search by your preferred country, dates, budget and trip duration; click again for a detailed itinerary, dates and rates, plus links to travellers' message boards. In most destinations you can choose between budget tours or the more expensive "Time Out" tours. Although the largest choice is in Europe, the range is vast. Accommodation, sightseeing and, by all accounts, as much heavy drinking as you can manage, is included. No online ordering; email direct for bookings. Check the "Specials" for bargains.

Dragoman

www.dragoman.co.uk

Based in the UK, Dragoman provides worldwide overland journeys from 2–42 weeks in length. Classic overland routes include the old Hippy Trail from London to Kathmandu, as well as hardier trans-Africa expeditions. The one North American itinerary runs from Alaska to Mexico; as with most trips, you can extend it with a variety of add-ons through central and South America. Prices are a little higher than elsewhere, but then the trips aren't aimed exclusively at young backpackers. Email the form to register your interest and hold a place.

Encounter Overland

www.encounter-overland.com

The youth-oriented arm of Dragoman (see above), organizing trips of 2–26 weeks across Africa, Asia and South America. Its Website asks "r u 1 of us?" (in your twenties or thirties, basically), and insists that its expedition leaders (one per trip) "are NOT tour guides because you are not a tourist". The actual trips are as inexpensive as possible, with extra activities ("Wildside adventures") such as rafting or climbing priced separately. Full details are given online and you can fill in an email form to hold an option.

Exodus Travels

www.exodus.co.uk

Among its many adventure-travel options, this British company arranges overland expeditions in the Americas, Australia, Asia and Africa. Most travel in relative comfort, and are priced accordingly. Although the Website supplies the barest onscreen details about individual trips (brief overview, daily itinerary and prices) – download the Acrobat version of the brochure to learn more – you can, nonetheless, complete online bookings with the minimum of ceremony.

Suntrek

www.suntrek.com

Californian tour company that offers low-budget, long-distance expeditions across North America and Mexico for participants of all nationalities, travelling in customized 4WD "maxi-vans" (motorcycle tours, using Harley Davidsons, are also available). On the Website, trips are arranged by duration, ranging from one week up to thirteen weeks; some are exclusively camping, while pricier alternatives ("comfort tours") use cabins and hotels instead. Electronic reservations are taken, though it isn't possible actually to pay online. For details of their Mexico trips, see p.281.

Trekamerica

www.trekamerica.com

Trekamerica is a UK-based company that runs more than fifty overland camping itineraries across Canada, the USA, and Mexico, for small groups of travellers aged 18–38. Their separate "Footloose" programme, for people of all ages, offers a combination of walking, camping and lodging tours in North America. The Website, featuring a jaunty animated banner of a van rolling through classic red rock scenery, provides full details of itineraries and prices, provides online availability checks, and accepts online bookings.

Skiing

For a company that specializes in Alpine skiing holidays and instruction for mature and senior travellers, **see www.classicski.co.uk**, reviewed on p.149.

1 Ski

www.1ski.com

Excellent UK-based site offering useful information on hundreds of worldwide resorts, with user reviews, webcams, weather and snow reports and piste maps. The main draw is the searchable database of winter ski breaks and accommodation-only deals. You can specify country, resort, accommodation type and preferred dates of travel (there's a convenient box to tick if you want fourteen-day flexibility, or simply to leave on any Saturday or Sunday in a given month). Options come up gratifyingly fast and in ascending order of price; bookings can then be made over the phone. Special offers and last-minute bargains are highlighted on the home page.

Bigfoot Travel

www.bigfoot-travel.co.uk

UK-based agency Bigfoot Travel run this highly informative Website to sell its programme of skiing or snowboarding breaks on the slopes of Chamonix in the French Alps. It operates five chalets, five hotels and some self-catering apartments in the region. Accommodation details, and booking forms, are downloadable.

Colorado Resort Net

www.toski.com

Representing all Colorado's ski resorts, this Website offers destination information and links to every resort and city in the state. Its Vacation Planner invites users to fill in a detailed form specifying their holiday requirements; you are then emailed back with the best deals. Alternatively, click an individual resort on the map to read about ski packages and a full list of accommodation, dining and activity options.

Crystal Ski

www.crystalski.co.uk

Specialist UK ski operator that sells holidays in eight European countries, plus the USA, Canada and Chile. Its Website has a high standard of information (click on Quick Search), not only on the 130 or so resorts it represents, but also on specific accommodation options within those resorts. You can check availability and complete your booking online.

Go Ski

www.goski.com

US ski site that provides copious information on over 2000 resorts in 38 different countries, from Lesotho to Greenland. Not surprisingly, it's strongest on US destinations, with great details on all the domestic resorts (including first-hand reports, not always positive, from ordinary skiers) and a host of travel deals available online. Specialist interests are well catered for, and there's plenty of equipment on offer too.

If You Ski

www.ifyouski.com

Part of a small family of British Websites (others include Ifyoudive and Ifyougolf) designed to sell reasonably priced activity-oriented package holidays. Choose from its list of resorts to summon up informative written details; finalize your plans by telling the straightforward search engine where you want to go and when, plus where you want to fly from. Bookings, however, have to be done over the phone. Other site features include forums, resort reviews and a regular newsletter complete with equipment reviews.

Ski Central

http://skicentral.com

The premier online skiing directory is a vast compendium of ski-related sites, centring especially on North America. For destination information it's unbeatable, with links to each resort's own general sites as well as specific accommodation options and other businesses. Other categories include equipment suppliers and up-to-the-minute snow reports, plus plenty of fun stuff like snowcams, chat rooms and competitions.

Ski Club of Great Britain

www.skiclub.co.uk

Certain areas of this top-quality information site are only accessible to enrolled club members, but any skier or snowboarder can use its search facility to find a travel operator to suit their needs, or access the Which Good Skiing and Snowboarding Guide for detailed resort reviews and Website links. The site covers resorts around the world, with snow reports, feature articles and an email newsletter. Join the club to benefit from discounts from all the featured operators.

Ski New England.com

www.skinewengland.com

This companion site to the general New England travel site **www.seenewengland.com** covers skiing possibilities throughout the region, with easy links not only to each resort's own Website but also to individual accommodation options within that resort. You can set about finding your dream holiday either by searching for the perfect resort to match your chosen priorities, or by using the excellent lodging finder to find the ideal property anywhere in New England.

Snow.co

www.snow.co.nz

All the information you could possibly need about skiing in New Zealand, covering every resort in the country with live Webcams, plus forthcoming events, up-to-the minute snow reports and details of which roads and ski lifts are currently open. Links to each resort make it possible to plan your entire trip online.

The Snow Team

www.ski.co.uk

A very useful UK-oriented directory of ski- and snowboard-related Websites, arranged (and many of them rated with marks out of ten) according to several different criteria, including "Late Availability" and "Short Breaks" as well as the basic "Travel". It also lists resort sites and equipment retailers, and offers an advice service if you email your requirements for a skiing break.

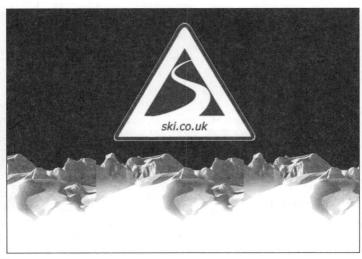

UptoYou.com

www.uptoyou.com

Travel agency specializing in bargain Alpine skiing breaks, combining good-value accommodation with cheap flights from net airline easyJet (see p.38), who part-own the site. You can choose a chalet from the home page and then check availability, or else search to see what's on offer on your chosen dates. To book, fill in the online enquiry form or simply call them direct. Subscribing to their newsletter keeps you updated on ski break offers and relevant easyJet flight deals, snow reports and resort information.

Surfing and windsurfing

A1Surf

www.a1surf.com

The A1Surf site is primarily devoted to surfing in the UK. Its up-to-the-minute Surfcheck relays conditions from all the country's major beaches, while the busy bulletin board is filled with equally up-to-date reports from surfers. You can pick up cheap secondhand boards and suits via the small ads.

About.com

www.surfing.about.com

The surfing and bodyboarding section of the massive North American about.com site is well up to the usual standard (see p.12), packed with links to online resources such as instruction sites, equipment sales, destination guides, topical forums, surf cams and weather reports.

Las Olas

www.surflasolas.com

This irresistible specialist site is devoted to promoting an all-women surf school located near Puerto Vallarta on Mexico's Pacific coast. It offers luxurious surfing vacations for anyone from beginners to experts, in idyllic conditions, with yoga, massage and spa treatments also available. Complete and submit the onscreen form for full details.

Maui Windsurfari

http://windsurfari.com

Custom vacation packages in the world's premier windsurfing destination – the Hawaiian island of Maui. This simple site lets you put together your own "windsurfari", with flexible choices of accommodation, tuition if needed, car or board-adapted van rental, and also equipment rental – though you'll have to arrange your flights yourself. Submit the onscreen form once you've decided what you're interested in.

Surfing Australia

www.surfingaustralia.com

At first glance, the Surfing Australia Website appears to have a very heavy bias towards news and features about competitive surfing. Delve a little deeper, however, and you'll find a wealth of listings and links covering every aspect of surfing in the country, including surf schools and tour companies in every state.

Wavehunters

www.wavehunters.com

This full-service surfing travel agency, based in California, has a lavish, memory-gobbling Website. If you're in the market for an all-inclusive surf vacation, pick a destination from the interactive global map – options include little-known South Pacific and Indonesian spots, as well as the more famous North and Central American resorts – swoon briefly at the photos, then call or complete the onscreen booking form. You can also check out assorted world surf reports and maritime weather sites.

Walking and trekking

Note that in addition to the sites listed below, most of the companies listed in the "General adventure holidays" section on p.101 offer walking and trekking holidays.

Active Journeys

www.activejourneys.com

While this Canadian operator also arranges biking, rafting and kayaking trips, its speciality remains walking, with an unbeatable programme of well-priced hiking tours in all parts of the world (except the US). Its easy-to-search Website swiftly unveils a diverse range of trips, from comfortable inn-to-inn walks in Britain and Europe to high-altitude treks. Many are available both as self-guided strolls, which you can take more or less when you choose, and as scheduled, but only slightly more expensive, guided small-group expeditions. Email for full details, then download and mail the reservation form.

Community Action Treks

www.catreks.com

Specialist trekking company, owned by mountaineer Doug Scott, offering eco-friendly and responsible trips to Nepal, India, Pakistan, Bhutan and east Africa. Each trek is accompanied by porters, sherpas, cook and helpers and a local trek leader, and is covered in detail on the site. They are graded from easy to very strenuous; a separate section covers more gruelling mountaineering trips and also pilgrimage treks.

Headwater Holidays

www.headwater-holidays.co.uk

Family-run British firm that arranges a year-round programme of "soft adventure" walking tours in Europe and North Africa, from guided inn-to-inn hiking holidays to one-centre independent walks. Some are purely scenic, others take in historical and archeological sites. Via its easy-to-use Website, it sells holidays to travellers from all parts of the globe, quoting prices with and without air or ferry fares. Specific dates are listed for each tour; email the onscreen form to check availability and make a provisional reservation, and someone will call you back.

HF holidays

www.hfholidays.co.uk

Established UK operator offering self-guided and escorted walking holidays for all levels, plus cycling, cross-country skiing and special interest tours. Self-guided itineraries tend to stay close to home, in the UK and Europe; guided tours, which follow trails in Morocco, Barbados, Chile, Peru, South Africa, North America and Australasia, balance time spent on foot – from two to eight hours per day – and using transport (a minibus), staying in comfortable hotels along the way. You can check availability and book online.

The Ramblers' Association

www.ramblers.org.uk

As well as offering detailed news and advice on walking in the UK, including guides to long-distance footpaths and updates on legal issues, the Ramblers' Association Website links to the Association's sister company, Ramblers Holidays, at **www.ramblersholidays.co.uk**. This organizes walking holidays in Britain and many other destinations, from the Alps to the Himalayas – and including a forty-day around-the-world walking tour – with accommodation usually in family-run hotels.

Sherpa Expeditions Online

www.sherpaexpeditions.com

UK company that offers trips for walkers of all abilities, from gentle self-guided hiking excursions in Europe and inn-to-inn walks in the Atlas Mountains of Morocco to guided hut tours in the Icelandic wilderness or full-scale trekking in the Himalayas. Most trips are within Europe, and many within Britain itself, including coastal walks. The Website holds full details and itineraries, all clearly and neatly presented. Self-guided trips can be arranged whenever you like; for guided tours, check availability by email or phone. To make a booking for any tour you will need to fill in a form and send a deposit.

Sherpa
Expeditions

February 23, 2004
about sherpa
Booking with Confidence
Testimonials

Read the good book and
you'll go to heaven

Webwalking.com

www.webwalking.com/hiking.html

The home page of this American walking and hiking portal holds an extensive menu of features and reviews of interest to hikers, including articles from about.com (see p.12) and lots of equipment bargains. Its greatest value, however, comes in its huge directory sections, with vast lists of tour operators and hiking organizations that either cover specific destinations or operate worldwide.

World Walks

www.worldwalks.com

British company that arranges both guided and self-guided walking tours in the UK and most of Europe, plus a more limited selection in Kenya, New Zealand, Indonesia and the USA. Submit the online form to make your booking.

Water-based activities

Adrift White Water Rafting

www.adrift.co.uk

UK operator that runs well-priced white water rafting trips in Turkey, Nepal, Ecuador, Chile, Ethiopia, Uganda, Zimbabwe and Zambia. Its Website carries full details and itineraries, quoting prices either on a river-only basis – for international customers – or inclusive of flights from Britain. Email or phone to make a reservation.

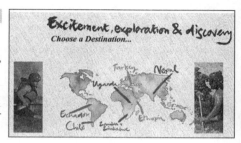

Excitement, exploration & discovery
Choose a Destination...

Blakes Boating Holidays

www.blakes.co.uk

Blakes began life in 1908 renting out wherries on Britain's Norfolk Broads; it now arranges boating holidays of all kinds throughout France, Ireland and the UK. Vessels vary, but the most popular choice remains a barge (narrowboat) trip along the canals of England. To search for a suitable holiday you can either browse a list of possibilities in your preferred destinations or check to see what's available on your dates. No online booking.

British Waterways

www.british-waterways.org

A superbly informative site devoted to "the hidden world of Britain's inland waterways". With help from its sister site **www.waterscape.com**, to which it is linked, it meticulously maps out the UK's canal network and traces its two-hundred-year history. You can search for tour and rental companies that operate on each individual segment, as well as attractions, museums and other facilities along the way.

Ecosummer

www.ecosummer.com

Canadian operator providing crewed yachting trips and cruises in its home waters of British Columbia and Alaska, including wildlife expeditions in pursuit of whales and bears, as well as canoeing and kayaking (with a range of destinations including the Canadian Arctic, Mexico, Belize, the Bahamas and Tonga). Reserve via email or phone.

Far Flung Adventures

www.farflung.com

Specialist rafting operator with a programme of white water trips throughout the Western US. You can join expeditions along the Arkansas River (in Colorado) and the Rio Grande, but the real highlight has to be the musical jaunts near its home of Big Bend, Texas, on which participants are serenaded around the campfire by top-name country musicians such as Jerry Jeff Walker or Butch Hancock. No online bookings, as it insists on customers speaking with staff first.

Far Flung Adventures

"Putting People And Rivers Together"
*

Whitewater river rafting trips, scenic river rafting trips and canoe river trips on the Rio Grande in Big Bend Texas and the Rio Grande and Rio Chama in New Mexico, the Arkansas River in Colorado, the Salt River in Arizona and the Rivers of Veracruz Mexico.

Find Your Far Flung Adventure

| Arizona | Colorado | New Mexico |

GORP Paddling

www.gorp.com/gorp/activity/paddle.htm

As ever, the North American GORP site (see p.103) provides an invaluable resource on "paddling" – which covers canoeing, kayaking and rafting. As well as instructional articles, travel features, bulletin boards, links and equipment sales, it holds a database of vacation operators all over the world, searchable by destination, many of which are available for online booking.

The Moorings

www.moorings.com

Although based in Florida, the Moorings has set up its sailing vacations Website to accommodate customers from all over the world. Beginners can learn to sail in the Virgin Islands or join crewed charter excursions in the Caribbean or the South Pacific. If you can demonstrate the necessary experience, you can also charter your own vessel. The site shows what's available, but you can only book via email or phone.

Neilson Holidays

www.neilson.com

Thanks to its school at Brighton Marina, this British operator can teach you to sail in the English Channel, but its more enticing activities centre on flotilla and bareboat yacht-charter holidays in Greece, Croatia and Turkey. They also offer cycle/surf/sail breaks, combining mountain biking, windsurfing and dinghy sailing in the Mediterranean and Caribbean. Reservations by phone or email only.

Sunsail Holidays

www.sunsail.com

Based in the UK but offering separate Websites depending on the country you're in, Sunsail Holidays arranges crewed, flotilla and "bareboat" yacht charters in the Mediterranean, Caribbean, Indian, Pacific and US coastal waters. Work through all its destinations, checking availability and receiving price quotes for specific dates, then secure a booking by submitting payment online.

Western River Expeditions

www.westernriver.com

Western River Expeditions, whose base is in Moab, Utah, launches rafting trips onto the rapids of mighty rivers such as the Salmon, Green and Colorado, with three enticing options (3-, 4- or 8-days) in the Grand Canyon, setting out (by road) from Las Vegas. All details are clearly and enticingly laid out on screen, and there's online booking available.

Special requirements

Children's holidays and camps

ActionQuest Worldwide

www.actionquest.com

ActionQuest Worldwide offers summer live-aboards for teenagers, with camps and courses for all levels in sailing, scuba diving, wakeboarding, water-skiing, windsurfing, and adventure sports. Kids come mostly from the US, but there are campers from South America and Europe, too, and programmes are available in the Caribbean, Galapagos Islands, Mediterranean, Tahiti and Australia. The site features lots of purple prose, with rave recommendations from past clients and idyllic photos. If you can afford it, download an application form to book.

British Activity Holiday Association

www.baha.org.uk

The British Activity Holiday Association sets safety standards and minimum requirements for facilities and staff training in activity centres – including children's camps and family attractions – around the country. The site is simple and fast, allowing you to pull up a list of its members, with full contact details and Websites for more information.

Camp Beaumont

www.campbeaumont.com

A stalwart in the children's holiday field, with four residential and seven day camps in England, with lots of outdoor activities, creative endeavours and character-building for kids as young as three (day camps) and six (residential). The site covers everything in colourful detail. To reserve, fill in the detailed online booking form (with space for up to four children).

Camp Channel

www.campchannel.com

Searchable summer camp directory from the US, with hundreds of options including adventure camps, family camps and retreats, adults-only camps, specialist camps, camps for people with special needs, and some twenty camps outside North America. Browse the lists under each category and click for full details, including programmes, capacity, average prices and the like, following swift links to Websites where available, and the option to contact them direct for more details. You can also keep a tally of camps that interest you and then compare them all at the end. Check the Camp Store, too, which has links to all sorts of useful outfitters for camping and outdoor gear.

Camp Page

http://camppage.com

Comprehensive, speedy directory of North American summer camps (many of which accept kids from abroad). Either search by state, or decide if you're after a wilderness programme or a boys', girls', or co-ed camp, then click on a map to choose a region or province (there's also a separate section for Canada). Up comes an alphabetical list, with brief reviews and contact details, together with links to the individual sites.

Cross Keys

www.xkeys.co.uk

Cross Keys runs reasonably priced day and residential camps in North London and East Anglia. There are two kinds of day camps, held in the school holidays and at half-term:

Cross Keys Activities, for the 4–12s, allow the kids to specialize in art, drama or sport, while Mini Minors, every Easter and summer, are for the 3–8s, and geared more towards free play. Residential camps (called XUK) are held in Norfolk during the summer. They cater for 6–17 year olds, with clay pigeon shooting, cookery, woodwork, computers, fancy dress competitions and the like, plus lots of free time and day-trips. To book, you can call, send a hard copy form, or download an online form.

Kids' Camps

www.kidscamps.com

Huge Internet directory of summer camps in North America (and a few beyond), including day camps, residential camps, family camps, teen tours, sport camps, art or academic camps, special needs camps, leadership programmes, weight-loss camps – the lot. You can't browse the full list, but search by region or by keying in a few preferences. Up comes a list of the relevant camps, with logo, blurb, and contact details including Websites.

National Camp Association Inc.

www.summercamp.org

Useful American site that will help you choose the best summer camp for your child, either in the US or abroad. First, it gives a rundown of the questions you need to ask yourself before sending your darlings off for a month or so; you can then go on to use its free advisory service. Simply key in your needs and you'll be sent a list of summer programmes that meet your requirements by email, post or fax. You will also receive information from each camp, including brochures and videos if you wish. The form is simple, but covers all the bases: you need to be as specific, and as flexible, as possible. You can also ask for an opinion on any camp that you might be considering.

PGL

www.pgl.co.uk

PGL ("parents get lost") is the UK market leader in kids' camps, offering a wide range of activity holidays in the UK and France (plus one each in Austria and Spain) for kids aged 7 to 17. Search by holiday centre or by activity; the imaginative choice – from acting holidays, surfing and ski trips to themed weeks such as "secret agent" and "pop star", all geared towards different age bands – is great. Booking online gets you a discount of £25 off the brochure price.

Disabled travellers

Able To Go

www.abletogo.com

Database of UK holiday accommodation suitable for people with mobility difficulties. You can either browse a list of all the properties available in your preferred area, or use the advanced search to specify price range, type of property, and the purpose of your trip. Results come with full details, photos and Web links where available. You need to register to use the advanced search, but membership is free and gives access to a number of special offers and promotions.

Access-Able Travel Source

www.access-able.com

Amazingly useful information site, produced in the US, with links to travel resources – accessible hotels, tour operators, equipment rental outfits and so on – around the world. There's a searchable cruise section which reviews individual ships according to their accessibility. Plus FAQs, trip reports, travel tips on a variety of subjects from travelling with oxygen to taking guide dogs on taxis, and a good range of general disability and travel-related links.

Accessible Journeys

www.disabilitytravel.com

US operator, with offices around the world, offering a wide variety of touring holidays for slow walkers, wheelchair users and their companions. As well as fixed-base holidays in places such as southern Spain, Switzerland, London and Devon, it leads trips around the national parks of the American West and as far afield as Nepal, South Africa and Australia. There are also many custom-designed possibilities, from adventures in China and the Philippines to luxury villa stays in the Caribbean. The Shopping link gets you to online suppliers of medical supplies, wheelchair accessories and such like, and there's an intelligent set of links ("Travel Resources") to a variety of travel sites. Unusually, the travel tips section comes up trumps, and you can subscribe to a monthly newsletter for more of the same.

All Go Here

www.allgohere.com

This UK-based site includes help for people using speech systems or who cannot see the screen clearly, and has two very useful features: the database of more than 2000 mainstream hotels (all in Britain), rated for accessibility and listed with contact details; and the directory of disability-friendly world airlines, complete with reviews covering carriage of wheelchairs, oxygen provision, boarding procedures and the like. Each has been vetted in person.

Disabled Holiday Directory

www.disabledholidaydirectory.co.uk

Exactly what it says – a UK-based directory of services, holiday centres, adventure/activity holidays and specialist agencies in Britain and further afield. A large section of the site is devoted to accommodation options, including self-catering, in Europe and the USA. Just click on a link to read full details, including links to websites where available.

Microtel Inns and Suites

www.microtelinn.com

Inexpensive American hotel chain that strives to be "the preferred chain for travelers with disabilities". You can take a 360° tour of a typical disabled access room, check each motel for facilities such as roll-in showers and hearing-impaired guestroom kits, and then finalize availability and rates before booking online.

Society for Accessible Travel and Hospitality

www.sath.org

Major lobbying organization, based in New York, whose aim is to "remove physical and attitudinal barriers to free access and expand travel opportunities in the United States and abroad". The site provides guides on how to travel with various disabilities or illnesses, news stories – including details of regulations affecting disability – and scores of useful links to tour operators, newsletters and other disability websites.

Transitions Abroad

www.transitionsabroad.com/listings/travel/disability/index.shtml

This bi-monthly alternative tourism magazine has a very good list of resources for travellers with disabilities, from educational programmes to home exchanges and diving trips.

Each entry gets a brief review and contact details, including links to websites where available.

Travelin Talk

www.travelintalk.net

Password-protected directory of thousands of travellers with disabilities, most of them in the US, willing to offer advice and assistance – from researching hotels to recommending equipment repair shops – to other members who are visiting or passing through their home towns. Lifetime membership costs $19.95, for which, as well as a monthly ezine filled with news, access information and resources, you get discounts of up to 50 percent at hotel chains and on equipment and travel publications.

Tripscope

www.tripscope.org.uk

UK charity offering advice and information to travellers with impaired mobility. There's no actual database on the site – all requests are responded to personally over the phone or by letter, fax, or tape – but it does provide useful and detailed checklists for things to consider when planning your journey and booking accommodation, insurance policies and transport.

Virgin Holidays

www.virginholidays.co.uk/home/specialneeds/special.html

Virgin do an admirable job of making their special needs policy clear – all flights have an onboard wheelchair, travellers to the USA can rent cars fitted with either left or right hand controls, and accommodation options suitable for disabled travellers are denoted with wheelchair symbols. Clicking onto this page of the site you can also read detailed tips and airport information for disabled travellers.

Family travel

For children's holidays and camps, see p.136.

British Youth Hostel Association

www.yha.org.uk/sctn_fami/intro.html

The British Youth Hostel Association offers a good deal with its "family-friendly" hostels. With kids older than three you can breeze past the dorms to your private bunk-bedded room, complete with washbasin, and for families travelling with babies there are cots and highchairs for hire. You're given your own keys and all-day access to the hostel. Most hostels have a games room, and organize activities from wildlife-watching to treasure

hunts. For details of YHA's family activity packages, look at
www.yha.org.uk/sctn_acti/intro_fam_breaks.html; options include biking, walking and
climbing, along with paint-ball weekends and seasonal celebrations. A year's YHA membership
costs £27 (£13.50 for one-parent families), with children under 18 free. You can join online.

Butlins

www.butlins.co.uk

The classic British holiday camps (sorry, resorts) may not have quite shaken off their enduring
image – all hyperactive Redcoats and hearty bootcamp activities – but they certainly know
their stuff when it comes to reasonably priced family holidays (and, for a small fee, day
visits). The resorts, in Skegness, Minehead and Bognor, have splash pools, crazy golf, funfairs,
bowling alleys, tennis courts, cinemas – even Burger King franchises – with special features
for different age groups. The live entertainment isn't to be sniffed at, either, with themed
weekends and big pop acts – Atomic Kitten, Blue and the like – doing the rounds. The site
details a wide variety of last-minute and seasonal deals. Online booking is available, and
you save £5 for your trouble.

Centerparcs

www.centerparcs.com

Centerparcs' Website has plenty of information about its forest "villages" in the UK
(Longleat, Elveden, Oasis Whinfell and Sherwood) and northern Europe, but the online
booking facility, though secure, is disappointing: currently you can't book for any stay
longer than a week, nor can you book more than one villa (for these you need to phone
them direct). You can, however, read about the villas, the "Aquadomes" with their "subtrop-
ical swimming paradises", the sports facilities, and the spas. Everything at Centerparcs is
family-oriented, with play areas, adventure playgrounds, swimming classes, children's
menus and the like. The only way to find out how much things cost is to set off on the
online booking trail: key in your details to access a list of what's available on your chosen
dates, with the price per villa per night. Prices vary widely according to season and villa type.

Esprit Ski/Esprit Alpine Sun

www.ski-esprit.co.uk and www.sun-esprit.co.uk

UK-based family-holiday specialist offering alpine holidays in France, Italy and Austria all
year round. Both sites are clear and useful, with details of all resorts, facilities and
accommodation, and the holidays are great, with tons of childcare facilities. Sun-Esprit has
"Alpies" clubs for kids (summer tobogganing, biking, rafting and circus skills, for example),
along with nurseries, babysitting, and children-only meals. Meanwhile, the Ski-Esprit site
details a number of resorts, with a great range of activities including ski classes for children
as young as three ("spritelets"), and clubs for over-8s ("Super Sprites"), who receive instruction
in skiing, snowboarding, ski-touring and snowblading. You can check prices online, then
download a booking form or call direct to make a reservation.

Keycamp

www.keycamp.co.uk

Up-market camping holidays in palatial mobile homes and four-bedroom "super tents" throughout Europe. Though you have to click around a bit to get where you want, the site eventually comes up with all the salient details: photos, ground plans, information about the local area and so on. All sites have restaurants, sports facilities, games and TV rooms, and pools; the children's clubs are free, and there's an emphasis on hearty outdoor activities. Many throw in use of canoes, windsurfers and barbecues for free, and offer special offers and short break deals. The campsite search allows you to key in your requirements to find the best matches; you can then check availability and book online.

Thomson Family Adventures

www.familyadventures.com

US operator offering creative adventure holidays for families. The range of destinations is inspiring, with holidays in Alaska, Australia, the Galapagos, Costa Rica, Ecuador, Africa, Turkey and New Zealand, and the site covers each trip in detail, including itineraries, photos and costs. Everything is well-planned, from the activities – rafting, safaris, rainforest tours and snorkelling, among others – and the accommodation (family-owned guesthouses, villas, safari lodges and campsites) to the "pen pal" visits to community projects and schools where kids can hook up with local children. Prices are, not surprisingly, high. No online booking; contact them direct.

ukparks.com

www.ukparks.com

The British Holiday and Home Park Association (BHHPA) Website is a searchable database of more than 2600 holiday and residential parks in the UK. You can search by name, town, county or type of park – and there's a separate search tool for special deals. Each park has their own page on the site, with full details of facilities, and, in many cases, photographs. The Virtual Brochure link allows you to add whichever park you are interested in as you go; you'll then be sent an email with full information on the parks contained, with hot links back to the relevant pages on the site. Special conservation award icons denote parks that David Bellamy has pinpointed as having positive eco-policies, as well as being in particularly lovely countryside – you can search for the award-winners direct.

Single parents

Opfholiday

www.opfh.org.uk

Though the site design is clunky, the concept – reasonably priced group holidays (camping, self-catering and in hotels) for single parents and their kids, geared around the school holidays – is so good that it's well worth a look. Options include France (including Disneyland Paris), Spain, Malta, the USA (more theme parks) and Australia, and it even offers a world tour. Head straight for the calendar to see what's on offer when, then check the index for full details (including costs) and "vacancies" for availability. It's a charitable organization, and offers good deals. US travellers can join groups in Florida and on French camping/caravan holidays. Online booking available.

Small families

www.smallfamilies.co.uk

Bare-bones site from a newish UK-based operator that organizes group holidays to family resorts in Tunisia, Portugal, Spain (the Universal Mediterranea theme park, near Barcelona) and Cyprus, along with skiing trips and "Santa" breaks in Finland. Groups are made up of between five and fifteen single-parent families, and resorts are selected for their children's activities, evening entertainments, and good value. Prices, which start at around £450 for adults, include flights.

Family holiday advice

For a rundown of the family programmes offered by the major cruise lines, check **www.cruiseinformationservice.co.uk** (see p.162). And for information on health precautions for children travelling, go to **www.tripprep.com** (see p.81).

CyberParent

www.cyberparent.com/trips

Forthright US family site with a subsection on travel. Short, focused articles emphasize the need to make family travel relaxing and spontaneous, keeping in mind the needs of both children and parents. The content is perceptive, covering subjects such as cruises, flying with children, and the particular problems faced by single parents. And it throws in a couple of suggestions for lifesaving travel games for good measure.

Family.com

http://family.go.com/travel

Disney-owned site with a large section devoted to family-friendly holidays, primarily throughout the US and the Caribbean. Lots of Disney ads, of course, with information about and links to the parks – which is useful in itself – but it's gratifyingly broad-focused, with articles, trip reports, sensible travel tips, pre-departure checklists and lots of links.

Family Travel

www.family-travel.co.uk

This stylish, independent UK site – no adverts! – deals with everything you need to know when planning a holiday with kids, whatever their age and whatever your budget. Content ranges from the fairly obvious to what, in this field, is relatively hard-hitting (pointing out, for example, that so-called "child-friendly" hotels can be a real nightmare for adults). With news on deals, offers and events around the world, along with scores of articles on immunization, independent travel, round-the-world trips and the like, it also features a monthly special report. These are incredibly detailed, with numerous articles, links to operators, and so on. When their month's up they're stored in a database, which it will cost you £14.95 per year to access. There's also a moderated noticeboard, filled with recommendations.

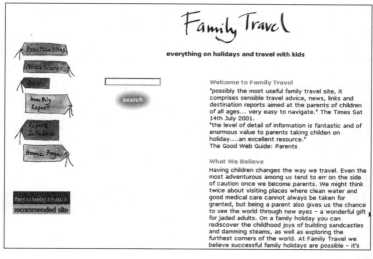

Family Travel Forum

www.familytravelforum.com

"Have kids, still travel!", chirrups the logo of this excellent US subscription-based site. Joining online (around $4 per month or $38 per year) gets you a trip-planning service, access to special deals and tried and tested family-friendly agents around the world, and a monthly FTF ezine (trip reports; book, toy and travel gear reviews; resort ratings and so on). Non-members can read a selection of stories and post on the open forums.

GoNomad

www.gonomad.com/family/familyTravel.html

If theme parks and French campsites don't appeal, turn to the excellent GoNOMAD site, which details alternative holidays across the spectrum. The ambitious, eco-friendly options recommended for families include horse riding in Mongolia and sea-kayaking in Ireland. See p.103 for more on GoNOMAD.

Theme Park Insider

www.themeparkinsider.com

Handy site reviewing the world's major theme parks. (Most are American, but there are listings for Canada, Japan, Australia and Europe as well.) Each ride, restaurant and hotel is ranked and reviewed individually by site users, with separate sections reviewing rides for toddlers and for kids, plus tips for thrill-seeking parents wanting to maximize their own fun. There's also a good section on safety, with regular news updates. You need to register to log your votes and reviews, and to post a comment on the message board. Note that the major American theme parks are reviewed in our USA section; see p.342.

Tiny Travelers

www.tinytravelers.net

Brought to you by the same people as Family Travel Forum (see above), this slick US site specializes in the issues raised when travelling with kids younger than four. Beautifully easy to navigate, it's one to bookmark, with a range of articles subdivided into clear sections. "Trips" is devoted mostly to reviews of American and Caribbean resorts, with some general info on flights, cruising, home swaps and so on; "Tips" tackles common problems (car journeys, flights, tantrums and the like); "Health" has advice on things like preventing motion sickness and ear pain, while "Gear" not only features gear reviews and articles but also links to the Family On Board shop, which sells such things as laptop games, strollers and air-turbulence protection vests. You can read more gear reviews, along with destination reports and general discussions on the message board ("Share").

Gay and lesbian travellers

For a gay guide to Australia, see p.198. And for the same writer's take on gay Thailand, see p.311.

Damron

www.damron.com

The publishers of the leading gay guides to the USA (and, to a lesser extent, Europe), have a useful, if not wholly freely accessible, Website. You need to subscribe (around $10 for three months or $32 per year) to access the online guides: doing so allows you to search a database of destinations, with thousands of listings for bars, clubs, restaurants, stores, helplines, Websites, community centres, magazines, and sex clubs around the world – including places not yet in the printed guides. Non-subscribers don't do too badly, either, with free access to the online calendar, detailing circuit parties, Pride events, AIDS fundraisers, etc (all in the US), and also a set of links to US tour operators offering men-only, women-only, and mixed holidays, in all sorts of categories. Ordering the guides online gets you a 20-percent discount.

Man Around

www.manaround.com

Large UK-based operator offering gay-friendly packages in Cape Town, California, Australia, New Zealand, South America, Europe (city breaks and beach resorts) and Thailand. Choose your destination and then your accommodation (some, but not all, of which is exclusively gay). Holidays come priced with flights from London or on a room-only basis. Call or email to make a booking, or to order a hard copy brochure. A link on the home page takes you to their sister company, Alternative Holidays, who organize gay ski weeks, cruises and party holidays; you can get there direct on **www.alternative-holidays.com.**

Planet Out

www.planetout.com

Huge gay lifestyle portal, produced in the US, with an excellent travel section. It's very user friendly, with articles on anything from gay ski vacations to lesbian rodeos, and handy tour- and event-finders. Much of the site is devoted to the worldwide destination guides; search by region, then use pull-down menus to fast-track to the most popular cities or resorts. For each place you get reviews of accommodation, restaurants, nightlife, shops, sightseeing and so on, and, in the major destinations you can filter listings further, choosing to view only "very gay" hotels, say, or "renowned cuisine". Plus message boards, travellers' tales and news stories.

Respect Holidays

www.respect-holidays.co.uk

British travel company specializing in quality package holidays to popular gay resorts in Spain – including Gran Canaria, Ibiza and Sitges – Mykonos, and Cape Town. The site features an edited version of its hard copy brochure, with lots of detail on its rather good accommodation (from basic to very luxurious, gay-friendly to exclusively gay), plus destination reports and last-minute deals. Whether you can book online or not depends on where you choose to stay; for some places you will need to call them direct.

Toto Tours

www.tototours.com

Men-only US operator that takes gay men on small-group adventure tours. Activities, including rafting, horse riding, trekking and sailing, are moderate to soft, with the exception of the high-adrenaline "Macho" tour in Costa Rica, which includes mountain biking, paragliding, body surfing and rainforest trekking. Destinations – among them Vietnam, China, Panama, the American Southwest and the Virgin Islands – are superb. Each holiday is covered in detail on the site, with photos of the accommodation and full itineraries. Bookings are made by printing out a form, which you then need to send with a deposit.

UK Gay Hotel and Travel Guide

www.gaytravel.co.uk

Wide-reaching directory of worldwide travel services, all of which claim to be either gay-owned or gay-friendly. Sometimes the "gay" tag is tenuous: clicking the link for "car hire", for example, or "flights", brings up the usual big-name Websites, and many of the hotels listed mention nothing whatsoever about gay credentials, but if you stay specific, choosing "lesbian accommodation", "gay holiday weeks" and so on, you'll do OK. Categories include accommodation in the UK, Europe, USA, Canada and worldwide; travel guides; UK travel services; and worldwide tour operators.

Walking Women

www.walkingwomen.com/lesbians.htm

UK company (see p.156) organizing women-only walking holidays in the Lake District, Scotland, Ireland, Madeira, Crete, Lesbos, France and Italy – and occasionally in South Africa, too. Though all women are welcome, it does encourage lesbian ramblers, and a couple of breaks per year – as yet only in the UK – are exclusively gay. In the past these have included murder mystery weekends and seasonal celebrations.

Senior travellers

Classic Ski

www.classicski.co.uk

Starting on the premise that you're never too old to ski, Classic Ski organizes small-group (six people maximum) holidays to the French Alps, with five hours instruction per day, whether you're a complete beginner or more experienced. Participants tend to be aged between 40 and 70, though they have had some in their eighties; you can even fix up to go paragliding, snow scooter riding or ballooning.

Elderhostel

www.elderhostel.org

This US-based, not-for-profit company offers an extraordinary range of adventure/educational holidays in more than 90 countries – open to people over 55 and their travelling companions. Some trips, labelled "inter-generational", are open to entire families. Programmes range from visits to the Hopi tribal villages of Arizona to 22 days trekking in Fiji, Tonga and Samoa. Frustratingly, though, because there are so many hundreds of options, you have to instigate a search by destination, season or keyword only, and nowhere can you browse a full list. You can, however, check availability and book online – if you manage to decipher the byzantine security code system. Flights are priced from US airports only; you can, however, book programmes by themselves. You'll need patience to get the best out of this site, but the trips themselves are well worth it.

ElderTreks

www.eldertreks.com

Toronto-based company running small-group walking and adventure trips for the over-50s (plus companions of any age). There are more than fifty exciting destinations, from Easter Island through Bhutan to Iceland, and you can choose your own pace depending on your stamina and interests. Although most trips have you sleeping in guesthouses, you could choose to camp, or bunk up in a tribal hut, and some trips involve canoe trips, bike rides or (moderate) climbs. However, even the most challenging holidays are not meant to be a strain, and each one employs local guides, cooks and porters for support. You can browse a list of tours, with full details including photos, itineraries, testimonials and activity ratings, and then book online. Prices include everything but the flight; solo travellers share with others of the same sex.

Saga

www.saga.co.uk/travel

The leader in travel for the over-50s in the UK – also offering insurance and financial services – has a frustratingly slow-moving, image-heavy site. It's divided into ocean cruises and "touring", which covers bus and train tours, river cruises, short breaks with city break specialist Travelscene, and special interest breaks (bridge, historic houses, walking). You can view a list of holidays by destination (and there are many, from the Rocky Mountains to Sri Lanka), with full details. You can make a provisional reservation online, but bookings have to be made by phone.

Senior Women's Travel

www.poshnosh.com

Upbeat US site "for the 50+ woman with a passion for travel", offering pricey European city tours – usually including food tastings and a cooking class, literary tours, and shopping trips – for older women who don't want to go it alone (there are no single supplements and no sharing required). They have a good range of grandmother/granddaughter packages, and outside Europe a few tours in New York City, the Berkshires, Peru and Costa Rica. No online booking, but you can read about the trips and email to make a reservation. Plus book reviews, trip reports and travel news.

Student travellers

See also p.72 for hostels. For interrail and train passes see p.50, and for bus passes see p.58. And if you've come out of college with a yen to do good … turn to the volunteering sites reviewed on p.182.

American Institute for Foreign Study

www.aifs.com

AIFS organizes educational trips, cultural exchange and study abroad programmes for American students, while foreign students can apply to live with an American family and attend high school for a year, or offer their services as an au pair while studying at an American college. The Institute also oversees employment opportunities in summer camp programmes (the site links through to **www.campamerica.co.uk**) and major US resorts (**www.resortamerica.co.uk**).

Backpack Europe on a Budget

www.backpackeurope.com/other/students/

Bursting with useful links, Kaaryn Hendrickson's excellent budget travel site, though written mainly with Americans in mind, is perfect for any young person embarking on the "grand tour". This section, devoted to students, features study/work abroad programmes and volunteer agencies and is particularly useful to travellers from the US.

BUNAC (British Universities North America Club)

www.BUNAC.org

Information site for BUNAC, the work/travel programme specialist. Best known for its US summer camps, BUNAC also offers schemes in places such as China, Australia and Ghana, many of which are teaching programmes, and not all of which are exclusive to students. The site gives details of the possibilities, along with downloadable application forms.

International Student Travel Confederation

www.istc.org

The ISTC, which brings together a number of international student travel organizations, was devised to develop travel, study, and work exchange opportunities around the world. If you're a student, or a teacher, or under 26, you're eligible for one of its ISIC identity cards, which give discounts on travel, hotels, theatres, restaurants, shops and attractions in more than 100 countries. The speedy, user-friendly site has information on the cards, and where to get them (if you want to buy you'll be directed to your local student travel office), as well as details on work and study exchanges.

STA

www.statravelgroup.com

Worldwide specialists in under-26 and student fares, STA has a huge Website that leads you to different pages depending on which country you are in. Wherever you're looking from, you'll read about STA's deals on tickets, tours, insurance and accommodation, with offers from a number of operators and pop-up windows advertising last-minute deals. Most services are available online, including ordering an ISIC card (see **www.istc.org**) or procuring certain visas. With ideas for gap year and graduate travel, competitions and articles, there's a lot here to read.

Study Abroad

www.studyabroad.com

Comprehensive listings of study programmes in more than 100 countries. You can search first by subject or destination or from categories including summer schools, intern/volunteer, TEFL courses and so on; course descriptions come with email addresses so you can contact them direct. Elsewhere on the site you're linked to organizations offering student fares and discount cards. Original content includes plenty of practical travel and cultural information, and there's a good set of links. You can sign up for the ezine *Express!* to receive details of special offers, news, and links to organizations that can give financial aid, and browse the message boards.

Youthtravel.com

www.youthtravel.com

Beefy, one-stop online travel agency offering discounted scheduled airfares, charter flights, accommodation, weekend breaks and package holidays for 18-25 year olds. One handy feature is the round-the-world flight-planning map; simply hover your cursor over the place you want to go to see a network of routes serving that destination. You can then click to see dates and pricing details of a particular route. They also offer bus and train passes, travel insurance and car hire, student travel cards and all manner of advice, with destination news, medical tips, useful contact numbers and web addresses.

Weddings and honeymoons

www.cruiseinformationservice.co.uk (see p.162) provides a fact sheet for honeymooners and anyone planning to get hitched at sea.

About.com

http://honeymoons.about.com/travel/honeymoons

More from the monster US directory about.com, which consistently comes up with quality links and strong content. The honeymoon channel can hook you up to sites arranged into categories including planning, destinations, all-inclusives, "weddingmoons" (the destination wedding package where absolutely everything is included), budget honeymoons, cruises and train journeys. Clicking each section might get you straight to a list of reviewed links, or to one of the specially written about.com articles, which are themselves peppered with even more links.

Absolute Asia

www.absoluteasia.com

Luxurious custom-designed tours in Asia and the South Pacific offered by a classy New York company. Look under "Special Interest Tours" for a choice of ten honeymoons. Fiji, Indonesia, Vietnam, Bora Bora, the Philippines, New Zealand, Australia – all of them sound fabulous, but few can match the "Maharaja's Honeymoon". Among other treats, this throws in a traditional Indian wedding ceremony, a horse-and-carriage ride to the Taj Mahal, Ayurvedic treatments and massage, elephant rides, and three nights at a top beach resort in Goa, all for $6000 each (excluding flights). These romantic plans are only suggestions: you should call direct to benefit from the pampering personal service.

Destination and Specialty Wedding Page

www-personal.umich.edu/~kzaruba/wedding.html

The site is tired looking (as Karen, the host, readily and unashamedly admits) and maybe too chummy for some tastes, but overall it's a gem: devoted to unconventional, themed and destination weddings, it's well written and informed, with hundreds of indispensable links, many of which apply to honeymoons too.

Hawaii Weddings

www.hawaiiweddings.com

Unusual wedding packages in out-of-the-way Hawaiian beauty spots performed by the non-denominational Reverend Howie and his flamboyant parrots. The emphasis here is on spirituality: no orders to "obey", no parting through death, three blasts on the conch shell and much Hawaiian chanting ... though all the usual things, like photographs, flower garlands, cakes and videos are taken seriously, and you can even get a drop-dead gorgeous make-up job (check the entertaining before and after photos). A handful of video clips let you see the Reverend in action, performing weddings by a waterfall, on a boat, and under the ocean.

! ! ! Above Heaven's Gate

Waterfall & Beach Weddings ! ! !

41-1010 Laumalo St., Waimanalo Bay, HI 96795
voice: 1-800-800-2933 (2WED) toll-free fax: 1-888-463-6933 (INFO-WED)

Honey Luna.com

www.HoneyLuna.com

American wedding gift registry service that allows you to demand romantic honeymoon activities (dinner cruises, scuba and sailing trips, spa treatments, candlelit dinners), and chunks of your honeymoon (contributions to airfare, lodgings, tours), instead of the usual pillowcases and toasters. Look at the site's sample registries, and then contact HoneyLuna direct to have one designed for you.

The Knot

www.theknot.com

The Knot – "Weddings, Gowns, Gifts" – is a slick US information site and directory for anyone about to tie just that. Go straight to "Ideas and Advice" and then "Honeymoons" for links to the major cruise companies and resorts, plus articles on the Caribbean, Europe, Hawaii and the Pacific, Mexico, Central America and North America. Destination weddings are also dealt with, with real-life stories, question-and-answer lists, and practical "dos and don'ts". "Travel Smarts", in addition to dull old airline sites and hotel groups, features a flurry of frothy articles on beauty products and packable "romance enhancers".

Sandals Resorts

www.sandals.com

The big name in all-inclusive Caribbean resorts, with eleven luxurious complexes, "created exclusively for couples in love", in Jamaica, Antigua, St Lucia and the Bahamas. It was Sandals that patented the "weddingmoon" (which "speaks of love forever true"), and its sun-and-sand weddings – including champagne reception, flowers, cake, photos, candlelit dinner and "Just Married" T-shirts – are now among the most popular in the world. You can check availability and final pricing online. Sweethearts from the UK are directed to **www.sandals.co.uk**

Women travellers

See p.88 for **www.christinecolumbus.com**, where you can shop online for all manner of ladylike travel gizmos, and **www.surflasolas.com** (p.129) for an all-female surf school in Mexico.

Adventures in Good Company

www.goodadventure.com

Eco-friendly tour company that arranges splendid outdoor and wilderness trips for women of all ages. Most of the trips take place in the wild areas of the US, but you can also choose from vacations in Canada, Mexico, Europe and Nepal. Trips are organized on the site by season or activity; a few require a high standard of physical fitness. Discounts are available for single mothers and early bookings. Call or email to check availability, then register by fax, phone, email or online.

GoNOMAD

www.gonomad.com/womens/womensTravel.html

The alternative US-based travel site comes up trumps with its directory of women-only tours worldwide. If you're after anything from sea kayaking in Mexico through cultural tours of Provence to yoga retreats, you'll find something here. Each operator comes with a short review plus email and Web addresses. Plus travellers' tales and handy articles on women's safety, adventure travel, tour operators and the like, with hotlinks.

HERmail

www.hermail.net

International directory of more than 10,000 women travellers in 35 countries worldwide who are happy to advise others coming to or passing through their home town. There is no list to browse, you simply add your details and request a contact in your chosen destination. Email addresses are kept private, and all initial communication is channelled through the site. You'll also find travel articles, a good links page (check under "Classifieds", too), and some genuinely useful travel tips (loved the one about lavender oil and Chinese toilets) – but we could do without the site's disarming practice of using the third-person feminine at every possible opportunity ("Sign Her Up!").

Journeywoman

www.journeywoman.com

"Gal-friendly" quarterly travel ezine, produced in Canada, full of travel information provided by female travellers for other female travellers the world over. With a lively message board, plenty of practical tips – from how to buy tickets for Egyptian trains to where to dine solo in Calcutta – and entertaining anecdotes from intrepid adventurers, it's a really good read. There are also links to dozens of companies that specialize in women-only travel, though these tend to be pricey, and you can sign up for an e-newsletter, which pulls together highlights from the site. One caveat: like HERmail, the incessant use of the third-person feminine –"Try our search engine. You'll love her!" "What should she wear?" – comes across as a little bizarre.

Walking Women

www.walkingwomen.com

UK company organizing women-only walking holidays in the Lake District, Scotland, Ireland, Madeira, Crete, Lesbos, France, Italy and even South Africa – for all levels of fitness. It also offers trips that combine walking with photography, skiing, natural history or quiet contemplation, women-only Murder Mystery Weekends, and a couple of lesbian breaks – all of them reasonably priced. The site provides full information about each trip, with photos, and there's an email booking form.

Wild Rose

www.wildroseholidays.co.uk

When it comes to all-women holidays in the UK, walking holidays rule the roost. This UK operator offers women-only breaks that entail walking (for all levels), plus creative writing, wildlife tours, tennis or watersports. Most are based in the sunny south of England, though there are some trips to Mallorca, southern Spain, France and Gozo. You can read a schedule of trips on the site, but brochure requests and bookings have to be made direct.

Women Traveling Together

www.women-traveling.com

American travel club offering women-only trips – from long weekends in San Francisco and New Orleans to longer stays in safe-bet destinations in the US, Caribbean, Europe and South America, plus adventure trips, sailing, spa holidays and retreats. Membership costs $45 per year and the vacations aren't that cheap (especially if you want a room to yourself), but accommodation is generally top-notch, and most tours and many meals are included in the price. Members receive discounts on trips, and also earn "travel dollars" which are redeemable against future travels. You can make space reservations and join online.

Women's Travel Club

www.womenstravelclub.com

North America's largest travel club for women – membership, which costs $35 a year, gives you access to some thirty holidays in many quirky and off-the-beaten-track destinations around the world (art trips in Mali, anyone?). Each trip involves around 15–20 women. Non-members can read travel tips, book reviews, links and trip reports on the site, and even, if there is space, join the holidays for a premium. Members receive a monthly newsletter and access to password-protected areas of the site; to join, fax the form or phone them.

Women Welcome Women World Wide

www.womenwelcomewomen.org.uk

"Circle the world with friendship", says the "5W" logo. It's a simple concept: a directory of some 3500 women from seventy countries around the world, from as far afield as the Arctic Circle and Argentina, who are willing to invite other members to stay in their homes. It's not so much a hospitality exchange as a cultural one: many members are not wealthy enough to travel far, and are simply interested in meeting women from other cultures. You can download an application form and send it; there is no formal subscription fee, but it asks that members donate at least £25.

Specialist holidays

General specialist holidays

A number of operators offer country-specific special interest holidays. We've reviewed the best of these, where relevant, in our individual destination sections, which start on p.193. See also the UK-based **www.holidaybank.com/holcosp.asp** for a directory of companies offering specialist holidays around the world.

ACE Study Tours

www.study-tours.org

ACE (Association for Cultural Exchange) arranges very good study tours around the world, and, as an added bonus, donates part of its profits to the communities it visits. Specializing in art, architecture and history, it also covers archeology, music, natural history, houses and gardens, theatre and literature; each tour is led by expert scholars. Search by subject, world region or date to read details, itineraries and costs: prices are not unreasonable considering the quality of tuition, standard of accommodation, and range of trips. This is a British company, so prices are quoted in sterling, and most flights, included in the cost, are from London.

Infohub

www.infohub.com

Fantastic US site detailing more than 11,000 specialist holidays around the world, with menus that allow you to specify destination, activity, and lodging. Its activity selectors are superb, with hundreds of options including fashion trips, camel riding, Egyptology and tearoom tours as well as the more usual cookery schools and painting workshops. Destination-wise, it claims to have more choices than any other site – life's too short to try and prove otherwise, especially when you pull up 199 tours for Italy alone, 212 for China,

23 for Kyrgyzstan and ten for Papua New Guinea. Once you've chosen, click the link to submit an email request form direct to the operator.

Martin Randall

www.martinrandall.com

Up-market UK operator offering escorted tours in a variety of countries, from Australia to Uzbekistan via Lebanon and Sweden, focusing on music, art history, archeology and gastronomy. This is serious stuff – a Le Corbusier tour promises an "exploration of the origins of the look of the modern world", for example – and prices aren't low, but you're undoubtedly paying for more than just a holiday. Browse the list of tours by country to get the full range – some available trips simply don't appear if you search by category only. To book, download the form and send with a deposit after calling to check availability.

MARTIN RANDALL TRAVEL LTD

ART · MUSIC · ARCHITECTURE · ARCHAEOLOGY · HISTORY

Click on the image above or click here to enter the site

The air holidays and flights shown within are ATOL protected by the Civil Aviation Authority. Our ATOL number is ATOL 3622. ATOL protection extends primarily to customers who book and pay in the United Kingdom. Registered Company no. 2314294 England. VAT no. 527758803

Shaw Guides

www.shawguides.com

This phenomenal directory covers thousands of study- and hobby-based vacations. Whatever you want – arts and crafts courses, cooking schools, creative writing workshops, cultural tours, language vacations, photography, movie-making, sport – you'll find something here. Browse through lists organized by subject, then search by month, destination or keyword; reviews come with all the relevant information (type of programme, group sizes, costs, location and so on) plus contact details with Website where applicable. Searches can sometimes pull up inaccurate results – selecting England as a destination may well get you a smattering of courses in Maine and Massachusetts as well as in the UK – but that's surely forgivable in such a huge endeavour.

Voyages Jules Verne

www.vjv.co.uk

Enticing site run by up-market UK travel operator, darling of the Sunday supplements, with a long list of options pointing you towards specialist themed trips on every continent. Steam trains, exploration cruises, music and opera, art and history, scenery and landscape ... there's lots to choose from here, from a star-gazing Indian ocean cruise to a week following the Silk Route to Samarkand or twelve nights on a train across rural China to the walled city of Xian. Reservations can be made online; you will be contacted by email or telephone to reconfirm.

Cruises

Alaska's Marine Highway

www.alaska.gov/ferry/

The legendary Alaska Marine Highway System (AMHS) operates perhaps the most spectacular programme of scheduled sea voyages in the world, with its service along the "Inside Passage" complemented by trips across the Gulf of Alaska, into Prince William Sound, and out to the Aleutian Islands. With the exception only of very complex itineraries – for which you have to submit a very detailed reservation request and await confirmation by phone – the Website enables you to plan and pay for journeys between any ports on the network.

Celebrity Cruises

www.celebritycruises.com

Celebrity Cruises is a major player in the world cruise market – "Celebrity" is just a name, you don't get to share a cabin with your favourite soap star – sailing in the waters of the Caribbean, Mediterranean, South America, Alaska and Hawaii. Once you've checked out the cruise descriptions onscreen, booking via the Website is extremely easy; successive pull-down menus guide you into the relevant region, show all available dates, then offer different classes of accommodation; if you like the price, email your full details and you're done.

Cruise.com

www.cruise.com

North American cruise discount site offering savings of as much as 69 percent on a wide range of possibilities – with more than 70 lines represented – including adventure and river cruises. They provide lots of information on which lines and ships are best for you – whether you're an expectant mother or a wheelchair user, or if you're after "lean cuisine",

All the cruise lines included in these listings maintain high-quality Websites. The following other operators also run Websites, but be warned that on the whole they're nothing like as useful; most simply enable users to request printed brochures.

Bergen Line www.bergenline.com
Carnival Cruise Lines www.carnival.com
Crystal Cruises www.crystalcruises.com
Disney Cruise Line www.disneycruise.com
Fred Olsen Cruise Lines www.fredolsen.co.uk
Holland America www.hollandamerica.com
Norwegian Cruise Line
  www.ncl.com (North America) and www.uk.ncl.com (UK)
Orient Lines www.orientlines.com
P&O Cruises www.pocruises.com
Princess Cruises www.princesscruises.com
Swan Hellenic www.swanhellenic.com
Thomson Cruises www.thomson-holidays.com
Windjammer Barefoot Cruises www.windjammer.com

kids' activities, or a honeymoon. If you're not entirely convinced, they challenge you to find a cheaper deal elsewhere, and then promise to beat their competitors' prices. Hot deals and last-minute offers are shown on the home page.

Cruise2.com

www.cruise2.com

Non-profit, ad-free Website that holds an unbelievable amount of cruise-related information. Search its vast database by any permutation of destination, date, price, cabin type, cruise line or specific ship, to find exactly who's doing what; read objective reviews by journalists and comments from passengers; or use the free "Cabin Exchange" to connect with cruise companies offering specific bargains. Above all, Cruise2 is a wide-ranging portal, with links to an endless array of cruising sites arranged as responses to questions such as "Where can I find Discount Prices for Cruises to a particular Destination?" and "Where can I find Websites that have Auctions on Cruises?"

part two: themes and activities

Cruise Information Service

www.cruiseinformationservice.co.uk

Information resource set up by the UK's Passenger Shipping Association, providing helpful onscreen "fact sheets" for would-be cruise passengers, and covering topics like family cruising, river cruising, "repositional cruising" (that's when you can get a bargain cruise by joining a vessel that's voyaging between seasonal destinations), and which companies offer which destinations, with contact details and active links to the relevant cruise lines.

The Cruise Marketplace

www.thecruisemarketplace.com

Californian discount travel agency that sets out to offer bargain cruises the world over. Its Website is extremely simple: just search by cruise line and destination, and it offers you a rough price, with the invitation to call or email if you're interested. This isn't the place to find any useful information, so you'll have to do your research elsewhere, but once you know what you want there's no harm in doing a bit of comparison shopping here.

CruiseOpinion

www.cruiseopinion.com

Though it's basically a promotional tool for a Michigan-based travel agency that specializes in selling cruise vacations – call the phone number if you want to make an actual reservation – the CruiseOpinion Website is a valuable tool for anyone researching a cruise trip, holding five thousand lengthy, personal customer reviews of cruises taken with all the major lines. If you have a specific ship in mind, there's almost certainly a warts-and-all report here written by someone who's already done it.

The Cruise People

www.cruisepeople.co.uk

Shipping agency, with offices in London and Toronto, which takes the whole concept of cruising considerably further than you may ever have imagined. In addition to conventional big-name cruise trips, it sells an intoxicating array of long-distance ocean voyages. Separate sections are devoted to commercial freighters and scientific research vessels that carry paying passengers, and to sailings between Europe and North America (not all of them transatlantic – some head via Suez to California). With no online booking, you have to email or call to make an enquiry; in fact there are few onscreen gimmicks here, and the Website consists mostly of endless lists ... but what fabulous lists!

Geek Cruises

www.geekcruises.com

Geek Cruises are exactly what the name suggests: luxury cruises for computer nerds, devoted to such enticing themes as "Linux Lunacy", "PERL Whirl", and "JAVA Jam", and incorporating expert lectures and tuition. The "Convincing the Boss" section says to call it a conference, not a holiday; naturally, the ship is wired up for Internet access. Most but not all cruises are in the Caribbean, and two-thirds of the clients are said to be single females. Not everyone on board is a geek, as Geek Cruises typically lease around half the spaces on a 1500-passenger Holland America voyage. The Website offers useful links for all ports of call, and you can book and pay online by completing an endless form.

Royal Caribbean International

www.rccl.com

As the Website swiftly reveals, Royal Caribbean's activities are not restricted to the Caribbean alone; it also cruises to or around Hawaii, Alaska, Australia, Mexico and the Mediterranean. Using the "vacation search" facility, pull-down menus reveal every destination, itinerary and specifc vessel. Although it is possible to reserve online, you are strongly encouraged to use a travel agent, so that you can talk the whole thing through first.

Seaview

www.seaview.co.uk

UK-based site that both provides general information on, and sells, cruises and ferry travel, with an emphasis mainly but not exclusively on British and European waters. It offers news, features, destination guides, bulletin boards (in the "Funnel Vision" section), and an oddly flippant set of FAQs, which advise for example that if you don't like your table companions, "tip them overboard or poison them". Most important of all is a "Cruise Finder" facility that will find a trip by any combination of destination, price, date and company. You have to enter your name and email address to see the results, at which point you're told who to email or call to make a reservation.

Small Ship Cruises

www.smallshipcruises.com

Proclaiming itself "The biggest website in the world on small ships ...", this site sets out to cover small-boat trips of every kind, from barge rentals to diving operators. It's not exactly sophisticated (though the odd butterfly wings its way across the screen), and its reviews and listings are entirely uncritical, presumably taken from the operators' own press releases. However, there's a hell of a lot of them, with active links for most companies, and it also carries up-to-the-minute news on the latest routes and special offers. You can also book through Small Ships itself, though whatever you're enquiring about you have to complete much the same lengthy email form.

Star Clippers

www.star-clippers.com

Sailing cruises in the Mediterranean, Caribbean, and Far East on four- or five-masted clipper ships – or "mega-yachts", as the proud owner calls them. One, the *Royal Clipper*, which is based for much of the year in Barbados, is said to be the largest true sailing ship in the world; passengers caught up in the romance of it all can even help to haul the ropes. Though it's a memory-gobbler of a Website, however, packed with enticing images, you can't book online; you can only call, or contact a travel agent.

Eco-tourism

See p.71 for an accommodation reservation company dealing only in eco-lodges; p.182 for volunteer programmes and conservation schemes, and p.185 for wildlife and nature tours. Eco-tour operators that specialize in individual countries are reviewed with the relevant country in our "Destinations" section, which begins on p.193; for an account of Wales' Centre for Alternative Technology, the largest eco-centre in Europe, see **www.cat.org.uk** on p.335.

Ecotravel Center

www.ecotour.org

Produced in collaboration with Conservation International, a field-based organization with headquarters in Washington DC, the Ecotravel Center provides a number of online services. On the home page you're linked to Conservation International's own site, while a notice-board details local (in the US) eco-travel lectures and events. "Destinations" focuses on the exotic "biodiversity hotspots" where CI concentrates its efforts, with all the information you need to plan a trip.

Field Studies Council

www.field-studies-council.org

This British educational charity runs low-impact, culturally aware environmental study holidays across the globe. Scores of choices in Britain range from the seriously specialist –

half a dozen different weekends on mosses and liverworts – to more widely appealing visions like "exploring the seashore". Some combine eco-tourism with painting, photography or arts and crafts. If you're yearning for something more exotic, however – discovering the alpine flora of Sikkim, say, or meandering through the Seychelles – and have upwards of £2000 to spare, follow links to "FSC Overseas" and the world map. Read details on the site, then book using a downloadable form.

Planeta.com

www.planeta.com

Though its main focus is eco-travel in Latin America, this colossal information clearing house – a "global journal of practical eco-tourism" – has hundreds of articles, official reports and links to environmental groups and tourism providers, e-newsletters, forums and eco-journals across the Net. The home page details upcoming events.

Responsibletravel.com

www.responsibletravel.com

Brainchild of Body Shop magnate Anita Roddick, this well-composed site markets rigorously vetted eco-tours and accommodation around the world. You are linked from the home page to individual holidays, which are organized by destination, activity or late availability, and to a growing list of member-operators, which includes high-profile companies Sunvil, British Airways, and Eldertreks as well as a number of grass-roots organizations around the globe. All this plus feature articles, information on health and safety and human rights, trip reports, and travellers' tips. Sign up for a newsletter to be alerted to special deals and promotions.

Tourism Concern

www.tourismconcern.org.uk

UK-based charity that lobbies governments, the industry and travellers to raise awareness of the tourism industry's impact on the planet. Though it's a little scrappy design-wise, the site is worth a look for its invaluable links – covering, among other themes, eco-tourism and ethical tourism – and, under "What we Offer", the resources section: a bibliography of serious tomes, reports, research papers and magazines, some of which can be ordered online.

Tribes Travel

www.tribes.co.uk

This award-winning "fair trade travel company" – paying decent wages, promoting conservation and contributing to sustainable development of the areas it visits – offers small group (six to twelve people) cultural holidays, safaris, treks and special-interest breaks, with

set-departure trips and tailor-made itineraries. These are pretty luxurious breaks, putting you up in tented camps, lodges, characterful hotels or traditional tribal huts; the added benefit is that you know your money is going towards various good causes. You can browse a full list or search by budget, destination – African countries, mostly, but also South America, Jordan, India and Nepal – or interest, from rainforests to arts and crafts. There's an online booking form, but payments should be made off line; prices are quoted in sterling or US dollars.

Food, drink and cookery

For a site detailing accommodation around the world that offers organic food, see p.72.

Absolute Asia

www.absoluteasia.com/cul/index.asp

Up-market New York-based tour operator organizing gourmet private tours throughout Asia, Australasia, North Africa and India. There's a good choice, from family-run cooking classes in remote villages to formal feasts in Japan, each one emphasizing local cuisine and culture and with good attention to all the details. Each itinerary features accommodation at top-notch hotels and resorts, sightseeing, meals, market tours, tastings, cooking classes and demonstrations. Costs, though high (from around $3000 for thirteen days in the Philippines or eight days in Korea, to $10,000 for three weeks in India or one week in Japan) include everything except transatlantic flights.

Arblaster and Clarke

www.arblasterandclarke.com

Informative site managed by the UK specialists in wine holidays. Led by experts, all tours feature visits to top producers, chateaux and cellars, with lots of tasting along the way. Trips vary every year: along with France, Italy, Spain and Portugal, you can also visit Austria, Hungary and Switzerland, and the "New World" wineries of Australia, New Zealand, South Africa, Chile, Argentina and California. "Gourmet tours", which place as much emphasis on food as drink, include five days in a Provencal chateau or a southern Italian fishing village, or you could choose a Ceylon tea tour, taking in regional Sri Lankan dishes. Champagne weekends start at around £300. Also vineyard walking holidays, picnicking and wine tasting as you go, and week-long wine cruises around remote Italian islands. Arrangements are flexible; you can book your flight separately, or opt to add on a variety of extras. No online payment; call or submit the online form to reserve your place.

Bike Riders Tours

www.bikeriderstours.com

Boston-based company offering small, up-market culinary-cycling holidays – find them under "Guest Chef" – for all levels of fitness (most itineraries don't exceed 35 miles a day). Tours, of Burgundy, Provence, Tuscany, Umbria and Sicily take in open-air markets, cookery demonstrations, hands-on classes and feast preparations, plus plenty of tastings. At around $3000 a go, they're not cheap, but everything is top quality, and accommodation, in inns, palaces and elegant hotels, is invariably stunning. To order online, submit the reservation form.

Epiculinary

www.epiculinary.com

North American culinary tour company whose opening page welcomes you to "distinctive cooking journeys". It specializes in trips to France, Italy, Spain and the US, with one trip to Mexico. All trips include classes, meals, market trips, vineyard tours and the like. Tours are arranged on the site by country, with full details of itinerary, cost, dates and everything that's included. Secure online booking.

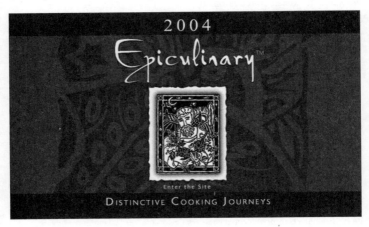

Flavours of Italy

www.flavours-foodiehols.co.uk

UK operator offering up-market small-group holidays in lovely old villas in Lazio, Puglia and Bologna. Prices, from £650 to £1400, cover cookery classes, all food including restaurant meals and wine, luxury accommodation, and visits to local food producers and places of interest. Flights to Italy are not included, though the company can help with your travel plans. No online reservations; instead it provides a downloadable booking form.

Happy Cow's Global Guide

www.happycow.net

Online guide to vegetarian restaurants and health food stores around the world. As you'd expect in an undertaking this large, the listings aren't comprehensive (ten for the whole of Africa), but when it comes to Europe and North America (which includes Canada, and, rather more oddly, the Caribbean, Costa Rica, El Salvador, Guatemala, Mexico and Panama) it's not at all bad (94 in London, 21 in Poland, 87 in New York City), and each country/region offers up a couple of relevant links. There's also space for users to post their own reviews, and an open forum.

Kitty Morse

www.kittymorse.com

Cookbook author Kitty Morse organizes a couple of two-week deluxe culinary tours of her native Morocco – taking in Casablanca, El Jadida, Essaouira, Fez, Marrakech, Rabat, Ouarzazate and Tinerhir. The emphasis is on local cuisine and culture, with two days of classes with Morse at her gorgeous old house south of Casablanca. You also get trips to meet local artists, culinary demonstrations, excursions to mosques, ruins and monuments, shopping jaunts in medinas and souks, and lots of nice dinners in restaurants, working farms and family homes. Unsurprisingly, it's not cheap: the $4995 cost doesn't include airfare. You are linked through to a travel agent to make bookings.

The Mexican Home Cooking School

http://mexicanhomecooking.com

Five-day holidays, comprising B&B and traditional cookery classes, in a lovely old house in the countryside near the colonial city of Tlaxcala, central Mexico. Groups are limited to one to four students (with no single supplements), and there are special vegetarian classes. The $1000 fee includes lodging, three meals a day, and five classes. Non-students pay $500. In keeping with the mom-and-pop style of the venture, there is no online ordering, and no credit card payments; all fees are received by bank-to-bank wire transfers. The site also features sample recipes, which sound very tasty indeed.

Mi Casa - Su Casa

Your Accommodations

Shaw Guides

http://cookforfun.shawguides.com

Specializing in educational and hobby-based holidays, Shaw Guides here offers a directory of more than eight hundred companies and 3000 cooking classes and tours around the world. Tuscany and Provence dominate, but you can also try your skills in less established foodie destinations including Laos, Norway and Fiji. Search by month, or cuisine, or where in the world you want to go; you're then linked to individual reviews with all the relevant informaton plus contact details with Website where appropriate.

VegDining.com

www.vegdining.com

User-friendly guide to vegetarian restaurants around the world, with more than 2000 reviews. It's a US site, so clicking on North America (which includes Canada, the Dominican Republic, Mexico, Panama and Puerto Rico) brings most joy, and though it looks far more professional than Happy Cow (see p.168), some countries bring up fewer listings (just 33 in London), so it's as well to look at both sites. Send an email for details of how to buy the VegDining Card, which offers a ten-percent discount on food and non-alcoholic drinks at vegetarian restaurants around the world (again, by far the majority are in the USA – just six in England). Users submit their own restaurant reviews, which are then vetted and edited.

History, art and archeology

If you're interested in **volunteering for a dig**, see the international archeological organizations reviewed on p.182. See also the specialist operators **www.study-tours.org** and **www.martinrandall.co.uk** reviewed on p.158 and p.159 for their art history and archeology holidays. For tours in individual countries, see reviews of sites for that country.

Andante Travels

www.andantetravels.co.uk

Andante can take you to the world's archeology hotspots – among them southern and eastern Europe, Latin America, Libya, Syria and Jordan, North Africa, Turkey, Sri Lanka and Britain – on tours led by lecturers, travel writers and active archeologists. Prices vary, but as an example you're looking at £2400 for twelve days in Libya, exploring the extraordinary Roman ruins of Leptis Magna, or £3650 for eighteen days following the Ruta Maya in Mexico. A couple of days bussing around prehistoric Wessex, with walks around Stonehenge and Avebury, will set you back around £150 (no accommodation included). Generally, costs include full-board accommodation, admission fees, guides and tips, and on foreign tours include flights from the UK (which you can opt to forego). The site has all the details you need to plan a trip, including availability checks and an online booking form (though you need to call with credit card details).

Holts Tours

www.battletours.co.uk

Established operator offering historical breaks and walking tours of battle sites: whether you're interested in the Hundred Years' War, the Knight Hospitallers, Napoleonic campaigns or the Western Front, you'll find a trip to suit you here. Prices vary from around £330 for two days seeing the sights in York to £2600 for twelve days exploring Anglo-Zulu war sites in South Africa. The site, which you can search by historical period or calendar month, has full details of all the options, but no online booking. Call or send an email, quoting the code of the holiday you're interested in.

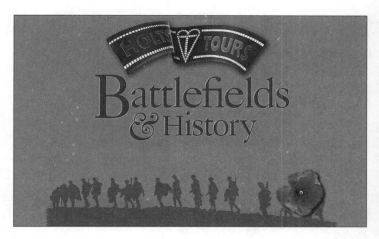

Plantaganet Tours

www.plantagenettours.com

Very good selection of historical tours of Europe, many of them focusing on different figures – Eleanor of Aquitaine, Richard III, the Medicis, and even – stretching the "historical" somewhat – King Arthur. Although they're led by a learned Dane, Peter Gravgaard, who now lives in England, prices are quoted in dollars and may seem rather high to British travellers. The quality of the research, however, and the scope of the tours, are undeniably impressive.

Stephen Ambrose Tours

www.stephenambrosetours.com

Despite charges of plagiarism, the late Stephen Ambrose was one of America's key historians, and his company, managed by family members and friends, is an admirable venture. Ambrose designed the itineraries himself, and his presence is very strong on the site: the trips, naturally, reflect his areas of expertise. Options include a Civil War tour, which starts in New Orleans and takes a week to work its way up the Mississippi via Natchez and Vicksburg into Tennessee; an outdoorsy jaunt following the pioneer footsteps of Lewis and Clark (including a canoe trip down the Missouri); and a D-Day fortnight. It's not cheap – prices start at $1600 for the Civil War tour, and are as high as $6300 for the "Band of Brothers" trip, on which participants are accompanied by Easy Company veterans and get to cross the English Channel in an authentic C47.

Trail of Many Spirits Journeys

www.gonativeamerica.com

The very flash Flash intro, all drum beats and chants, sets the scene for this enterprising UK-US collaboration. On offer are fascinating historical and cultural itineraries of various Native American territories, drawn up in collaboration with the tribal nations themselves.

Whether you're interested in the Sioux of Dakota, the Cheyenne of Wyoming or the Hopi of Arizona, these trips (or "trails") – "Walk in Beauty", "Cheyenne Autumn" and "Seven Council Fires" – offer sightseeing and cultural interaction, crafts workshops, storytelling sessions and cookouts, and each is led by a Native American guide. It would be difficult to create these types of journey independently. Transport is by jeep, minivan or on horse trails; you're looking at around £1895 for two weeks, with no supplements for single travellers.

Language holidays

All the schools below offer courses for all levels, and each one welcomes students from around the world.

AmeriSpan

www.amerispan.com

Highly rated educational travel company with a variety of immersion, volunteer and language programmes, many of them homestays. Though they concentrate mainly on schools throughout the Hispanic world, they have more than 80 schools and languages include Italian, German, French, Arabic, Japanese, Chinese, Thai and Russian. The site couldn't be more user friendly: click a country, select a school and read no-holds-barred reviews (note that the quoted costs don't include the $100 registration fee). If you're not sure where to start, the "Choosing" search lets you specify all sorts of preferences, including safety, political stability and creature comforts, while the site recommends the best programmes for seniors, families, or professionals. It's possible to register and pay online.

Center For Study Abroad

www.centerforstudyabroad.com

Seattle-based company offering flexible, reasonably priced language programmes in Austria, France, Germany and Italy, Costa Rica, Mexico, Chile and Spain, Japan, China and Hong Kong, Brazil, Russia, Vietnam, Australia and New Zealand, Ireland and England. Most are summer schools – from one to nine weeks – but you can sometimes choose to stay on for another semester or even a year. Students live with local families or in guesthouses, or are free to make their own arrangements. To apply, fill in the online form; they also require a $45 deposit (cheque or money order only), deductible from the total cost of a programme.

Language Studies Abroad

www.languagestudiesabroad.com

Whether you want to learn French in Canada, Cantonese in China or Portuguese in Brazil, there are lots of countries, schools and languages to choose from here. Hundreds of classes, too, many of which can be combined with lessons in music, sports, cultural studies, cooking and even fashion history, and which range in length from one week to one year. Browse a full list or use the search, which lets you choose the city you wish to study in, the language, the school and the programme. You can book with or without accommodation, most of which is homestay. Prices vary widely, but the application fee is always $100, and there's a $100 deposit on top of that; fill in the online application form and phone with your credit card details.

Languages Abroad

www.languagesabroad.com

This North American company has a classy site detailing probably the widest selection of language courses and holidays available, with all the usual destinations in western Europe and Latin America, plus places like Guadelupe, Morocco and Yemen, Croatia and Indonesia. Courses can last anything from a week to a year, and accommodation is in university dorms, self-catering apartments, hotels, guesthouses or with host families. There's aboutely tons to read about each destination, school and course – the downside is the registration fee, which at (a non-refundable) $200 is a bit steep.

New Age, religious and spiritual

For Ayurvedic and healing holidays, see Health Breaks and Spas on p.117.

Confraternity of St James

www.csj.org.uk

Based in London, the Confraternity of St James is a non-profit, non-denominational group of people who have completed the pilgrimage to the shrine of St James in Santiago de Compostela, northern Spain. Organizing conferences, lectures and "practical pilgrim days", where you can meet up with experienced pilgrims, it also runs this useful, unadorned site. Head straight for the FAQs, which cover everything, linking to relevant pages on the site and to tour operators, pilgrim stories and pilgrim associations across the Web. There's also an English-language bibliography and a secure online bookshop selling CSJ guides – and even a list of Internet cafes that you'll come across along the trail. The American pilgrims' association has a garish site at **www.geocities.com/friends_usa_santiago**, with basic information, recommended reading, and a forum.

Godserver.com

www.godserver.com

Search engine for more than 80,000 alternative health, spiritual and religious Website, including more than 1000 sites devoted to travel. They're organized into categories including retreats, pilgrimages and indigenous spirituality, so whether you're after traditional ayahuasca ceremonies in the heart of the Amazon jungle, or discovery of self-identity through Ho'oponopono (that's an ancient Hawaiian healing and forgiveness process), you'll find something here. It has to be said, though, that some of them – the directory of Native American Studies, for example – are pushing the "travel" aspect a bit.

Heritage Tours

www.heritagetoursonline.com/jewish_heritage.html

Up-market New York-based operator offering cultural and adventure tours of Morocco, South Africa, Turkey and Spain, with an emphasis on Jewish heritage. The Moroccan itineraries, in particular, are strong on the country's Jewish history and the tradition of Muslim-Jewish co-existence. No online booking; contact the company direct for more details.

Huzur Vadisi

www.huzurvadisi.com

Peaceful retreat in a mountain valley in southwest Turkey. Guests (a maximum of twenty) stay in traditional tents, or yurts, with beds, electricity and wooden floors (on hot nights the tip of the roof is left open, so you can stargaze from your bed), and spend their days practising yoga and swimming in the natural stone swimming pool. Week-long yoga, pilates and walking breaks start at £390, not including flights. The Website has lots of tempting photos of whitewashed courtyards and leafy vistas, and includes dates of courses and all costs. You'll have to make contact direct (or via Huzur Vadisi's agent in Wales) to make a booking, however.

Infothai.com

www.infothai.com/itm

Information site for the International Training Institute of Thai Massage in Chiang Mai. This is one of the most highly regarded Thai massage schools, offering English-language courses for all levels, from five to fifteen days. Study includes yoga and meditation and the giving and receiving of supervised Thai massage. Fees start at US$65 for five days.

International Sivananda Yoga Vedanta Centre

www.sivananda.org

Kindly faced gurus and sage quotations on the subject of bliss and inner peace dot this impressive site – lots of content, lots of links. Eighty or so ashrams offer retreats and yoga holidays year-round, all of them offering two yoga classes, meditation sessions and vegetarian meals per day. Costs vary, depending on whether you want to stay in a beachfront room in Nassau or in a tent in Kerala, but at each one guests are encouraged to participate in karma yoga (or "selfless service" – volunteering and offering donations). Click "Our Locations" or "Yoga Vacations" on the "Om page" (it's pronounced ohhm ...) for information.

Iona Community

www.iona.org.uk

Founded in 1938, the Iona Community, an ecumenical Christian fellowship marooned on a tiny island off the west coast of Scotland, works to explore inclusive approaches to worship and spirituality. The community welcomes up to 100 guests a week, along with pilgrims, to stay either in a restored medieval abbey (bunk-bedded rooms for between two and five people), a conference centre (dorms for four, six or ten), or at an adventure camp in stone-built cottages on the moors. At each centre, meals, prayer, activities, chores and social occasions are shared. The site is detailed and well-illustrated, but you need to call or email the Community for full information.

Kalani

www.kalani.com

Part cultural centre, part fabulously luxurious oceanside "wellness resort", Kalani Honua, on Hawaii's Big Island, offers a wide range of vacations and activities including yoga, lomilomi massage, watsu (water shiatsu), traditional hula and Hawaiian healing. Women can energize their feminine fire, for example, while men spend a week celebrating the Body Erotic – the range of options is gratifyingly wide. Accommodation ranges from tent space to a gorgeous tree house with private bath.

OmPlace

www.omplace.com

Large, well-organized US directory and information site for all things alternative and spiritual. Click on "Travel" to access a searchable database – organized by destination – with links to retreats, workshops, holiday rentals and hotels, eco-tours, vegetarian vacations, adventure travel and the like. Whether you want to take a vegan tour of the rainforests of Costa Rica, visit shaman in Russia, swim with the dolphins or discover the warrior within, you can find someone to help you here.

Pax Travel

www.paxtravel.co.uk

Established operator, based in London, offering individuals and groups the chance to make pilgrimages to a wide variety of centres including Rome, Santiago de Compostela, Chartres, Lourdes, Bruges, Finland, Malta, Mexico, Egypt, Jordan and Peru. Though most pilgrims are

Christian, the site is keen to point out that "religion is hard to separate from culture in most pilgrimage centres and most of our tours have a healthy mix of both". You can read blurbs and check prices here, but you'll need to email for full details and a booking form.

Peng Travel & Peng France

www.pengtravel.co.uk

Anyone of the belief that "naturism is a way of life in harmony with nature, expressed by communal nudity with the aim of furthering the respect of oneself, of others and that of the environment" will want to check this site. Britain's largest naturist tour operator, Peng offers naked package holidays in the south of France, Croatia, Spain, the Canaries, Crete, Florida, Mexico and the Caribbean. The site, all happy blonde families frolicking on sandy beaches, comes up with the information you need about each resort. There's a downloadable booking form, which you can print and send off by fax.

Naturist holidays

France • Spain • Canaries • Croatia • Crete

United States • Caribbean Islands • Mexico

The UK's biggest naturist tour operator

The Retreat Company

www.retreat-co.co.uk

The Retreat Company produces a bi-annual directory of holidays, getaways and courses that promote spiritual health and wellbeing. This online version lists organizations and operators (most of them, but by no means all, in the UK), with contact details and links. As well as the directory itself, organized by destination, you can browse an events diary, plus sections on tailor-made and eleventh-hour retreats. Bear in mind that the companies featured elect to be included on the site, and that there appears to be little vetting involved: if you want to know more, click "Focus On" to read personal reviews (always positive) of a featured retreat, venue or workshop, or call the Retreat Company direct.

Sacred Journeys for Women

www.sacredjourneys.com

Women-only retreats and pilgrimages to England, Ireland, Crete, Hawaii, and India, with a number of programmes (red tent circles, tantric wisdom weekends, full moon rituals and such like) in the company's home base of Sonoma County, California. The site provides lots of day-to-day details, and photo-galleries, but in most cases you have to email them for prices. The one cost that is detailed here, $495 for the three-day women's writing retreat in California, gives you some idea.

Skyros

www.skyros.com

Best known for its two holistic holiday centres – Skyros and Atsitsa – on the eponymous Greek island, Skyros also has a winter holiday home on the Thai island of Koh Samed. Between them, they offer some 250 courses, many of them taught by big names in their field, and each one – be it yoga, writing or clowning, windsurfing, art or singing – with an emphasis on self-development. Each course runs for one week; you can take one (or, at Atsitsa, three) in the first week, choosing either to take the same one (or three), or continue with something different in the second. The Thai centre has a few special courses on fruit carving, Thai massage and the like. The "guestbook" – where you can ask questions of old Skyros hands, arrange taxi-shares, etc – is a great touch, and there's secure online booking.

Soul of India

www.soulofindia.com

Very good UK operator, run by ex-Church of England minister Kenneth Wilson, offering escorted and self-guided cultural and spiritual tours of the subcontinent. Itineraries follow the footsteps of spiritual leaders, cover themes such as Ayurveda and yoga, or are simply arranged according to religion – Hindu, Sikh, Buddhist, Jain or Christian. For an independent itinerary – which gets you car and driver, local English-speaking guides, and all hotels and trips booked in advance – you're looking at paying anything from £1465 (seventeen days following the footsteps of Gandhi) to £2170 (a fortnight from northern India into Tibet), including flights from UK. Enthusiastic without being gushing, the site gives you all the details you need, plus a handful of travel articles. To book you need to print out a form and send it with a deposit.

Painting

See also **www.andalucian-adventures.co.uk** (p.304) for walking/painting breaks in Spain, **www.industours.co.uk** (p.251) for painting tours in India, **www.filoxenia.co.uk** (p.242) for Greece and **www.skyros.com** (see above) for Greece and Thailand.

Art in Provence

www.artinprovence.com

American-French operation offering workshops en plein air for all abilities in that most painterly of French destinations, Provence. These are luxury trips – painters stay in gorgeous chateaux (with pools) or a three-star hotel, and receive six hours instruction per day; extra-curricular activities, such as cocktail parties and trips to galleries and concerts, are also laid on. You're looking at $2650 for nine days, based on two sharing a room, everything included; non-painting guests are welcome for a lower rate. You can reserve online and call with your credit card details. Their sister sites, **www.art-in-ireland.com** and **www.art-in-holland.com**, cover the same kind of set-ups in Ireland and the Netherlands.

ArtStudy

www.artstudy.com

Based in Florida, Art Study offers the chance to study painting or photography in a dream of a location: Claude Monet's gardens in Giverny. You can sign up for eight or eleven days, from May through October; classes are limited to eight students, who are permitted to wander the gardens at will for one full day and six afternoons a week. The site, dotted with inspirational waterlily pictures, tells you that all instruction, lodgings, field trips and meals are included in the price, which, maddeningly, it withholds – you'll need to send off for the "free information package" to get the full low-down.

Horizons to Go

www.horizons-art.org

True to its promise of "global artistic travel", this excellent US-based company runs intriguing small-group workshops in painting, textiles, sculpture, ceramics, photography, glass-blowing, silversmithing, mask-making and more. Most of the world's artistic hotspots are on offer here – France, Italy, Ireland, Vietnam, Thailand, Guatemala and Belize, Mexico and the American Southwest among them – and students are encouraged to find inspiration in local landscape, culture and history. Courses, which draw upon folk traditions and experimentation, include field trips and workshops with local craftspeople. To register, fill in the email form and call them with credit card details.

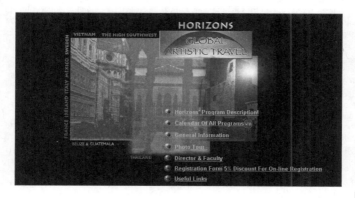

Taos Institute of Arts

www.tiataos.com

One-week arts workshops in Taos, New Mexico, where for years New Agers, artists and Native Americans have lived side by side in an extraordinary desert landscape. Classes, which are held between April and October, incorporate rigorous classical techniques with the rich cultural traditions of the Southwest, including painting, weaving, ceramics, folk art, silversmithing and jewellery-making; groups tend to be small. You can search the schedule on the site, or browse a full list of courses, clicking to see examples of tutors' works. Costs hover at around $400, but you're expected to book your own accommodation. Register by phone or email.

Photography

See also **www.artstudy.com** (see p.179) and **www.tiataos.com** (see above) for art programmes that include photography.

American Photo Mentor Series

www.mentorseries.com

Organized in association with the popular US photography magazines *American Photo* and *Popular Photography*, these holidays (or "treks") allow students of all abilities to join professional photographers – "mentors" – on trips around the world. The site is clear, confident and no-nonsense, telling you what to bring, what to expect, and what you'll need to pay – which is between $650 for a weekend in Seattle to more than $3000 or so for a week in the Galapagos (including tuition, accommodation, meals, local transport). Destinations change each year, but all trips involve daily talks, slide presentations, and personal critiques. Check the gallery to see the impressive – very commercial – results from previous trips, and to email past participants.

Essential India

www.essential-india.co.uk

Specialist operator offering a number of study tours to India, including a sixteen-day photography trip to the Himalayan foothills tutored by a professional anthropological photographer. Emphasis is on "creative risk and cultural understanding", and as well as exploring the extraordinary local landscapes groups work with Tibetan and Gaddi communities to create individual artistic projects. The tour costs £785 (excluding flights); you'll need to send an email to book.

Photo Explorer Tours

www.photoexplorertours.com

Starting its days as a China specialist – the annual China tour, which features field trips with local professionals, is still its most popular – this US-based operator, run by award-winning travel photographer Dennis Cox, now offers trips to a stunning range of destinations. It's a long list – including Ireland, Russia, Iceland, the Greek Islands, Turkey, Tibet, Nepal and Bhutan, Newfoundland, Costa Rica, South Africa, Namibia and Botswana – so browse the thumbnail details (under "Tours Schedule") before clicking for fuller accounts. As well as tuition and guides, prices include three/four-star accommodation, local transport, and most, if not all meals. Download the booking form and send with a deposit of $500 per person.

Wildshots

www.wildshots.co.uk

Nature and landscape photography trips in the Scottish Highlands, Norway, India, Tanzania and the US. The widest choice is in the company's home base of Scotland, where you can focus on all things wild from owls through reindeer to coastal landscapes and autumn light. You're looking at paying anything from £345 for four days photographing Highland raptors to considerably more for a fortnight in the national parks of Utah or India – and close on £3000 if you long to shoot migrating wildebeest on the Serengeti plain. Send an email for a print brochure or download the booking form to make a reservation.

Welcome to Wildshots

WILDSHOTS
wildlife photographic adventures

Hello and welcome to the Wildshots web site.

- Home
- Mailing List
- Special Deals
- All About Us
- Our Home Base
- Guides
- Highland Holidays
- Overseas Holidays
- Pro-Tours
- Gallery
- Contact Us

Wildshots Photographic Adventures is a small Scottish-based tour company that offers a range of photography holidays and workshops in the Scottish Highlands as well as in Yellowstone, Norway, Tanzania, Florida, Utah, New Mexico and India.

To join our email mailing list please provide your email address below and press 'join'

[Join]

Our new 2004 programme of holidays continues our theme of providing a photographic adventure in friendly, informal surroundings for beginners and experts alike. Each holiday has been carefully researched and structured so that you can relax and fully indulge in your passion for wildlife, nature and landscape photography.

Volunteering

See also **www.discoveryinitiatives.com**, reviewed on p.186, for a selection of wildlife-related volunteering and study holidays.

Archaeological Institute of America

www.archaeological.org

The AIA publishes the annual *Archaeological Fieldwork Opportunities Bulletin*, which contains detailed information about two hundred excavations around the world that are open to volunteers. Each entry tells you about the excavation site, dates, costs, contact information (including links to Websites), and summaries of work needed. You're also linked from here to the publisher so you can buy the print edition (which features extra info) online.

Archaeology Abroad

www.britarch.ac.uk/archabroad

London-based organization that publishes a twice-yearly bulletin and a number of factsheets detailing around a thousand fieldwork opportunities outside the UK. They're available to subscribers only (£14 for UK citizens, £17 for individuals living abroad). The site has information on how to subscribe, as well as useful general tips, and links, related to digging abroad.

British Trust for Conservation Volunteers

www.btcv.org

More than five hundred conservation holidays around the world. UK holidays last from two days to a few weeks – a weekend tackling drainage problems on a Pennines path, say, or dry-stone walling in the Scillies. For most projects no experience is needed. International holidays, open to over-18s only, entail living and working with the local community; you might spend a week bear- and wolf-tracking in Slovakia, six weeks monitoring Leatherback turtles in Grenada, or six weeks maintaining trails in the Grand Canyon. You can select a project by location, month, type of work, or simply browse a full list – before booking (it's a secure server), check the offers detailed on the "Discounts" page.

Council for British Archeology

www.britarch.ac.uk

The first stop for professional archeologists and enthusiasts in the UK. Click "Fieldwork Opportunities" for a list of projects around Britain that accept volunteers; make sure to read each carefully, however, as some are open to students only.

Earthwatch Institute

www.earthwatch.org

With offices in the US, England, Australia and Japan, Earthwatch places volunteers on conservation research expeditions in around fifty countries. Most need no skills, and whether you fancy charting changes in the Gobi desert, tracking macaw activity in the Peruvian Amazon, or researching nutrition and child health care in South India, Earthwatch has something for you. Trips last between one and three weeks, and each volunteer pays something for food and lodging (which could be in anything from a mud hut or campsite to an up-market lodge). Prices can seem high, but these are bona fide scientific expeditions, among the best in their field. You can search for a project by location, date or subject, and reservations can be made online.

Global Service Corps

www.globalservicecorps.org

California-based organization offering community service holidays in environmental, health and education projects in Tanzania and Thailand. Short-term projects (14–28 days) cost around $2000–2500, not including flights; longer programmes incur further daily costs. In Tanzania, projects revolve around AIDS awareness and sustainable agriculture, while Thai projects concentrate on helping students, teachers and Buddhist monks with conversational English. To apply, fill in the downloadable application form and send with a deposit. All trips are also open to non-Americans.

i-to-i

www.i-to-i.com

There are some really exciting trips on this well set-up, slick site. It's divided into two sections: one for TEFL (Teaching English as a Foreign Language) training and the other for volunteer projects. Anyone aged over 18 can join projects in 23 countries around the world – from preserving petroglyphs in the Dominican Republic to working with a film production company on community development projects in South India. They also have a number of "Escapes", which last from one to three weeks; in these cases everything, including food and accommodation, is arranged and included in the placement fee. Secure online booking.

Idealist.org

www.idealist.org

Excellent Website set up by the New York-based non-profit group Action Without Borders. Use the speedy, well-designed search facility to browse 8000 volunteering opportunities in 165 countries: search by name, location, mission, dates or skills, or a combination of all those. There are hundreds of opportunities in the USA and the UK, as well as further afield. You can also create a "volunteer profile" and sign up for personalized email updates about upcoming volunteer opportunities. Good links page, too.

La Sabranenque

www.sabranenque.com

This non-profit French organization restores medieval structures, paths and monuments throughout Provence. You can choose from volunteer sessions pure and simple, or combine them with sightseeing or technical training in traditional construction techniques including stonemasonry, rubble clearing and roof-tiling. Accommodation is in a medieval stone village near Avignon, with time off for sightseeing and tasty home-cooked meals provided. Send an email for full details of costs, or to request a brochure.

National Trust

www.nationaltrust.org.uk/volunteers

The National Trust, which protects outstanding rural areas, houses and gardens around England, Wales and Northern Ireland, has a good-looking site detailing its 370 working holidays at more than 100 rural locations. Anyone can volunteer for a weekend, week, or fortnight – no experience necessary – to do anything from maintaining woodland paths, surveying hedgerows, clearing rhododendron bushes, rounding up goats, or restoring the gardens of stately homes. Searching by region and/or date, or pulling up a complete list, brings you accounts of the holidays, with dates and costs and a rundown of tasks; check the "Holiday Types and Costs" page to identify which category you should be looking out for ("Acorn" holidays, for example, are particularly suited to volunteers over the age of 35, while anyone who prefers "the finer things in life" should look out for breaks labelled "Premium"). Secure online booking.

Sense

www.sense.org.uk

British charity that organizes about 25 holidays a year for small groups of deaf-blind people – mostly children – in England and Wales. Lasting a week each, during the school summer holidays, they vary from stays at outdoor activity centres to farm holidays and boat trips. All accommodation and food expenses are paid for volunteers, each of whom is paired with an individual holidaymaker; training is offered, and there is support available throughout the week. Schedules are available in text or PDF format; to apply, contact them direct.

Voluntary Work Information Service

www.workingabroad.com

UK-based networking service for international volunteers and volunteer organizations, with opportunities in social and community projects, environmental groups, English teaching, human rights campaigns, wildlife expeditions, health care, housing and organic farming around the world. For anyone not sure which direction to take, click on "Voluntary Work Opportunities" to use its personalized search service. Simply fill in the form stating your interests, experience, time available, preferred countries and the like, and, for a fee, you'll be sent a report on at least twenty relevant organizations. If you'd rather do your own research, click on "Volunteer Organizations" to pull up a selective list of outfits, with accounts of their programmes and contact details. "News from the Field" features trip reports and feedback from volunteers, campaign and charity news, and urgent calls for volunteers.

Volunteers for Peace

www.vfp.org

Thousands of opportunities, in more than eighty countries, for American volunteers. The work varies widely, from insulating orphanages in Ukraine to teaching English in Beijing or assisting surgeons in Bangladesh. Most camps are for over-18s, though a few accept younger volunteers and some take families; the site's slightly hectoring tone – lots of directives underlined and in bold italics – perhaps reflects the fact that the average VFP volunteer is in their early 20s. The bulk of the directory is finalized in March each year, though many programmes are posted before then; choose by date, destination and camp type to see what's available, and then sort the resulting table of options by date, country, age limits or type. You can then click on each camp for details, and again to apply for a place. The registration fee is usually $200 per workcamp plus $20 VFP membership. Volunteers from the UK should register with Youth Action for Peace (**www.yap-uk.org**), or the International Voluntary Service (**www.ivs-gb.org.uk**).

Wildlife and nature

For a good range of birding and wildlife safaris, see also **www.footprint-adventures.co.uk**, reviewed on p.102. And if you're after an African safari, check the individual African countries detailed in our Destinations section.

Destinations and Adventures International

www.daitravel.com

Californian consultancy that offers a fine array of safaris and wilderness experiences throughout Africa, ranging from the merely expensive to the positively luxurious. Most of the continent is covered, with mobile luxury tented safaris in Kenya, flight-seeing tours of Namibia and Botswana, and Nile cruises in Egypt. You can read all about the trips on the site, but there is no online booking.

Discover the World

www.discover-the-world.co.uk

This British tour operator offers more than twenty different wildlife- and whale-watching holidays in seven continents, including island hopping in the Galapagos in search of albatrosses and giant tortoises, or a train safari through Namibia examining dinosaur footprints and visiting a seal colony. You're presented on the home page with clickable versions of their print brochures to destinations including the Bahamas, New Zealand and Sweden, among other places, along with whale-watching and Arctic cruises – their Arctic Experience brochure, specializing in Iceland and Greenland, is covered on p.247. Unless you have a particular destination in mind head for "Wildlife Encounters" (also accessible by simply typing in **www.wildlife-encounters.co.uk**) for the widest selection. All tours are fully described on screen; you have to fill in an email form, or download a PDF file, to request reservation details.

Discovery Initiatives

www.discoveryinitiatives.com

Really good holidays, and a nice user-friendly site, from this British eco-tourism operator. Users can search a great range of options by country, animal (more than 20, ranging through elephants, tigers, rhinos and whales), habitat (from rainforest to desert) or activity (including walking, riding, cruising and rafting). As well as tailor-made tours and the more relaxed "Footprint" trips, "conceived to blend in with nature's rhythms", you can also search for "Discoverer" study tours or volunteer work – with orang-utans in Borneo or on a game safari in South Africa, say – or "Insight" trips, which offer in-depth cultural perspectives of the places visited. It suggests trips all over the world, setting out full itineraries and prices; email if you're interested in making a booking.

Nature Expeditions International

www.naturexp.com

North American company that arranges wildlife and natural history tours in Africa, Central and South America, Asia, and Australia and New Zealand. It caters to both escorted groups and independent travellers, attracting older, more affluent participants by promising high-standard accommodation and "elective and low-intensity" adventures. Itineraries in such places as Nepal, Bali and India include conventional sightseeing as well as expeditions in pursuit of local flora and fauna, and also optional academic lectures. Choose your goal from the home page's antique world map, study complete tour details, and then fill in the email form of call the toll-free number to discuss your trip.

Out of the Blue

www.wdcs.org

The British-based Whale and Dolphin Conservation Society is a charity that promotes the welfare of whales, dolphins and porpoises throughout the world. As well as news, information and links, its Website contains full details of the society's travel-operator offshoot, designed to set an example to less eco-sensitive operators. Out of the Blue runs a select and heavily subscribed programme of whale-, shark- and dolphin-watching trips to Scotland, Wales, Iceland, the Azores, New England, California, Canada, Alaska, Patagonia, South Africa and Antarctica. Read full itineraries on the site, check out what previous participants have said about the trips, and then if any appeal, fill in and download a booking form.

Safarilink

www.safarilink.com

Although its home is in the UK, the Safarilink portal serves as a comprehensive directory of British, North American, and African tour companies that offer African safaris, lodges and travel services. Click on the map of Africa to pull up a list of companies that operate in whichever country interests you.

Vintage Africa

www.vintageafrica.com

Attractive and easy-to-use site, run by a British operator to publicize its extensive programme of African safaris, which goes well beyond the typical Botswana and Kenya itineraries to include expeditions through Ethiopia and further afield. Some of the trips are absurdly luxurious, offering for example the chance to eat fresh sushi and sip champagne cocktails as you watch chimpanzees beside Lake Tanganyika, and some are more beach holiday than safari, but it does offer budget alternatives as well; if you don't want a full package, you can also just arrange accommodation in specific lodges. Online booking is available.

Windows on the Wild

www.windowsonthewild.com

Beautifully simple site from this UK operator, with an exciting range of wildlife trips to Canada, USA (including Alaska), Sweden, Mexico, Costa Rica, Argentina, Chile, the Falkland Islands, Ecuador and the Galapagos, the Seychelles and New Zealand. The long list of search criteria includes beaches, grizzly bears, polar expeditions, sea kayaking, dog sledding, volcanoes or wolves; click on your favourite to be shown on the world map where they offer these tours. Itineraries come with photos, details and costs – return flights from the UK are included in all the fares, but they can be arranged without flights if you wish. There's an online booking form for reservations, though payment has to be made by phone.

Bird-watching

Birdquest

www.birdquest.co.uk

Promising "The Ultimate in Birding Tours", this long-established British operator offers around one hundred superb trips each year, from a repertoire of around 150 different itineraries. All regions of the globe are covered, including cruises to Antarctica and such little-visited destinations like the Nusa Tenggara islands of Indonesia. Detailed tour descriptions are packed with accounts of specific birds you might encounter, and illustrated with appealing line drawings; there's also a substantial set of links. Though all the holidays are set up to be as comfortable as possible, they may entail some hiking or long days in the field; anyone who wants an easier time should browse the less demanding "Easybird" itineraries. Check availability by email, then book online or using a downloadable form.

Eagle-Eye Tours

www.eagle-eye.com

By and large, this Canada-based bird-watching specialist concentrates its activities in the Americas and the Caribbean, but it also runs trips as far afield as Namibia, Papua New Guinea and Australia. Tours are arranged here both by date and by region; some are even devoted to particular birds, such as Kirtland's Warbler. There's a downloadable registration form.

Naturetrek

www.naturetrek.co.uk

British wildlife tour operator that takes twitchers all over the world to see birds such as the white-necked Jacobins of Trinidad, but stresses that its clients spend more of their time on foot appreciating their chosen destination than they do scurrying off in the minibus in pursuit of the next species on the checklist. Botanists and naturalists accompany each expedition, with European regions such as the mountains of Spain figuring as prominently as exotic tropical locations. Each trip has a brief itinerary online; you can download the hard-copy brochure page and/or detailed trip reports as you choose. Fill in the secure online form to make a reservation if anything catches your eye.

Writing

See also **www.skyros.com** (p.178) for creative writing classes in Greece and Thailand and **www.tiataos.com** (p.180) for courses in the southwest USA.

The Arvon Foundation

www.arvonfoundation.org

Arvon offers hugely popular week-long residential courses in lovely old houses in Devon, Shropshire, Yorkshire and Scotland. Themes run the gamut from comedy to poetry to songwriting; time is divided between workshops, private study, readings and socials. Taught by leaders in their field, most courses are open to anyone over 16, and the atmosphere is relaxed, with students sharing the cooking and chores (food is provided). They cost £435 per week (£325 for untutored retreats), and there are a few grants available. You can browse a full calendar, or search for courses by genre, location or tutor (though this can be a bit tricky as they are not, for some reason, listed in alphabetical order). Send off the downloadable booking form, with a deposit, to reserve a place.

Essential India

www.essential-india.co.uk

Specialist company (see p.250) offering a nice variety of creative study tours to India. The writing course, based in Himachal Pradesh in the Himalayas, involves three-hour workshops every day, with writing trips to Tibetan monasteries, Hindu temples, street markets and mountain villages. It costs £695 for two weeks, not including flights; book by email.

Literary Traveler

www.literarytraveler.com

Patchy online magazine filled with articles about Great American Writers and the places they travelled. Whether you want to follow in the path of Hemingway, Twain or Melville, or if you're an Anglophile with a hankering for the works of Austen or Agatha Christie, its useful directory of literary tour operators links you to walking tours, academic trips and custom-designed holidays.

Natalie Goldberg

www.nataliegoldberg.com

Minimal site from America's favourite writing guru, famed for her passionate belief in writing as a practice with the power to free "wild mind". Click on "Workshops" to read testimonials about her hugely popular week-long seminars at the Mabel Dodge House in Taos, New Mexico – frustratingly, you need to call the centre direct to get a full schedule – and on "What's News" for details of other upcoming courses around the US.

Nightwriters

www.nightwriters.com

Small seminars and writers' retreats in "creative settings" – among them a sixteenth-century villa in Tuscany, an antebellum inn in Virginia and a mountain lodge in the foothills of the Sierra Nevada. The tutors, all professional American writers, each have a slightly different style – you can read about them on the site – but every course includes exercises, writing time, feedback and social events. If you like what you see and have at least $1250 to spare, you can fill in and print the downloadable registration form.

"Every human being lives in the middle of a landscape. Writing illuminates it. And when we write from the truest, most authentic part of ourselves, the spotlight widens. Other people can see where they live, too."

– Phyllis Theroux

Nightwriters

Go to Home Page

part three

destinations

Antarctica

Abercrombie and Kent

www.abercrombiekent.com

Up-market adventure operators offering two- to three-week cruises of Antarctica and the Falkland Islands. Cruises are taken on the *Explorer II*, which carries just under 200 passengers, plus 146 crew (which includes the expert guides and lecturers). You can read all about the vessel, and the various itineraries, before submitting an email form to make a provisional booking. You're looking at paying from around $6000 for an all-inclusive trip, flying from Miami.

International Association of Antarctica Tour Operators

www.iaato.org

Click on "Membership Directory – Contact Information" for links to a variety of environmentally responsible operators offering Antarctic cruises. Other pluses include the general information (including a history of tourism in the area, and guidelines for visitors), plus links to Antarctica resources, information sites and organizations.

Quark Expeditions

www.quarkexpeditions.com

Specializing in polar expedition cruises, this groundbreaking operator offers a variety of Antarctic trips, lasting from around ten days to four weeks and taking in the South Shetland, South Georgia and Falkland Islands; some even include scuba diving. Prices start at around $3000, not including flights to and from the various embarkation points in South Africa, Australia or New Zealand. If you've got $36,000 to spare, you can take a luxury cabin for a month-long tour of the "Far Side of Antarctica". Itineraries of each trip are detailed on the site, along with costs. To book, however, you need to call one of their (listed) international offices or go through an agent.

Antigua

Caribbean Holidays 4 Less

www.caribbean-holidays4less.co.uk

UK-based online consolidator offering package holidays and discounted flights throughout the Caribbean, plus links to major all-inclusives such as Sandals. Holidays in Antigua start from around £600 for seven nights, including international flights. Although there are pictures and room descriptions for each hotel, the information isn't hugely detailed, so you might want to check out the newsgroup on **www.antigua-barbuda.org** (see below) to get first-hand reviews before you complete the email form to pursue your chosen trip.

Island Inns

www.islandinns.com

Up-market hotel and villa reservations at select properties throughout the Caribbean. The Antiguan collection includes the romantic all-inclusive Jumby Bay resort, where staff outnumber guests nine to one and nightly rates start at $700 per room. The site has all the details you need, with long reviews, tempting photos, rates and a Specials page. Email direct to request a reservation.

Official Travel Guide to Antigua and Barbuda

www.antigua-barbuda.org

The official site of the Antigua and Barbuda Department of Tourism is well put together, packed with information and intelligent links. You can read anything you need to know about the islands here, including historical snippets, features on food, drink and cricket (as befits the home of Viv Richards), and a good accommodation section complete with links to all the major properties and a handy rates comparison table. The lively newsgroup is restricted to travel and tourism questions.

TourScan

www.tourscan.com

North American Caribbean specialist agency that allows you to find the best offers available for packages, flights and accommodation. Use the "Vacation Finder" to hunt by season, price range (rates are per person including mid-week airfare from NY) and destination, refining your choice if you want to stay by the ocean, in all-inclusive or self-catering accommodation, or whatever. Options are listed in ascending order of cost, with little written information, but with links to Websites where available. If a place has no site you might find yourself wanting more details before booking (which is done via Tourscan).

Argentina

Argentina Travel Net

www.argentinatravelnet.com/indexE.htm

The major portal for Argentine tourism, featuring English translations and links to a host of small companies and adventure-tourism operators throughout the country. Search facilities enable searches by region as well as interest, and suggested Web links, to the sites of hotels and travel agencies in Buenos Aires, for example, make it clear which are available in English.

Galapagos Holidays

www.galapagosholidays.com/argentina.htm

Canadian travel agency that specializes in customized South American tours. Their four Argentine offerings range from "Cosmopolitan Buenos Aires" to "Spectacular Iguazu Falls" and trips to the country's lakes and mountains, and include accommodation in high-quality hotels. Email the lengthy form, and someone will call you back to firm up your plans.

Grippo

www.grippo.com

Wide-ranging compendium, completely in Spanish, covering all matters Argentine. The tourism section is strong on destination information, with dossiers on each region that include 360° images of beautiful beaches, and there's also plenty of history, news, sports and literature; a search for cult writer Jorge Luis Borges, for example, found 326 relevant pages.

Kon-Tiki Tours and Travel

www.kontiki.org/argentina

Calling themselves "The Argentina Specialists", this Miami-based travel agency offers a wide variety of tours to South America, including several either exclusively to Argentina, or adding a visit to Buenos Aires onto trips to neighbouring countries. As you look through the site, you can assemble your own "trip planner" by adding such components as a set of tango lessons, or a tour to Iguazu Falls or Patagonia, to a basic Buenos Aires package. Then either phone or email for further information, or simply complete your booking online.

South American Explorers

www.samexplo.org

This non-profit organization, based in upstate New York, is a member-supported clearing house for travel information and advice for South and Central America. Its Website includes bulletin boards, news updates, health and safety tips, and discount offers on accommodation. Sign up as a member to receive regular email and printed newsletters.

Sur del Sur

www.surdelsur.com/indexingles.html

The English version of this Argentinean Website – run by the National Department of Culture, its name translates as "The Southernmost South" – sets out to portray the country in all its "magnificence" and "idiosyncrasy". For beginners, it includes a potted history from first migrants through the Bering Strait, plus sections on "where we are" and "the way we are". Other pages cover art, the economy, literature, and of course tango. There's little of great practical use for travellers, but if you want to bone up on the basic facts, including detailed accounts of individual provinces with links to local papers and government offices, this is the place to start.

Traveland

www.traveland.com

General Latin America tour agency, based in California, which offers full online booking for short-break packages to Argentina, including six nights in Buenos Aires, including a tango lesson, for $699 flying from Miami, plus flight-only deals from all over the US.

Australia

Adventure Center

www.adventure-center.com

US operator, active worldwide, that offers around thirty different personalized tours in Australia, ranging from three days' kayaking up to a 28-day expedition around the continent.

Trips cover all aspects of Australian life, including Aboriginal culture or wildlife, and can involve both hotel accommodation and camping. The Website provides full itineraries and prices, but not online booking.

Australian Tourist Commission

www.australia.com

This official Website tends to be rather feverishly overwritten, but with so much information on offer – over 10,000 pages of it – it's an essential first stop for anyone planning a trip. Promising "Australia in as little as two weeks", it's packed with suggestions like "pat a koala" or "camel trek", and offers a phenomenal array of links to tour and adventure operators in every conceivable destination, as well as other government sites that offer practical advice or details on visa and health requirements. The "Ozplanner" section makes devising a two-week itinerary a real joy.

Australian Explorer

www.australianexplorer.com

Travel agency with offices in Australia, England and the US, whose comprehensive Website offers online booking for flights, tours, and hostels, and includes a travel forum.

The Big Banana

www.bigbanana.com

Exactly what it claims to be – a giant yellow banana – which typifies the Australian phenomenon of big garish roadside things. Unless you're planning to drive the 1000 km Pacific Highway between Sydney and Brisbane – in which case you'll spot it roughly halfway along – you can visit the banana online instead. For that matter, you can also email it, while if you email the Bunyip, at Bunyip Billabong, you're promised a nice surprise.

CitySearch Australia

www.citysearch.com.au

Comprehensive online guides to fourteen major Australian destinations, including Tasmania and the Gold Coast as well as cities like Sydney, Melbourne, Canberra, and Brisbane. The level of detail and reliability is first class, combining searchable databases of restaurants, clubs and other businesses with reviews from local newspapers and good-quality maps. To make the most of it, it helps to know the cities well already, so it's more use for residents than for tourists, though the accommodation listings stretch to 47 hostels in Melbourne alone.

Culture and Recreation Portal

www.acn.net.au

This official government-sponsored gateway connects to around two thousand sites devoted to Australian cultural life, and a combined total of over a million pages. It holds links to every imaginable museum and gallery, from the Canberra Bicycle Museum to the Maffra

Sugar Beet Museum, plus sites that explain and/or sell Aboriginal art, sports sites ranging from cricket statistics to the latest football news, and the home sites of the nation's leading authors.

Dreaded Ned

www.oz.dreadedned.com

The home page of this one-man gay guide to Australia proclaims it to be "the Website with a bucket on its head"; disappointingly, page two continues "Obviously this Website doesn't really have a bucket on its head". Once past the whimsy, however – the Dreaded Ned in question is of course folk hero Ned Kelly – it's a pretty good site, with detailed listings of gay-friendly accommodation, clubs and other services across the continent, a lively users' forum, and plenty of links, including to the official (but sadly somewhat lacklustre) Mardi Gras site.

OzOutback

www.ozoutback.com.au

OzOutback deals primarily in images of Australian landscapes, wildlife, and especially Aboriginal culture, which you can email to friends as electronic postcards or buy for your

own use. The captions hold some useful destination information, and you can also get a free email address to use as you travel. The main reason to visit, however, is to work your way through the full set of outback-related links, which include lots of back-country tour operators and vehicle rental agencies.

Puffing Billy

www.puffingbilly.com.au

This lovingly compiled and appropriately noisy site details schedules and fares for the century-old Puffing Billy steam train, still chugging through the scenic Dandenong mountains 40km east of Melbourne; email or phone for bookings.

Qantas Holidays

www.qantas.com.au/qantasholidays

The holidays section of the Website of Australia's national airline invites users to choose from an enticing array of tailor-made packages. They'll take you from pretty much anywhere within the country to anywhere else, focusing especially on accommodation but also including car or motorhome rentals. They don't offer online booking, as yet, and neither, oddly enough, can you book your ticket to get to Australia in the first place.

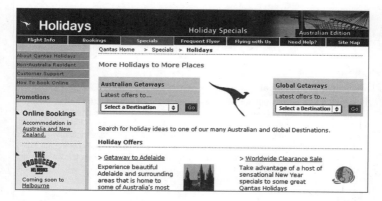

Travelmate

www.travelmate.com.au

The Travelmate site belongs to the petrol company Caltex, which explains its emphasis on driving in general and petrol prices in particular, but it's one of the very best online travel guides to Australia, enabling you to select from over 20,000 hotels across the country and request reservations online. The "Map Maker" facility will sketch out an itinerary between any two locations, highlighting whatever features you request (such as museums or national parks as well, of course, as Caltex petrol stations), while "Trip Talk" is a frank message board with a lengthy and much-debated "Never Go To ... " section.

TT-Line

www.tt-line.com.au

Owned by Tasmania's state government, the TT-Line operates a regular ferry service across the Bass Strait to the island from Melbourne. One vessel is a high-speed catamaran, the other more of a cruise ship. The Website provides full schedules and fares, plus online booking.

Wilkins Tourist Maps

www.wilmap.com.au

Abounding above all with maps and photos, the Wilmap site holds a massive database of Australian destinations. Once you've picked a spot that appeals to you, you can read about it, look at photos, search for accommodation, and – which is where they hope to make their money – ask them to mail you a large-scale map. Or, you can simply take advantage of their full set of links to get whatever information you need.

Austria

Austrian Tourism

www.austria-tourism.at

Promising "here you will find everything you need to know for a smooth holiday!", this official Website devotes separate sections to visitors of different nationalities. If you fail to specify your country of origin on the home page, it'll only give you generic information, but once it knows where you're from, it reels off useful practical details, including lists of operators who can arrange your Austrian vacation. Activities such as golf, fishing, hiking, cycling, horse riding and, of course, skiing are well covered, while North American users get a special section on Arnold Schwarzenegger.

Austrian Travel Network

www.tiscover.at

Part of www.tiscover.com, which also covers Germany and Switzerland, in Austria itself the Austrian Travel Network enables online searches and booking for over 5000 accommodation options, categorized by region, price and facilities. It also carries details of special all-inclusive packages, as well as listings of upcoming events.

Herzerl Tours

www.herzerltours.com

Specialist Austrian operator based in the US, which offers a very wide array of themed personal tours, covering wine, music, and cuisine as well as more strenuous activities such

as ballooning and cycling. Pick up full details on the Web, then phone or email to book.

Virtual Vienna

www.virtualvienna.net

Aimed primarily at Vienna's English-speaking community, these listings include rather too many plumbers and too few restaurants for most tourists' needs. Virtual Vienna nonetheless provides a good basic guide to the city, and holds a multitude of links to other Austria sites.

Barbados

Barbados Tourism Encyclopedia

www.barbados.org

The official site of the Barbados Tourism Authority is a great resource and lively to boot. It's particularly strong on travel information, with links to airlines, travel agents, car rental companies, and ground operators, with an extensive searchable accommodation database that lists everything from guesthouses to luxury villas, detailing rates, facilities and links to Websites where available. You can also read about restaurants, activities and shopping, with a schedule of music, theatre and carnival events.

Belgium

For tour operators that offer short breaks in Brussels and other Belgian cities, see the "European city breaks" section which starts on p.33.

All The Restaurants in Belgium

www.resto.be

The largest Belgian restaurants site may not boast every restaurant in Belgium, but it has 10,000 or so to be getting on with. You can search by location, price and style (which ranges from "mussels and chips" via "from Madagascar" to "Tex-Mex" and even "erotic"), and then take a look at menus and photos. An interactive poll section reveals that of the top hundred in the country, only four are categorized as Belgian. Sadly, although almost all the site is translated into English, the customer reviews are not.

Bed and Brussels

www.bnb-brussels.be

Excellent, simple accommodation site for the Belgian capital. Enter your criteria and dates, and it will put you in touch with B&B host families anywhere in the city.

Belgian Tourist Office

www.visitbelgium.com

The superbly detailed official Website of the Belgian Tourist Office in the Americas – slogan, "A country the size of Maryland" – covers every imaginable aspect, from "Belgium for the eclectic art nut" to "Belgium for chocolate lovers", with dozens of additional links from every page. It's great for setting you up with package tour operators – a typical special offer would be a city break in Brussels from New York for just $500 – or making your own travel arrangements on Belgian railways. Rather than handling accommodation reservations online, however, it simply links you to specific hotels.

Belgium Travel Network

www.trabel.com

So long as you can put up with its consistently drab grey screens, this site provides a clear and efficient online guide to the country. Working methodically through its multitude of menus is rewarded by all the destination information you could need on Belgium's monuments and churches, beers and lace, while the associated **www.hotels-belgium.com** site offers easy-to-use searches and email bookings for hotels.

Famous Belgians

www.famousbelgians.net

Enthusiastic amateur site that finally puts the lie to the notion that there are no famous Belgians. In fact, there are 248 of them, ranging from jazz guitarist Django Reinhardt to Joseph Plateau, inventor of the stroboscope.

Tourism Flanders

www.visitflanders.com

The official English-language Flanders Website opens with a nice animated intro of cyclists cruising down a Flemish road (though sadly Ned Flanders is nowhere in sight). The information beyond includes details of "historic cities" such as Brussels, Antwerp, Ghent and Bruges as well as the sandy Channel coast, while there are useful practical links to international and domestic train, ferry and flight operators. By combining the hotel

search facility with the connections to local sites, you can book an entire vacation online.

Belize

Belize Online

www.belize.com

This joint Belizean-US enterprise is intended as much for potential investors in the country as for tourists, but it's still a great source of travel information, with links to tour operators as well as hotels and resorts, and also plenty of background information, plus a large bibliography for further reading.

Island Expeditions Company

www.islandexpeditions.com

US tour operator that specializes in small-group adventure-travel trips to Belize from any US city, arranging kayaking and diving along the barrier reef as well as white-water rafting on the inland rivers and expeditions to ruined Maya cities. The Website holds detailed itineraries, maps and tour descriptions, but recommends you speak with someone in the office before returning the downloadable booking form.

Reef and Rainforest Tours

www.reefandrainforest.co.uk

Eco-friendly British tour company that offers a choice of six tailor-made natural history Belize itineraries, ranging from the "Belize on a Budget" trip, which takes in a week's bird-watching, based in a rainforest lodge, and a week by the sea, with scuba diving available, to the three-week Grand Tour. You can pick up full information online, but to make a reservation you have to print out and mail a booking form.

Bolivia

Bolivia Web

www.boliviaweb.com

Bolivian portal with links to all manner of sites, including business, poetry, photography and food as well as travel; it even sells mouse mats and coffee mugs. A useful set of pages is devoted to hotels in each major city, with links to those establishments that have their own Websites.

Magic of Bolivia

www.magicofbolivia.com

British company that offers a standard three-week guided tour of Bolivia – taking in jungle, deserts and mountains – at regular intervals between March and November each year (thus avoiding the rainy season). The Website gives full itineraries, with photos and prices (typically around £1800 excluding international flights), and you can also customize individual trips. There's no online booking, however; fill in an email form, or call to discuss your needs.

Myths and Mountains

www.mythsandmountains.com

Worthy Nevada-based tour company that runs a fascinating array of Bolivian expeditions. They can take you out onto Lake Titicaca on a raft, or school you in the medical lore of the Kallawaya people, but they can't take credit card payments online; email for further details.

Botswana

Crocodile Camp

www.botswana.com

Based in the Botswana town of Maun, Crocodile Camp specialize in wilderness photographic expeditions, travelling by jeep, horseback or by *mokoro* (traditional canoe). How much you pay depends on how much of the hard work of a back-country trip you're prepared to shoulder yourself. Trips are priced in US dollars and sold to clients of all nationalities; payments cannot be made online.

Okavango Tours and Safaris

www.okavango.com

Although enabling tourists to experience the wildlife of the world-famous Okavango Delta is the main priority for this British tour company, they can also take small groups to meet with Bushmen in the Kalahari Desert, or onto the desolate Madgadikgadi saltpans. There are good descriptions on the Web, but you have to call or email with enquiries.

Brazil

A number of operators offer eco-tours to Brazil; see p.164 for a selection. And for conservation volunteer holidays, see the section starting on p.182, in particular **www.earthwatch.org.**

Amazon Adventures

www.amazonadventures.com

Texas-based operator specializing in trips to South America, who have a variety of packages to Brazil. Their cruises, which start at just under $600 for a week, involve activities such as jungle trekking, survival training, spear fishing and meetings with local tribes. Alternatively, you could study medicinal plants while staying at a lodge with a river family, go wildlife-viewing in the Pantanal, swimming in the crystal waters of Bonito, take cultural and historic tours of Bahia, and much more. Prices are reasonable – $2190 for a three-week package, not including flights, in the high season, or $545 for a week-long gaucho adventure. To book, fill in the email form and fax them your credit card details.

Brazilian Embassy in London

www.brazil.org.uk

Very useful, good-looking site with all the facts and figures you'd expect from an embassy site, plus fascinating cultural articles on everything from cinema and music to fashion and cuisine. The travel and tourism channel is extremely good, with informative regional guides, links to hotels all over the country, and carnival schedules and links. Kids will enjoy the animated feature, "Let's Visit Brazil with Monica's Gang".

Brazilinfo.net

www.brazilinfo.net

Useful Brazilian directory with general country information plus English-language links to travel operators, hotel directories, city guides and Brazilian maps.

Brazil Nuts

www.brazilnuts.com

Brazil specialists, based in Florida, who offer a wide range of packages throughout the country, including cultural itineraries ("Celebrate Life", for example, which explores African heritage in Rio and Salvador Da Bahia), off-the-beaten-track trips (canoe expeditions through the remote Pantanal waterways, say), Amazonian jungle lodges and city tours. You can also choose "budget" options that allow you to book flight and hotel only, leaving you free to arrange add-ons when you arrive. Most tours, though not escorted, hook you up with a guide who will take care of you for the duration of your trip; if you want to plan your own itinerary, fill in the online form and they'll suggest hotels and quote a price. Otherwise, to book, email them direct. There's also a travel forum, though more people post questions than reply.

Carnaval.com

www.carnaval.com

This gem of a carnival site, packed with information on all the world's great party cities, has large sections on Salvador and Rio. Quite apart from the pages of links relating to the carnivals – music files, video clips, historical background, parade schedules, samba schools and so on – you can glean huge amounts of travel information here, with links to city guides, accommodation, restaurants and bars, as well as a host of general background reading.

Insider's Guide to Rio

www.ipanema.com

There's an overwhelming amount of information on this phenomenal site, every other word, it seems, hotlinked to a useful database or a relevant cross-reference. With its straight-talking, common-sense advice, its lively tone and its palpable passion for the

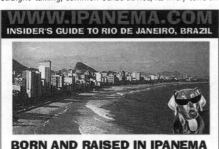

place, the guide gives you all the skinny on Rio's beaches, restaurants and nightlife, its drag queens and its samba parades, the thongs and the beach soccer, with maps and scores of photos. Accommodation reviews are honest and illuminating, and you can book rooms – and local tours – online. Your guide to Ipanema, incidentally, is Fred, a wisecracking dog; if you've got a spare moment you can make him bark and growl.

Journey Latin America

www.journeylatinamerica.co.uk

UK operator covering Mexico and Central and South America. While offering a handful of escorted group holidays, which they divide into "journeys" (adventurous trips, using public transport and staying in simple accommodation) and "tours" (private vehicles, posher hotels, softer adventure), they also suggest a number of independent itineraries: many of them allow you to choose between "tourist-class" hotels or more up-market places, and you can decide whether to count your flight in, too. Don't forget to check for late availability holidays as well. They also publish lists of best-buy airfares, return and one-way, with details of passes. There's no online ordering; email them direct.

Lost World Adventures

www.lostworldadventures.com

US company organizing small-group itineraries which you can either book as is or customize to your own tastes. Their Brazil options include an adventurous ten-day Amazonian camping trip, exploring the rainforest, river islands and Lago Janauari Ecological Park, which will set you back around $1500. You can read full itineraries, and details of accommodation, on the site, but bookings, in the first instance, should be made by email.

Reef and Rainforest

www.reefrainforest.co.uk

This UK operator specializes in tailor-made natural history-oriented tours. The main Brazil trip, a "natural history highlights" tour, takes in a good deal, covering Rio, whale-watching in Abrolhos National Park, rainforests, Iguacu Falls and the Pantanal wetlands. There's also a 14-day "Pantanal: Kingdom of the Jaguar" tour. Once you've read the detailed itineraries and worked out if you can afford £2400 (not including flight) for either one, simply print off the form and send it, with a cheque, to book.

Worldwide Samba Home Page

www.worldsamba.org

Huge directory of samba links around the world, including samba schools in Rio, CD reviews, Carnaval schedules, audio and video clips and an email list.

Bulgaria

Balkan Holidays

www.balkanholidays.co.uk

British operator that sells flights, tours and packages to all regions of Bulgaria, as well as its immediate neighbours. There's online booking for everything, from ski packages to summer beach holidays or coach tours.

Canada

Bed & Breakfast Online Canada

www.bbcanada.com

This members' organization of Canadian B&Bs includes around 8000 properties; each has its own page with colour photos, written descriptions and prices. Search according to specific criteria or simply work through the regional lists, then email your selection direct.

Brewster Holidays

www.brewster.ca

Though based in Alberta, Brewster arrange holidays in each individual region of Canada, as well as multi-destination bus, rail and Discovery Drive (self-guided) tours, and also golf and ski packages. The "Trains" section of the site includes trips starting in several major cities, with fully costed itineraries; email or call with queries or reservation requests.

British Columbia Ferry Services

www.bcferries.com

Based in Victoria, British Columbia, BC Ferries provide online timetable and fare information for their sailings between Vancouver and Vancouver Island and the Southern Gulf Islands, and also along the Discovery Coast, to the Queen Charlotte Islands, and up the Inside Passage. Submitting the lengthy online reservation form does not quite guarantee your booking, however; availability will be confirmed within 48 hours.

Canadian Tourism Commission

www.travelcanada.ca

Canada's official national tourism site offers a picture-packed "Virtual Tour" of every province, and enables you to plan your itinerary by building up your own "Travel Notebook". Every individual destination abounds with further links, including not only general overviews and recommended routes, but also specific adventure operators, with sections devoted to such activities as horse riding, canoeing, cycling, and rafting.

Greyhound Canada

www.greyhound.ca

Greyhound's Canadian site works in the same way as the US version (see p.345), with a speedy fare and schedule finder. There is no online booking facility for individual tickets as yet, but it is possible to buy a Canadian Discovery pass, or a North American CanAm pass.

John Steel Rail Tours

www.johnsteel.com

Canada is one of the best countries on the planet to take a train ride, with all those vast open spaces. Canadian operator John Steel organizes guided rail journeys for groups, or individual itineraries for independent travellers, throughout the country. Useful charts give basic information of each tour and links to a full description of its highlights and price details. Call or email to book.

Just America

www.justamerica.co.uk

British tour company that sells a huge assortment of rail, motorcoach and self-drive Canadian holidays in conjunction with local operators, with twin emphases on the scenic Rocky Mountain and Eastern Maritime regions. They can even arrange weekend breaks from the UK to Toronto. The Website provides full itineraries and prices, together with lots of photos, and has details of a similarly wide programme of US trips; call or email to make your reservation.

Parks Canada

www.parkscanada.pch.gc.ca

Comprehensive and beautifully illustrated Website, run by Canadian Heritage and covering all Canada's national and regional parks. Find any park by name, type or just clicking on the maps, and you're given full details on fees and access as well as practical tips on hiking and camping hikes.

toronto.com

www.toronto.com

This thorough independent guide to Toronto features up-to-the-minute events listings, a searchable database of around 3000 restaurants – many with detailed reviews – and webcam views of the city. Most useful of all, however, is its online hotel booking facility. It also offers links to similar guides for Calgary, Edmonton, Montréal, Ottawa, Quebec and Vancouver.

Tourism Whistler

www.tourismwhistler.com

Top-notch site run by the premier ski resort of Whistler, north of Vancouver, which centres on a superb "Trip Planner" that enables you to specify exactly what facilities you're looking for in your accommodation, returns a list of properties available on your chosen dates, and then lets you book the whole thing online. A separate section holds current Hot Deals, public transport is outlined in detail, there's a good interactive map of the resort, and a huge list of FAQs to round things off.

Tourisme Montréal

www.tourism-montreal.org

The official city site for Montréal covers the city in painstaking detail, anticipating any information a visitor might need and devoting pages on end, for example, to every permutation of public transport. Like everything else, its hotel and restaurant listings are exhaustive, and come with hyperlinks wherever possible; there's also plenty of eye-candy to keep you browsing.

Vacations in Canada

www.vacationsincanada.com

Based in Ontario, this portal reels off links to operators and outfitters all over Canada, with a special affinity for outdoors activities such as fishing (a search for trout fishing throws up 64 options), skiing, dog sledding and even caribou hunting. Most of the accommodation on offer is in rural mountain lodges.

Vancouver Central Reservations

www.vancouver.com

Commercial site, devoted exclusively to Vancouver, and offering reservations for almost anything related to the city, from flight deals originating in all major US cities to car rental and hotels once you arrive, and tour companies, sightseeing attractions and even golf courses to keep you entertained. Users can bundle together all their requirements into a single package, though as companies pay to be included, the listings are not exhaustive.

VIA Rail Canada

www.viarail.ca

Comprehensive site of the Canadian rail network, with railroad maps, pass details, and a beautifully simple search system that details full schedules and fares for any journey you can imagine. They'll even arrange – given at least 24 hours notice – for you to be dropped off or picked up at places other than scheduled stops. The adventures section is particularly interesting, listing a set of services tailor-made for outdoor enthusiasts and adventurers. If you'd rather not use the full online booking facility, choose instead from the list of travel agents around the world that deal in VIA passes and tickets. There's also a good set of links to operators who offer outdoor activities that can be reached by train.

Chile

Anglatin

www.anglatin.com

This Oregon-based operator, which arranges tours for both leisure and business travellers worldwide, has an especially extensive programme in Chile, including trips out to Easter Island, tours of the deserts and mountains, and also bird-watching, fly-fishing, skiing and golf excursions. Their Website offers full online booking.

Cascada Expediciones

www.cascada-expediciones.com

Clear, straightforward English-language site run by a Santiago-based adventure-holiday operator. Trips are arranged by both activity and region, and range through trekking and riding in Patagonia or on Easter Island, climbing in the Andes, rafting and kayaking trips on the Maipo river, and wildlife expeditions on Robinson Crusoe Island. Make your booking by printing the form and faxing it to Chile.

Chile Hotels

www.chile-hotels.com

A comprehensive site run by an agency with offices in Chile and Florida. They offer online hotel booking for the entire country, and the site covers 500 hotels in 80 cities. The more up-market properties tend to have the most detailed descriptions and photographs. Car rental and tours are also available, and the site holds an impressive selection of general Chile links.

Chile Information Project

www.chiptravel.cl

As well as its thorough destination and cultural guide to the country, with separate sections devoted to its history and environment, CHIP offers online booking for hotels and adventure packages, from the northern Atacama Desert all the way to Antarctica. Its own sightseeing tours include a "historical memory" tour of Santiago, focusing on human rights issues.

Go Chile

www.gochile.cl

Large, well-illustrated bilingual Web guide to Chile, packed with destination information for the whole country; simply click on the relevant area for details of accommodation and packages.

Secrets of Easter Island

www.pbs.org/wgbh/nova/easter/

A fascinating interactive guide to Easter Island and its mysterious statues, presented by PBS in the US and bursting with photos, panoramas and TV footage as well as informative text and maps.

China

Asian Pacific Adventures

www.asianpacificadventures.com

Californian company that arranges a genuinely unusual programme of special-interest China tours. These include the 20-day "Ethnic Minority Explorer" itinerary, to experience the cultures of China's tribal peoples; expeditions into eastern Tibet and onto the Mongolian steppes; and also women-only trips. Complete the full online reservation form if you know what you want, or just send a basic email for enquiries.

China On Your Mind

www.chinaonyourmind.com

Travel brokers with offices in the US as well as Beijing, who invite customers planning vacations in China to state their requirements in as much or as little detail as they choose, and then negotiate direct with Chinese tour companies and hotels to come up with the best match and prices. A few standard itineraries are suggested on the Website, and you can also read other travellers' experiences or admire their photos.

China the Beautiful

www.chinapage.com

This entertaining and user-friendly site has nothing to sell, it's simply devoted to stimulating interest in all aspects of Chinese culture. Besides slide shows of painting and calligraphy, it holds translated poetry, fiction and philosophy, and a series of articles and pages exploring Chinese history from a general-interest rather than an academic perspective, with links to related sites. There's also a set of satellite photos, supposedly of the Great Wall, that finally prove you really *can't* see it from the moon.

China Travel System

www.chinats.com

Based in Beijing, the CTS makes it easy for prospective visitors heading from the capital to the rest of China to purchase well-priced tours and arrange hotel accommodation. Whether you want to use their service rather depends on whether you can stomach the propaganda on their Website, such as news stories celebrating the "50th anniversary of peaceful liberation of Tibet".

Chinaetravel

www.chinaetravel.com

The principal aims of the Chinaetravel site are to sell package tours to China from Hong Kong, geared towards all interests and budgets, and also flights, hotels and tours within the country; all are bookable online. It also provides a general introduction to visiting China, with an extensive and well-illustrated destination guide, plus good background material and vital statistics on Chinese history, culture, and geography.

Cross-Culture

www.crosscultureinc.com

US adventure travel company, based in Massachusetts, that beyond its rather tired line about "catering for travellers rather than tourists" offers a small but attractive set of guided Chinese tours, including a swing through Beijing, Xian and Shanghai, a Yangtze river cruise, and trips to Tibet. Prices are quoted with and without international airfares.

Haiwei Trails

www.haiweitrails.com

This small-group adventure-travel outfitter, based in Yunnan and run by US and British expatriates, organizes four-wheel-drive expeditions and trekking trips in southwest China and Tibet. The "trails overview" page on their slightly tricksy but visually appealing Website sets out the different experiences they provide, the actual itineraries come with good maps and mouthwatering details, and as the emphasis is never on luxury the prices are generally very reasonable. Email if something catches your eye.

People's Daily

http://english.peopledaily.com.cn

For the official voice of Chinese reason, check out the online version of the national newspaper, the *People's Daily*. The Website holds an archive not only of the paper's own articles, back to January 1998, but also such delights as the collected works of Deng Xiaoping. There's also a fairly outspoken message board, plus links to government sites.

REI Adventures

www.rei.com/travel

US adventure travel specialist, operating out of Washington state, whose Website lists a worldwide programme of small-group trips, rated according to physical difficulty. The focus of their activities in China tends to be cycling and/or hiking, in the southern and central areas of the country, with a particularly nice-sounding tour in Guilin. Email a $400 credit-card deposit to reserve any trip.

Shanghai-ed

www.shanghai-ed.com

Though the lack of a site plan makes it all a bit hard to find, this enjoyable Shanghai-based portal-cum-ezine holds plenty of useful information for anyone planning to visit, move to, or study in the city. Aimed largely at the city's expat community, it includes several interesting and amusing regular columns, horoscopes, a serialized crime novel, personal and job ads, a directory of restaurants with reviews, and a useful question-and-answer feature for specific enquiries.

Wild China

www.wildchina.com

Beijing-based company, committed to eco-tourism, that offers customized tours in interesting and often little-known regions of the country. One, for example, traces China's Jewish heritage, while several venture into Tibet; all are outlined with set itineraries, but can be customized to your requirements, once you've registered.

Costa Rica

For volunteer holidays in Costa Rica, see **www.globalservicecorps.org** (p.183), and check the other agencies reviewed in that section.

Costa Rica Accommodations

www.accommodations.co.cr

As well as providing links to more than 350 hotels, this clean, efficient site can also hook you up with car rental outfits and local tour companies. As it doesn't provide online booking, it's primarily useful as a research tool: you can browse the full A–Z accommodation list, click a region on the map, and search for historical hotels or for places geared towards certain activities (honeymoons, golf, fishing and so on). There's a separate section for rental villas.

Costa Rica Naturally

www.tourism.co.cr

General information site brought to you by Canatur, the Costa Rica National Chamber of Tourism. It's a great place to start, not only for its detailed destination guides and articles on all the essential stuff – national parks, outdoor pursuits, indigenous cultures, eco-tourism and so on – but also the good links to individual hotels and jungle lodges, tour operators, language schools and travel agents.

Costa Rica Travelweb

www.crica.com

Produced by an online travel agency in San José, this Costa Rica portal is an unabashedly commercial operation, eagerly pushing its own services, such as all-inclusive packages, while also linking to a number of ground operators and scores of hotels. Click on a map to search for hotels by region; if the copious details whet your appetite, you can contact most of them direct. If you want to use the agency to help custom-build a holiday, submit the detailed online booking form; if you're ready to pay, there's a printable credit card payment form.

Costa Rica's Travel Net

www.centralamerica.com

A very good Costa Rica one-stop shop produced by the online travel agency Travel Net. As well as offering package holidays and discounted flights (from North America), the site also provides good destination information and links. Browse the directories of hotels, car rental companies and ground operators (all of which you contact via the site), or work through the handy travel planning sheet, with its links to destination guides and accommodation options. Other features include reviews of all the national parks, detailed area maps, and domestic airline schedules.

Costa Rica Vacation Rentals

www.crvacationrentals.com

For anyone planning to self-cater in Costa Rica, this US-based agency, with a number of luxurious villas and lodges, is a good place to start. Click on the property name to find descriptions and tempting photos, along with weekly (and, in many cases, nightly) rates, then email them direct with enquiries.

Costa Rica Vacations

www.costaricavacations.net

Costa Rica specialists offering flight-included packages from the US for less than $1000 – they have a good variety covering, among other things, rainforest lodges, Caribbean beaches, bird-watching and fishing. Plus links to hotels and car rental companies, late availability deals and good prices on domestic flights, along with add-on tours from San José. Complete the large email form to request reservations.

Journey Latin America

www.journeylatinamerica.co.uk

This UK operator, which specializes in reasonably priced holidays to Central and South America, suggests around a dozen individual Costa Rica itineraries. As well as three escorted group trips (one exclusively within Costa Rica, and two also visiting neighbours like Honduras and Panamá), it offers adventure-based packages that take in biking, hiking and rafting. You can also check out best-buy flight deals – single and return – and air passes; email direct to make any arrangements.

Reef and Rainforest Tours

www.reefandrainforest.co.uk

UK operators specializing in small-scale, natural history-oriented tours. You can read full itineraries and reviews of each tour on the site, and there are plenty of photos. These aren't budget holidays, starting at around £1600, without flights, for a 17-day 4WD itinerary and climbing to £2200 for two weeks "nature deluxe" – bird-watching, snorkelling, river rafting, exploring pre-Columbian ruins and jungle trekking. You could also choose a family-friendly option, a gently paced wildlife-viewing trip, or a romantic break. For scuba diving, you need to contact them direct. To book, print off the form and send a cheque.

South American Experience

www.southamericanexperience.co.uk

UK specialist operator with a good range of short packages in Costa Rica. Options are clearly laid out in tables, with thumbnail descriptions of the various accommodation options available; combine more than one to make a complete vacation. Although they quote ground costs only, you can check airfares and, after registering, book flights through the company. Call or email them to book the tours, or to get help with a customized itinerary.

Croatia

Croatian National Tourist Board

www.croatia.hr

This excellent official Website, maintained in both English and German versions, boasts a useful accommodation search engine that will find hotels, campsites, private home and even lighthouses (of which it holds 11) in any specified town or according to your chosen criteria, and provide detailed lists plus Web links and email addresses. Other features include sections on climate and currency, and transport and activities. It also provides extensive listings of Croatia's many naturist centres.

Dalmatia Touristic Pages

www.dalmacija.net

A good, well-illustrated, general site for tourists planning to visit the region of Dalmatia, along the Southern Adriatic coastline. The home page is entirely in English, but after, as you pursue the multitude of links to hotels and other local businesses, you never know whether the text will be in Croatian, English or German. Many hotels offer online booking; in fact you can even charter a yacht online. There's also plenty of background information on food, sport, history and culture.

Generalturist

www.generalturist.com

Croatia's leading travel agency runs an office in New York to cater for North American travellers. The Website promotes a wide range of detailed holiday packages, including the 9-day "Dalmatian Sunshine" tour, but they can also draw up an itinerary to suit your own requirements or simply arrange flights. Possibilities include food- and wine-themed vacations or simply short city breaks. There's no online booking, but you can email or phone to discuss your plans.

Holiday Options

www.holidayoptions.co.uk

UK package-holiday specialists who offer an extensive programme of holidays to Croatia and other Mediterranean destinations, including week-long trips to any of nineteen Croatian resorts and longer combinations. Independent travellers can also book seats on one of their charter flights, from London, Birmingham or Norwich to Split or Dubrovnik. Complete your booking by phone or email.

Istra

www.istra.com

An impressive site promoting the delights of Croatia's Istrian region, with good English translations throughout. Full details of hotels include current prices in Euros and email forms to make reservations, while the food listings include some appetizing photos of the regional seafood speciality *brodet*. If you really need it, you can even pick up a rundown of petrol stations in every town.

Cuba

AfroCubaWeb

www.afrocubaweb.com

An amazing compendium of anything related to Afro-Cuban history and culture, including life in modern Cuba as well as contemporary music and dance. The site also offers general advice on the legal side of travelling to the island, aimed primarily at US citizens, and links to other pages of interest.

Captivating Cuba

www.captivating-holidays.com

Simple, easy-to-navigate site operated by a British company that arranges inexpensive island tours of all lengths and levels of luxury. Aided by basic destination information, you can search for holidays in any preferred location, or perhaps combine Havana with a stay by the beach. They also provide links to climate charts, currency converters, and official British government advice on travel to the region. All bookings are made by phone.

Casa Particular Lodging Service

www.geocities.com/casaparticular

English- and Spanish-language site designed to connect prospective visitors with private homes and apartments for rent in Havana and elsewhere on the island. Rates are very reasonable, with no agency fee; in some properties you lodge with a Cuban family, others you have to yourself. Most are fully equipped to a high standard, and all include airport pick-up and drop-off, so if you're looking for "two rooms and warm family" you can't go far wrong.

Center for Cuban Studies

www.cubaupdate.org

Site run by a New York-based non-profit organization that arranges tours for groups and individuals. To adhere to US regulations – which are carefully detailed on the Website – all trips have to conform to pre-planned, pre-approved itineraries. These include regular Cuba

Update trips as well as visits that coincide with specific festivals or events, or are tailored to suit particular professional interests such as health care or education.

Cuba – Consular Information Sheet

http://travel.state.gov/cuba.html

The official Consular Information Sheet, issued by the US government, provides full details on the current US attitude towards Cuba and the ongoing travel embargo; an essential update for prospective US visitors to the island.

Cuba Flights

www.casaparticular.com

UK agency that offers email booking for charter flights from London Gatwick to Havana via Holguin, plus car rental and hotel reservations. They also arrange a much more elaborate package deal that enables budding film-makers to shoot a movie in Cuba, and includes tuition, plus pre- and post-production, in London.

Cuba Solidarity Campaign

www.cuba-solidarity.org

The UK's Cuba Solidarity Campaign is sufficiently devoted to the Cuban Revolution to enlist volunteers to join three-week "International Work Brigades" on the island. *Brigadistas* pay around £800, including flight, to carry out agricultural or construction work in a purpose-built camp outside Havana, and to undertake a full programme of educational and political events and visits – as well as the odd trip to the beach.

Cuba Travel Services

www.LAtoCuba.com

In itself, the CTS Website holds little of interest, with some rudimentary listings of hotels and attractions in major Cuban cities, but they do run direct non-stop charter flights each week from Los Angeles and New York to Havana, and from Miami to five separate Cuban destinations. Tickets for all can be booked online.

Directorio Turístico de Cuba

www.dtcuba.com/eng/cuba_turistica.asp?

Navigate an interactive island map to obtain copious destination information and practical listings. As well as holding links to hundreds of hotels all over the country – bookable a minimum of 15 days in advance – the Website also enables you to contact car rental and other agencies, and even local music venues.

Highlife Holidays

www.highlifeholidays.co.uk/cuba.htm

London-based travel agency that provides assorted conventional package trips to what it calls "the most beautiful island in the Caribbean", with an emphasis on beaches rather than *brigadistas*. Their "Pearl of the Caribbean" tour takes in Havana, Trinidad, Cienfuegos and Varadero. All holidays, as well as flights and car rental, can be booked online.

Marazul Charters

www.marazulcharters.com

US agency that runs charter flights from New York and Miami to Havana; US citizens are of course subject to their government's regulations concerning trips to Cuba. They also arrange personalized packages to the island, concentrating, for example, on professional events and conferences.

Worldwide Quest Nature Tours

www.worldwidequest.com

Canadian tour company that organizes cycling and hiking expeditions in Cuba each winter, with an emphasis on eco-tourism. Their ten-day, $1500 "Cuba by Bike" option, using hotel accommodation, tends to be booked up way in advance. Email for details.

Cyprus

Cyprus Tourism Organization

www.cyprustourism.org

Produced by the CTO in New York, this minimal site gives short, rather bland guides to every region in southern Cyprus, with snatches of history (no mention of the Turkish invasion) and practical information on how to get here. It will also fill you in on "surprise visitors" to Cyprus through the ages, such as Cleopatra and Richard the Lionheart.

Sunvil

www.sunvil.co.uk/sites/sunvil-cyprus/

British company offering a range of holidays around the island, many of them off the beaten track. You need to know where you're going, however, or at least have a map in front of you, as the site is laid out on a search basis only. The safest bet is the destination search, where you select from a pull-down menu; the holiday type menu (beach, multi-centre, traditional village and so on), which asks you to specify a month, often fails to come up with a match and offers no alternatives. The real strength is in the fantastic selection of villas in southern Cyprus, but they also have plenty of hotels too. Read about accommodation options, check rates and add any potential places to a personalized list, then email for availability and to make a provisional booking.

Czech Republic

For city breaks in Prague, see also the operators listed on p.33.

Czech-It-Out

www.goaway.co.uk

Sister company to British Goa specialists Goaway (see p.250), handling all aspects of short-break travel to the Czech Republic from the UK, including flights, accommodation in one- to five-star hotels, Prague bus tours, and rental of cars, bikes, and even sports equipment. You can't check availability online, but email the form and they'll be in touch.

Czech Tourism

www.czechtourism.com

The official site of the Czech Tourist Authority offers plentiful descriptions of destinations throughout the country (especially "sacral monuments"), plus practical planning information, and links for operators who offer all kinds of activity holidays, such as skiing or horse riding.

Greenways Travel Club

www.gtc.cz

Czech-American joint venture designed to promote small-group and individual travel along the Czech Greenways, a 250-mile corridor of riverside trails that stretches from Prague to Vienna through Southern Moravia and Bohemia. The Website lists dozens of active vacation possibilities, including walking, cycling, horse riding or canoeing trips, and also self-drive and guided tours focusing on art, architecture, music, folklore, or bird-watching. Full itineraries and prices are given, plus contact addresses in both Mikulov (in south Moravia) and Brooklyn that you can call or email to make a booking.

Lanzotic Travel

www.praguetravelbreaks.co.uk

British tour operator specializing in short-break trips to Prague from the UK. A midweek trip can be a real bargain, while if you don't want a fully inclusive package you can also buy flights or accommodation, choosing from a long list of hotels. Phone or email to book.

Paul Laifer Tours

www.laifertours.com

New Jersey-based agency that sells all-inclusive packages from any US city to Prague and other Central and Eastern European destinations, including trips that combine the Czech capital with Berlin, Vienna and/or Budapest. Once you've settled on a flight and a hotel, complete the email form to pursue your reservation.

Romantic Czech Tours

www.romanticczechtours.com

US company, with offices in both Seattle and Prague, that runs an extensive programme of tours to the Czech Republic and beyond. Walking and hiking holidays are the twin specialities, with both rural tours and also one-way trips to Vienna or Budapest. Prices are quoted inclusive of airfares from North America, though they can also simply book accommodation. Call or email with your requests.

TravelGuide

www.travelguide.cz

This Czech site suffers in parts from rather poor translations into English, but for sheer level of detail its destination guide to the entire country is unparalleled. It also offers comprehensive hotel listings, searchable by region or individual city, and complete in most cases with email addresses for reservation enquiries, plus similar databases of restaurants and Internet cafes.

Denmark

BikeDenmark

www.bikedenmark.com

With its scenic coastline and network of cycle lanes, Denmark is ideal holiday territory for bicyclists. Hence the success of BikeDenmark, a Danish company that arranges self-guided cycling tours of the country, with accommodation in inns and hotels and van transportation for your baggage. Their Website offers full details of such trips as "10 Islands in 10 days", but you can't book direct; instead it provides Web links and/or phone numbers for tour operators all over the world.

Scandinavian American World Tours

www.scanamtours.com

Based in New Jersey, this tour company claims to have been "Traveling the world since it was flat"; their logo is a Viking longboat rocking on the open sea. As well as packaged vacations in Denmark and throughout Scandinavia, they also sell air tickets and arrange accommodation. Call or email to make your booking.

Scantours

www.scantoursuk.com

UK-based tour operator specializing in Denmark and the rest of Scandinavia, which uses its Website to display full itineraries and rates for all sorts of Danish holidays, including short breaks to Copenhagen and/or Legoland. Customers from all over the world are welcomed, but you can only make a reservation by calling or emailing their London HQ.

Visit Denmark

www.visitdenmark.com

The home page of the Danish Tourist Board site displays twelve national flags, so you can choose your country of origin and be shown full lists of tour and transportation operators who can take you to Denmark, plus contact details for your local tourist office. Wherever you're from, the site also holds a comprehensive introduction to visiting the country, plus a destination guide to the hotels, restaurants and attractions (with Web and email addresses but not objective reviews) of Danish towns. It will even pinpoint any chosen hotel on national and street maps.

Wonderful Copenhagen

www.woco.dk

→ Copenhagen – living is easy

The centrepiece of Copenhagen's official visitor Website is its vast alphabetical listings section, which ranges from Hans Christian Andersen and Søren Kierkegaard to Bungee Jumping and Miniature Golf, and covers the immediate vicinity as well as the city itself. You're most likely to be looking for accommodation here, in which case you can find and reserve a suitable hotel; they can also arrange transportation and guides.

Dominican Republic

Debbie's Dominican Republic Travel Page

www.debbiesdominicantravel.com

A personal site that's worth bookmarking? Strange, but true. Canadian Debbie's hugely impressive travel page, which invites readers to contribute their own comments, travelogues and reviews, now has more than 4000 amazingly frank and detailed guest reviews and testimonies about hundreds of Dominican hotels and resorts, with star ratings, contact information and links to Websites for each. Not only that, but diving and golfing reviews and links, a section devoted to weddings, a list of travel agents in North America and Europe, and a lively message board. And Debbie doesn't try to sell you anything!

Dominican Republic Treasures

www.drvacations.com/main.htm

This New York company specializes in escorted tours and all-inclusive packages, throughout the DR. They only sell air tickets from New York itself, so all prices are quoted on a land-only basis. Whether you're into hiking, diving, whale watching, biking, festivals, rubbernecking, honeymooning or just chilling out on the beach, you should find something here. Each itinerary detailed on the site gives only a starting price, however; you need to email them to get fuller details and a quote.

Iguana Mama

www.iguanamama.com

Highly rated DR-based adventure and eco-tour company dealing in ground-only packages. The jewels here are the mountain-biking tours, which include a twelve-day coast-to-coast itinerary, but the special family vacations ("pirates, beaches and waterfalls" for example), look great, too, as do the exciting day-trips – biking, hiking, mule trekking, canyoning, diving and so on. Schedules, highlights and costs are laid out on the site, and you need to email them to make a reservation. If you want them to create an itinerary just for you, fill in the form detailing your interests and requirements.

Ecuador

Ecuador Explorer

www.ecuadorexplorer.com

The best overall Web guide to the country provides thorough destination information, with plenty of history and culture thrown in. It's most useful, though, for its detailed descriptions of accommodation options of all kinds, and of specialist tour operators, arranged by region and/or activity. Wherever possible, all recommendations come with links to the relevant Websites.

Galapagos Adventure Tours

www.galapagos.co.uk

British operator that arranges small-group tours of all kinds to Ecuador. Take a luxury cruise to the Galapagos Islands, or fly there and then explore on a yacht or motorboat, with diving available on some vessels. Alternatively, take a Jungle Safari or bird-watching trek into the Amazon rainforest. Booking by phone or email.

Galapagos Travel

www.galapagostravel.com

California-based cruise specialist, which runs a busy programme of 11- and 14-day Galapagos tours, placing an emphasis on environmentally friendly travel. Groups are accompanied by naturalists and biologists, and also given guidance with photography. Reserve via email.

Egypt

Africa Point

www.africapoint.com

Visually speaking, this Nairobi-based travel agency site is not in the slightest bit exciting; there's nothing here to stimulate your imagination or answer your questions. What you do get, on the other hand, is a straightforward list of well-priced Egyptian guided tours, all starting from Cairo, plus a good set of links. Tour choices range from three-day city stays to luxury Sun Boat cruises. Reservations can be made by email at the click of a button.

Ancient World Tours

www.ancient.co.uk

Ancient World Tours, an agent of the UK-based operator Kuoni Travel, give full details of their mouthwatering programme of attractively priced special-interest historical tours of Egypt, guided by leading archeologists and academics. Besides the obvious destinations, and a good overview of scuba diving possibilities, there are plenty of unusual and little-known alternatives, including Roman sites, early Christian monasteries, and the legendary oasis of Siwa, as visited by Alexander the Great. Sadly, you can't make bookings online, just call or email with enquiries.

The Best in World Heritage Travel

UK 020 7917 9494
International: +44 (0) 20 7917 9494

Photographic Copyright owned by AWT & others. No commercial use, please.

Updated 1st February 2004 2100 GMT

The 2004 Brochure is out!

To receive the 2004 brochure and to be kept up to date with developments in our newsletter, make sure you register with us.

To Register For A Brochure
CLICK HERE

Bible and the Mars/Egypt Connection

www.mt.net/~watcher/pyramid.html

The kind of site the Web was invented for, using VERY LARGE TYPE to spread the word of Watcher Ministries, who believe that the Great Pyramid was constructed by angels from the city of Cydonia on Mars to represent the essence of the saving work of the Messiah. All kinds of abstruse facts, figures and Biblical quotations are marshalled to explain the mysteries of ancient Egypt, such as why there aren't two more pyramids at Giza, corresponding to the stars Rigel and Betelgeuse.

Discover Egypt

www.discoveregypt.co.uk

Quick, easy-to-navigate site run by All Leisure Holidays of London to promote its "Discover Egypt" tours, which include airfares from London or Manchester. Their cruises are less high-minded than some, featuring fancy dress parties and belly dancers, while they also have a full programme of diving holidays and monument tours, and offer useful illustrated guides to hotels. The site isn't interactive, but you can submit an instant online reservation request form.

Egypt Sphinx Pyramids

http://users.cihost.com/ata/egypt.htm

On first glance, this site appears to focus on the wackier side of ancient archeology. The closer you look, however, you realize that it's been forced to acknowledge "new evidence pointing to humans as the builders of the pyramids", and in fact offers a balanced view of current debates, with lots of links to different theories and conventional research.

Egypt: The Complete Guide

http://touregypt.net

This huge database, packed with all the latest news, makes an excellent resource for travellers. Endearingly, its accommodation listings are divided into "hotels" (with detailed prices and active links) and "hotels with little info", while there's a wealth of details on antiquities and monuments, including glimpses "behind the scenes", and a special section for budget travellers. Colourful extras include a "virtual dive centre" and a "virtual Khan-el-Khalili" – a simulated tour through Cairo's main bazaar, in which you can shop for souvenirs – plus discussion groups and recipes.

Egypt Tours

www.egypttours.com

Illinois-based agent with an extensive programme of Egypt tours, packages and cruises, mostly quite up-market. Egypt can also be combined with other Middle-East destinations. All trips are available to customers worldwide, who submit the same detailed online booking form but simply deduct the US airfare from the usual price.

Egypt Voyager

www.egyptvoyager.com

General Egyptian site that for once is stronger on modern tourism than ancient monuments. Its superb accommodation database enables you to search over 2000 hotels by price, location, and quality, with links to those that have Websites, and there's good coverage of Nile cruises and diving holidays too. You can also download Egyptian music and stationery.

Egyptology Resources

www.newton.cam.ac.uk/egypt/

Massive international database maintained by the Newton Institute in Cambridge, England. As well as links to dozens of specialist archeological and historical sites, you'll find virtual reality tours of the great monuments, and a few resources for modern travellers.

Guardian's Egypt

http://guardians.net

A virtual "cyberjourney" through ancient Egypt, which as well as serious-minded interviews with archeologists and the latest news of excavations, offers 360° panoramas of pyramids, temples and even individual tombs in the Valley of the Kings, to the accompaniment of sonorous booming and other sound effects. There's no practical information, but if you want to see the Sphinx "between the paws" – and buy a few souvenirs too – this is the place to come.

Homeric Tours

www.homerictours.com

Although this good-value US company specializes primarily in tours of Greece, it also offers some appetizing 8–14 day trips to Egypt, incorporating Nile cruises as well as visits to Luxor and Cairo. You can also combine Egypt and Greece into a single package. The details are all there to help you make up your mind, but as yet, the Website doesn't offer online booking.

Ker & Downey

www.kerdowney.com

Texas tour company that offers luxuri-ous, gourmet Nile cruises in smaller vessels than most other operators. Trips consist of either seven nights from Luxor or four from Aswan. The Website gives full prices and details, but only enables you to request brochures rather than make bookings.

Mistress of Magic

http://egyptmagic.bizland.com

Splendidly batty site offered by an American High Priestess who conducts New Age tours of Egypt in search of "sacred secrets". Channel the spirits of your ancestors, or pray for your pet at the temple of the cat goddess.

Museum Tours

www.museum-tours.com

The travel section of this Colorado tour agency's Website simply offers text summaries of their relatively up-market guided trips to Egypt. Most run for two weeks from New York; the highlight has to be the private small-group sailing trips on the Nile. You can't book online, just email for availability. The site also includes, however, a "Virtual Egypt Museum", with an interactive gallery of the Valley of the Kings.

Yallabina @ Cairo

www.yallabina.com

Under the slogan "We take your fun life seriously", the focus here is firmly on Cairo's nightlife. As well as restaurants and bars, it covers sport, movies, theatre, music (including opera and an "Online Salsa Guide"). Its more general Cairo Guide section lists hotels and attractions, but really the assumption is that you're already based in the city.

Finland

Emagine UK

www.emagine-travel.co.uk

British travel company that specializes in tours to Finland, serving as UK agent for several Finnish companies, and offering activities like hiking and skiing as well as city breaks. Their busiest season is midwinter, when they arrange excursions to meet Father Christmas (not the real one) in Lapland. Reservations by phone or email only.

Finnish Tourist Board

www.finland-tourism.com

Visually speaking, this official site is far from appealing, and you have to plod through some rather tedious menus to get anywhere, but there's a lot of information in there once you dig deep enough. Apart from the general destination information and lists of links, it's especially useful for booking accommodation, with links to individual hotels and hostels and also to umbrella organizations and lodging chains.

The King's Road

www.thekingsroad.com

Attractive site promoting the King's Road, a thirteenth-century route from Oslo to St Petersburg by way of the southern Finnish coast of Finland. As well as details on towns and cities along the way, including Helsinki, there's an invaluable page of links to the (surprisingly many) North American tour operators that now offer the road as an up-market tourist itinerary.

Virtual Finland

http://virtual.finland.fi/

The Finland Information Pages, maintained by the Finnish Ministry for Foreign Affairs, provide comprehensive details on all aspects of the country's life and economy, ranging from Santa Claus (who appears under "Famous Finns") to the national parks. For travellers, the best feature is a full set of tourism links.

Wild North

www.wildnorth.net

Very fancy site designed to promote activity trips to northern Finland, which dishes up stunning images of the Finnish wilderness and offers a wide range of accommodation in the region, from rustic cabins to luxurious lodges and eco-resorts. If trekking and fly-fishing isn't enough for you, you can even shoot a moose.

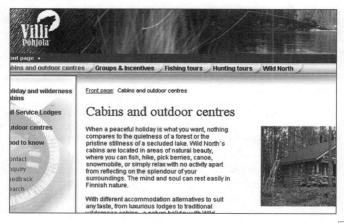

France

BCT Scenic Walking

www.bctwalk.com

California-based operator that offers up-market guided walking tours in different regions of France, staying in comfortable hotels and benefiting from a support vehicle. Download the booking form to make your reservation.

Brittany Ferries

www.brittany-ferries.co.uk

As well as providing information and online booking for their cross-Channel ferry services, as detailed on p.54, Brittany Ferries' Website enables users to find and book accommodation all over France. The excellent property search facility covers hotels as well as houses, cottages and chalets. Specify what type of lodging you prefer, when and where, indicate your budget and other requirements (such as being close to a beach), and it makes specific suggestions on which you can pick up further details. Ultimately, you can book the entire holiday, including ferry travel, online.

Brittany Tourist Board

www.brittanytourism.com

This regional Website is in principle available in English, though it's easy to stray into French-language areas, such as the travel forum. Pick you way carefully, and you'll find lots of readily digestible information, with a good set of links to complement its strongest feature, an easy search facility for local hotels.

Brittany Travel

www.brittany.co.uk

Superb site run by a British agency that arranges self-catering holidays in southern Brittany, in western France. The first words you see are "click here for current availability"; for every property, you can inspect interior photos, pick up full price details, and see whether it's free for the dates you want. Actual bookings are then confirmed by email or phone.

Corsican Places

www.corsica.co.uk

UK-based travel agency providing hotel, villa and apartment holidays on the rugged Mediterranean island of Corsica. Head first for the fine array of last-minute deals, then work your way through the pull-down menus to find full details of 150-plus properties, with prices for packages that include flights and car rental. Bookings are made by email or phone.

CybeVasion

www.cybevasion.com

General travel-related French portal, bursting with connections to hotels, campsites, agencies, and operators throughout the country. You never quite know whether a link will take you anywhere worthwhile, but there is absolutely masses of stuff here, and if you have a particular specialist interest it's well worth trying.

The Definitive Guide to Hotels in France

www.france.com

Colourful site, run by a Florida agency with an office in Paris, which besides selling flights from the US to France, focuses on a massive database of French hotels. Use the "Reservation Center" to find hotels that match your preferred criteria, and then read the objective guidebook and personal reviews (eg "small with a strong humidity smell, certainly not in line with the price paid"). There's also a forum for more general issues. Availability can be checked, but booking is not quite interactive; confirmation takes up to three days.

Discover France

www.discoverfrance.com

This US operator, based in Arizona, provides clear, succinct information on destinations throughout France, and promotes a wide range of all-inclusive cycling trips, both guided and self-guided, as well as other themed tours such as walking or cookery, and also offers simple accommodation-only deals. Prices exclude international airfares, while "booking" consists of sending an instant email without an interactive check on specific availability.

Eiffel Tower

www.tour-eiffel.fr/teiffel/tour_uk/index.html

Most of the best-known French monuments, such as the Louvre and the chateau of Versailles, run their own Websites, but the Eiffel Tower – "La Tour Scintillante" – has the best. Available in English, it offers a fully illustrated history and chronology of the tower, along with practical details for visitors. The best features, however, are the memory-crunching virtual 3D tour, which enables you to explore via cross-sections, and the streaming video views from the summit. You can even send a postcard from the Tower just to prove you've really been there.

France Afloat

www.franceafloat.com

A French company runs this English-language Website to promote its programme of barge and canal-boat holidays on rivers and waterways in three French regions: Central, South and West. Search by location, date and size of boat, then call or email to make your booking.

with *franceafloat*   Let's go!

the French Canal Specialists

France Tourism

www.francetourism.com

This useful complement to the main French Government Tourist Office site is run by the FGTO outpost in New York. As well as destination and practical information on France and its few remaining overseas possessions, it provides listings, and links where possible, to general and specialist US travel operators. The level of detail tends to be geared more specifically to first-time visitors to Europe, and business travellers.

France Vacations

www.francevacations.net

These Californian operators specialize in bargain travel to France from the US. The most eye-catching deals are on all-inclusive packages, with short Paris breaks at under $500, but they can also arrange separate accommodation, car rental, and flight-only deals. The Website carries full details; email with specific queries or simply request a brochure.

French Connections

www.frenchconnections.co.uk

Attractive and user-friendly accommodation portal that connects users with the owners of several hundred gorgeous French holiday homes, complete with enticing pictures. Options range from fifteenth-century chateaux to picturesque stone farmhouses, and the prices too rise from the very reasonable up to £7000 for a fortnight in a chateau near Bordeaux; some homes are also advertised for sale. The easy search facility allows you to see exactly what you're getting. Each property has its own page with photos and prices, and you contact the owners directly to make your reservation. Painting, cookery, walking and other specialist holidays are also on offer, as are discounts on Channel crossings, while the site holds an illustrated bibliography of relevant books.

The French Experience

www.frenchexperience.com

New York-based travel agency that offers a full programme of vacation packages in France, including inexpensive transatlantic flights. Having chosen from a long list of budget Paris options or the good week-long deals for Provence in the south, you can also add short self-drive or even chauffeur-driven tours in the regions, staying in hotels or chateaux. Booking requests are handled by email, phone or fax.

French Festival

www.frenchfestival.com/journeys.html

Small Californian travel agency, featuring a can-canning Mademoiselle on its home page. The main attractions are guided tours to Provence in southern France, where you travel from place to place by train, staying in village hotels and hiking in the hills, but they also offer walking tours in Paris. There's no online booking, but service is personalized and direct.

French Home Rentals

www.frenchhomerentals.com

Oregon agency that offers a small selection of rental properties all over France, available for periods between one week and nine months, and also runs its own French-language and cookery school in Villeneuve-sur-Lot in the southwest. Complete their online enquiry form, and you'll get a response within 24 hours.

Gîtes de France

www.gites-de-france.fr/eng/

The English-language version of the Website run by Gîtes de France, a government-funded agency that promotes and manages a vast array of B&B and self-catering accommodation in France. Their destination information is good, and the search facility enables you to find specific properties by region or département, and check their availability. A straightforward booking facility means that most, but not quite all, can be reserved online; there's also an online bookshop selling their own guides and directories.

Logis de France

www.logis-de-france.fr/uk/index.htm

Organization of independent French hotels, especially in smaller towns and villages, which are promoted together for their consistently good food and reasonably priced rooms. If none of the special offers grabs you, then search out hotels by area and specific characteristics. It only takes four clicks to complete a reservation, but it also takes faith; strangely, you have to go ahead without knowing the exact price.

Maison de la France

www.franceguide.com

Using the English-language section of the French Government Tourist Office's Website enables you to get up-to-the-minute news and details of forthcoming events, and access links to local and regional tourist offices, historic monuments and the like. The practical section promises accommodation searches and booking online, but tends to be complicated and largely unproductive; much better to work your way through the extensive lists of travel operators who run trips to France from your home country.

Matthews Holidays

www.matthewsfrance.co.uk

British operator with a straightforward speciality – inexpensive self-drive mobile-home holidays in French campsites – and an equally straightforward Website. Once you've opted for one of the three available regions on the opening map – Brittany, the Vendée or Southern France – and picked your precise spot, their impressive price calculator springs into action, factoring in whatever ferry crossings you need, as well as stopovers in hotels en route. You can then complete your booking online, though it's worth calling the office before you do to see whether any discounts apply.

New Frontiers

www.newfrontiers.com

The France department of this general North American travel and flight agency offers lots of good-value French package trips from the US city of your choice. Paris choices are legion, with $800 for five nights from LA as a typical price, but the selection elsewhere is more limited, with only certain odd, regional cities available. Email with full details to make a reservation.

Owners In France

www.ownersinfrance.com

A somewhat slow and cumbersome site run by an organization of British owners of around 800 French vacation rentals. There's some sketchy destination information, but the point of coming here is to search for specific properties by location, price, and facilities; if you find anything you fancy, contact the relevant owner to confirm a reservation. The umbrella organization can arrange discounted rates on cross-Channel travel.

Paris Hotels

www.parishotels.com

A Paris accommodation agency runs this very plain, simple site, that's almost entirely devoted, as the name suggests, to finding the perfect hotel out of the 180 Paris options on their books. Search by availability and/or neighbourhood (including close to the airport as well as in the city centre), click on detailed local maps to see photos and precise rates, and then email your reservation request to the relevant hotel. They also provide a database of around a thousand Parisian restaurants.

The Paris Pages

www.paris.org

This astonishingly detailed overview of all things Parisian holds links to two thousand hotels sorted according to price and location; prices, opening hours and descriptions for all the museums and monuments; a handy French glossary; and the opportunity to send electronic postcards to your friends.

Sherpa Expeditions Online

www.sherpaexpeditions.com

Although Sherpa are based in the UK, they sell specialist walking, hiking and cycling holidays to customers worldwide. Their trips, too, take place all over the world, but their France programme is especially large and appealing, including both escorted and self-guided tours, and accommodation in tents and mountain huts as well as in village hotels. Areas covered include the Loire valley, the Dordogne, the Alps and the Pyrenees. Bookings made online are provisional, and are only confirmed by mailing a deposit.

Ski France

www.ski-ride-france.com

The English-language version of this French portal, run by a marketing association that represents a hundred major French ski resorts, provides comprehensive links to resorts all over the country. You can find information on each by searching according to region or categories such as "traditional village" or "family" resorts; having chosen one you fancy, either connect to its own website or chose from an extensive list of operators who serve that particular destination.

SNCF

www.sncf.com/indexe.htm

Few fancy extras on this, the English-language Website of the efficient and user-friendly French rail network – assuming you want to plan and reserve a train journey in France, however, it does the job admirably. Specify the relevant stations, and your preferred departure or arrival times, and it comes up with a bunch of alternative schedules and prices, together with advice as to which rail passes can provide useful discounts. You can complete and pay for your tickets online; they'll mail them to you if there's time, otherwise pick them up at any SNCF station.

The South France Guide

www.le-guide.com

This comprehensive list of vacation rentals in southern France, especially in Languedoc and Roussillon, is maintained by the Home France and French Affair agencies, which operate from the US and the UK. Use the interactive regional maps, pinpointing specific properties, to find one that appeals to you, check the price is right, and then email the owner to complete the booking. The site also has a smaller selection of B&Bs, and connects to a database of properties for sale.

Tourisme en France

www.tourisme.fr/index2_uk.htm

This useful site centres on a handy database of almost four thousand of France's municipal and local tourist offices, arranged by région and département. In theory, each town's listings include practical and cultural information and links to local Websites, though many of the smaller ones simply offer their address and phone number. You can also search for destinations according to various criteria, such as those offering specific activities or historical attractions; peruse an online calendar of upcoming events; and get details of special offers, such as bargain weekend breaks.

VFB Holidays

www.vfbholidays.co.uk

Highly rated UK operator, exclusively specializing in French holidays, that can arrange all aspects of a trip to France, from accommodation to ferry crossings and fly-drives to Corsica. Their website also displays a fine selection of short breaks and special offers, and carries links to useful information sites. Online booking is only available for cottage rentals; for everything else, you have to phone or email.

Voyages Ilena

www.voyagesilena.co.uk

British operator that sells all-inclusive holidays both to the Mediterranean island of Corsica, and also to mainland Provence, with accommodation in hotels, villas and cottages. Follow their detailed destination guide, and if somewhere catches your fancy you can seek out details, with prices, of specific properties. Be sure to check out the cut-price last-minute offers, but you can't book or buy online, merely download and mail in a booking form.

Gambia

The Gambia Experience

www.gambia.co.uk

The only British operator to focus exclusively on holidays in the Gambia, with an emphasis on eco-tourism, activities including bird-watching, safaris and lazing on the beach, and weekly charter flights – also available on a flight-only basis – from Manchester and Bristol as well as London Gatwick. The "10 Reasons for going to The Gambia" on their Website don't amount to much more than "it's nice and so is the weather", but then that may well be all you want from a destination. If you're interested, call to book.

Germany

For spa holidays, see the operators listed on p.117.

DER Travel Service

www.dertravel.co.uk

A British travel agency that specializes in German holidays runs this Website to promote packages that include travel from the UK by rail, sea and air. It also covers resort or city accommodation, and activities such as walking and cycling. Reserve accommodation online, or fill in an email form to request a full itinerary.

Die Bahn

www.bahn.de

With a database of 150,000 rail stations in Germany alone, German rail network Die Bahn supplies online schedules for rail, road and sea connections all over Europe. Click "International Guests" on the home page for an English-language version.

Germany Info

www.germany-info.org/nf_index.html

Produced by the German embassy in the US, this slick site features all sorts of facts, figures and stats; thus it mentions that 47 percent of Germans are overweight. The travel section is good for practical information on driving, public holidays, customs, visa regulations and so on, with links to city and regional Websites and other relevant sources. They also suggest holiday ideas and itineraries arranged thematically – gay and lesbian, cultural heritage, music, history tours and so on – with plenty of good links.

Germany Wunderbar

www.germany-tourism.de

Exhaustive, Flash-enhanced English-language version of the official tourist board site. If you can trawl your way through the PR hyperbole, this is a fantastic resource, with links to state tourism boards, city sites, package holidays, ski resorts, accommodation groups and so on, all grouped intelligently by subject area. While you can read about states and cities under "Destinations", "Travel Tips" is perhaps the most inspiring place to start, organized into sections including youth vacations, culinary Germany (where you'll discover "there is no end to the praise of the potato"), national parks, cultural trips, spa breaks and active travel. Each combines original content, links, and a number of suggested itineraries. You can also search the "Events" for happenings, exhibitions, concerts and festivals up to 2003.

Hotels Germany

www.lodging-germany.com

It couldn't be simpler: click on one of the hundred-plus towns listed, select hotels from the chart (they're divided into three price categories), read the reviews, pore over the photos, and then use the secure server to make a reservation request.

Rhinecastles.com

www.rhinecastles.com

Searchable information site for the castle-obsessed. Here you'll find links to maps marking castles; castle travelogues; castle hotels; romantic hotels and country hotels with castle views; operators offering tailor-made and escorted castle tours; castles offering special "knight's meals"; companies offering castle-themed Christmas cards ... and a good range of general travel links, too, including general accommodation sites, city and regional sites. Oh, and some photos of castles.

Greece

Aegean

www.agn.gr

Well-presented, visually appealing site, run by Greek company OneWorld and covering all aspects of tourism in the Aegean. Navigating through its hierarchy of interactive maps, you can get full destination information on your chosen area, including climate details, and it's easy to find and contact hotels, and make online reservations. Although there are plenty of links to travel agents, for nitty-gritty transportation, such as trains and ferries, it provides phone numbers rather than actual timetables, let alone any booking facility.

All Greek Ferries

www.ferries.gr

The best of a number of sites that aim to cover all the ferry services in Greek waters, run by the Paleologos Shipping & Travel Agency in Heraklion, Crete. As well as international connections with Italy, Cyprus, Albania, Israel, Egypt and Turkey, with useful route maps, it details virtually all the countless domestic inter-island itineraries. Almost all the ferry companies maintain their own sites, but this is the place to choose which one suits your requirements, and offers immediate booking both online or by fax. You can also reserve train and air tickets, car rental, and accommodation.

Athens Survival Guide

www.athensguide.com

Written and maintained by American expat Matt Barrett, this very personal guide can be rather rambling at times, but it's the closest thing to having a helpful friend on the spot to give you whatever advice you need on visiting the city. "Athens is a fun place. It just looks like hell at first glance". As well as lengthy reviews of the eight hotels he recommends, he provides links to find others if necessary. He also offers comprehensive information on eating and shopping, links to recommended travel agents, and paeans of praise to the city's pristine new metro system and even to "George the Famous Taxi Driver". Once you're through with Athens, Matt's **www.greektravel.com** site provides a less all-embracing introduction to travel in the rest of Greece.

Dilos Holiday World

www.dilos.com

Travel agency with offices on Crete and, for some reason, in Belgium too, which specializes in cruising the Aegean. Their site presents full itineraries and prices for various vessels, and offers online booking. They can also arrange accommodation all over Greece, coach tours around Athens or further afield, and car rental, while their destination guides are strong on Greek history and culture.

Explore Crete

www.explorecrete.com

A general destination guide to the island of Crete, which for once isn't desperate to sell you anything. Instead, it holds lots of enthusiastic articles and colourful virtual guides. Busy message boards can provide feedback if you have specific questions about resorts or hotels, and there's also an immensely detailed comparison of the Rough Guide and Lonely Planet guides to the island. While there's not a great deal of concrete practical stuff in there, it's great for firing your enthusiasm.

Filoxenia

www.filoxenia.co.uk

British tour company that runs an extensive programme of special-interest holidays in both mainland Greece and the islands, including botany, history, archeology, painting and culture. Most of their site consists of a run-through of brochures you can then order, but they do illustrate some of their options in greater detail, and through their "Greco-File" consultancy they will answer queries, design tailor-made packages, and point you towards other operators who provide complementary trips. They also carry extensive listings of rental villas.

Friends of the Ionian

www.foi.org.uk

Lovely, and very enthusiastic site devoted to the six Ionian islands, with a particular emphasis on the healthy open-air life. The "Friends" are a membership organization, and paying the £12 annual fee to join entitles you to download detailed guides and hiking trail descriptions, but enough information is accessible for free online to thoroughly whet your appetite.

Gogreece.com

www.gogreece.com

California-based portal, aimed primarily at first-time American visitors to Greece, which provides an overview of every destination along with links to local tourist offices, plus air, rail and ferry services, and information from the simple to the technical about the country's language, history, culture and contemporary politics.

Greek Islands Club Online

www.greekislandsclub.com

Run by up-market British tour operator Sunvil Holidays, this site enables prospective visitors to search for their ideal vacation rental by island, holiday type (such as watersports, sailing or "traditional village"), by choosing from a long list of criteria, or simply late availability. All prices are detailed, and accommodation options come with 360° panoramas, but rather than booking online you have to make further enquiries by email or phone.

Hellenic Adventures

www.hellenicadventures.com

This one-(Greek)-man US outfit, based in Minneapolis, offers small-group hiking and sailing tours around Greece and its islands; makes reservations for cruises and yacht charters; and can also arrange self-guided itineraries for independent travellers. The six routes on the mainland include a 15-day Grand Tour and another designed to explore the origins of the Olympic games, while a further four explore the islands. Call or email for reservations.

Hellenic Culture

www.culture.gr

The official site of the Hellenic Ministry of Culture centres on an enormous gazetteer of monuments and museums, with full detailed descriptions of each, as well as opening hours, plus a calendar of forthcoming events and links to cultural organizations both in Greece and overseas.

Homeric Tours

www.homerictours.com

The largest specialist US operator to Greece, with a long and varied programme of vacations on the Greek mainland and islands, plus, of course, cruises in between. Some are geared towards ancient sights, others simply dedicated to hedonism, and the rates tend to be consistently low. For the moment, they haven't introduced online booking, so fill in the email booking form to secure the trip that interests you.

interkriti

www.interkriti.org

A comprehensive guide to Crete, the largest of the Greek islands, run by an agency in the capital Heraklion. In addition to its own content and sponsored links, it connects to assorted other municipal and commercial sites, so selecting any town or region calls up a database of hotels, car rental and other listings. A bulletin board carries details of other visitors' experiences.

Laskarina Holidays

www.laskarina.co.uk

A British company that specializes in high-standard apartment, villa and house stays on remote and unspoiled Greek islands. Their Website holds few photos, so it's very quick and easy to use, swiftly bringing up details and generalized prices for specific properties. However, it doesn't offer online availability checks, let alone booking, and serves primarily as a brochure-request service. It's included here simply because the actual holidays are so good.

Meander Adventures

www.meanderadventures.com

Promising "Innovative journeys for the Spirited traveler", Meander Adventures is a Utah-based agency specializing in holidays in Greece and Turkey. As well as preparing customized itineraries on the mainland, it organizes highly recommended small-group tours of Rhodes, Symi and Samos, and also yacht cruises. Browse the Website, then email or call to make a reservation.

Skiathos Island

www.skiathosinfo.com

Jazzy information site for the island of Skiathos, in which lots of pop-up menus chase you around as you track down every imaginable local business. Once you've got the destination information you need, you can link to **www.skiathos-direct.com** to contact specific hotels and travel operators. As well as arranging all-inclusive packages, you can also simply buy your ferry tickets.

Sunisle

www.sunisle.co.uk

London-based operator specializing in trips to six of the Ionian islands. Their Website enables you to check online availability for a wide range of villas and apartments, and either finalize reservations or simply hold dates for a few hours while you make up your mind. They also provide links to arrange flights and car rentals.

The Symi Visitor

www.symivisitor.com

A site run by the local English-language newspaper for the lovely island of Symi in the Dodecanese that enables you to bypass the major tour operators and make your own arrangements to stay in island villas and apartments. It also features satellite photos and real-estate ads, plus local gossip and a message board.

Travel à la Carte

www.travelalacarte.co.uk

Easy-to-use site set up by a British tour operator that arranges holidays on islands in the Ionian, Sporades and Dodecanese groups. You can search for accommodation to suit your precise requirements, or just browse the late availability offers. Having checked availability by email or phone, either email them or download and print your booking form from the site and mail it in.

Travelux

www.travelux.co.uk

British tour company that arranges packages both on the Ionian islands and on the mainland, staying in villas, apartments and hotels you can choose online. As well as simple sun-and-sand holidays, you can improve your mind or your body by joining special trips devoted to painting,

photography, trekking or tuition in the Alexander technique. The Website details all prices, but you have to email or phone to check on availability.

Valef Yachts

http://valefyachts.com

Valef Yachts is a US-based agency that specializes in private yacht charters and cruises around the Greek Islands. You can't literally book online, but email your choice of their set itineraries, or simply indicate how much you're prepared to spend on your own luxury voyage, and they'll take it from there, making all necessary transport arrangements.

Haiti

Haiti World

www.haiticentral.com

Somewhat chaotic Haitian portal, with text in both French and English, which despite the banner ad on the first page exhorting users to "step away from darkness, away from demonism!" carries forty separate links to sites on voodooism. You'll also find forums discussing Haitian topics, and a hotels and travel agencies section.

Hungary

Budapest.com

www.budapest.com

Locally based Web guide to Budapest, featuring a slide show of city attractions, listings of restaurants, shops and bars. Most useful of all is a hotel reservation service, under which you choose three preferred options from a long

illustrated list, submit an email request, and they get back to you once they've checked availability. Specific personal queries about visiting Hungary are also answered.

Hungarian National Tourist Office

www.hungarytourism.hu

The official site of Hungary's National Tourist Office provides a thorough overview of possibilities for visitors, including detailed recommendations of cycling routes; links to museums and galleries; a history of Hungarian baths; and even current cinema listings.

Paul Laifer Tours

www.laifertours.com

US tour company specializing in eastern Europe, which offers "classic" eight-day packages to Budapest from any US city (costing as little as $599 from New York); twin-centre holidays to both Budapest and Prague; and itineraries that take in Vienna, Warsaw and Krakow as well. Choose from several alternative hotels, then send the email form to make a reservation.

Travelport.hu

www.travelport.hu

Make your way to the English pages of this good general Hungarian site, and you'll find masses of information on destinations throughout the country, plus details of 2500 hotels, hostels and other accommodation options, of which around three hundred so far offer online booking.

Iceland

Iceland's geothermal Blue Lagoon is reviewed on p.117.

Arctic Experience

www.arctic-experience.co.uk

Environmentally conscious British tour company that in addition to basic weekend breaks in Reykjavik offers a huge assortment of active and adventurous trips to Iceland, both guided and independent, including hikes and jeep safaris through volcanic and geothermal wildernesses, or whale- and seal-watching in the fjords. The Website carries full itineraries, and includes an email booking form.

Icelandic Tourist Board

www.icetourist.is

The official Website for Iceland's tourism industry provides a colourful introduction to Europe's second largest island, with plenty of spectacular images and lots of cultural and historical information (including the true story of Gudrid Thorbjarnardottir, who founded a settlement in North America during the eleventh century, and later made a pilgrimage on foot to Rome, and also a page devoted to Björk). Its Yellow Pages section carries listings of hotels and restaurants, with Web links where available, though the lack of detailed reviews means it's not all that useful for making practical travel arrangements – and thanks to the idiosyncrasies of Icelandic typography, it can also be a little hard to read.

Iceland Virgin Earth

www.icelandholidays.com

Run by a British tour operator, this site announces itself as "the one-stop place to view and book your holiday in Iceland". Its bread and butter lies in long weekends or fly-drive holidays using inexpensive Icelandair flights from Heathrow, but additional pages detail longer adventure trips into the interior. Email or phone to pursue your enquiries.

India

See also our section on New Age, religious and spiritual holidays, which starts on p.174.

Chandertal Tours and Himalayan Folkways

www.chandertal-tours.freeserve.co.uk

In conjunction with its offshoot Himalayan Folkways, UK-based agency Chandertal Tours offers a stunning range of customized activity tours throughout India. The general trekking programme ranges up to a 30-day trans-Himalayan trek, plus walks geared towards wild flowers or geological features, and even one designed to induce weight

 loss. Several of the same routes, such as from Manali in Himachal Pradesh to Leh in Ladakh, can also be followed by pony, mountain-bike, motorcycle, or jeep safaris. In addition, you can fish for the legendary mahseer fish in rivers in both North and South India, take a yoga course, or tour spice and coffee plantations in the South. In fact, you're invited to suggest pretty much anything you fancy by email and they promise to do their best to arrange it. All trips are priced on a land-only basis, so participants from all countries are welcome.

Cox and Kings

www.coxandkings.co.uk

Large UK-based operator that's one of the major players in offering up-market guided tours of India, using internal flights and staying (wherever possible) in luxury accommodation. The Website provides details and prices of their dozen or so tours, which range from the 9-day Indian Experience exploring the Golden Triangle of Delhi, Agra and Jaipur, for £875 up to 18-day trips. You can then ask for their brochures and make your booking by phone or email. Typical prices, including return flight from Britain, are slightly over £100 per day.

Delhigate.com

www.delhigate.com

Specialist Delhi site with the added gimmick of offering a free online query service, which guarantees a personal email response to any question about the city. The site itself provides rail and air timetables, and lists rather than reviews Delhi's restaurants, hotels, and Internet cafes, with links where possible. One highlight is the section on "bad businesses", warning customers, for example, to steer clear of the restaurant that served a vegetarian kebab with a complete brass screw hidden in it. Limited coverage of the rest of the country includes online hotel bookings nationwide.

Discovery Initiatives

www.discoveryinitiatives.com

UK-based company dedicated to "Inspirational Travel that supports conservation worldwide", which offers tailor-made itineraries via its very glitzy Website, such as exploring rural Rajasthan on horseback or a "Tiger Insight Tour" in search of big cats. Tours are priced in both pounds and dollars.

Essential India

www.essential-india.co.uk

UK agency that offers courses of all kinds in India, largely in the Himalayan foothills, and including writers' workshops as well as learning local ceramic traditions. Warning that India "can be both frustratingly disappointing and breathtakingly wonderful", they aim to combine an experience of the atmosphere of India with the chance to develop new skills.

Explore the Taj Mahal

www.taj-mahal.net/

If you just want to say you've seen the Taj Mahal, this is the place to come. As well as providing a breathtaking 360° virtual tour of India's best-known monument, it also offers a plethora of links to further information, including details of its current environmental peril.

Geographic Expeditions

www.geoex.com

Active worldwide, but based in California, Geographic Expeditions run an extensive programme of small-group India tours, including conventional sightseeing itineraries as well as trekking in Sikkim, Ladakh and Zanskar, exploring the jungles of Arunachal Pradesh, or houseboating in Kerala. They're far from cheap, but they have a high reputation. If the extensive details on the Website give you enough confidence, you can email a reservation request; other-wise enquire further by phone.

Goaway

www.goaway.co.uk

The wittily named Goaway agency specializes in bargain packages from Britain to Goa, with options to combine the South Indian beach resort with a few days in Delhi, Mumbai or Kerala. Despite the low prices, they offer accommodation in luxury Goa hotels, and Ayurvedic treatments are also available.

Heritage Hotels of India

www.heritagehotels.com

Umbrella organization of hotels set in some of India's finest historical monuments, including magnificent forts in Rajasthan and the Himalayas, and palaces still used by Maharajahs. Most have their own Websites, offering online or email booking. The photos – and the prices – are all but irresistible, with luxurious rooms in places such as the Karni Fort in Udaipur or the Rohet Garh outside Jodhpur working out at well under £30/$40 per night.

Himalayan Kingdoms

www.himalayankingdoms.com

UK-based mountaineering experts that offer a very extensive programme of small-group adventure trekking and tours in regions such as Uttar Pradesh, Sikkim, Ladakh and Zanskar (where rafting is also available). As well as lots of photos, the Website carries details and prices for all tours: complete itineraries are downloadable as PDF files. Once you've decided, download the booking form and mail it in.

Indian Railways

www.indianrail.gov.in

The official site of Indian Railways – the world's largest railway system, carrying over eleven million passengers per day. Though you can't buy tickets online, it holds full timetables, with online availability checks and fares for services up to three months in advance, and details of Indrail passes for foreign travellers. There are no destination guides, nor illustrations of any kind, but if you need to look up practical information, you'll find it here.

Indus Tours

www.industours.co.uk

London-based tour company with a large programme of group and independent general-interest trips around India, covering lesser-known areas such as Orissa, Sikkim and Ladakh in addition to the well-trodden paths of Rajasthan and Goa. They also run specialist arts and textile tours of Gujarat. Complete the online booking form to pursue your enquiries.

Kerala.com

www.kerala.com

A colourful and exciting portal that abounds in links to all aspects of the tropical southern state of Kerala – "God's own country". As well as individual cities like Cochin and Trivandrum, it has extensive coverage of the major goal for most independent travellers – the Kerala backwaters. Thanks to its long list of hotels and tour operators, it's possible to book accommodation and boat transport.

Kerala Connections

www.keralaconnect.co.uk

Small, independent British tour operator that arranges all-inclusive packages in Kerala and other regions of southern India, including the islands, and also handles bookings for resorts and hotels. Their simple but attractive Website modestly calls the region "the best place in the world for a holiday". How much you pay depends on the level of luxury you prefer, but it's possible to arrange something on the tiniest of budgets. Email for further details.

Madhya Pradesh

www.mptourism.com

The enthusiastic official tourism Website of the central state of Madhya Pradesh holds an adequate rather than exhaustive guide to regional destinations such as the temples of Khajuraho. It comes into its own, however, in its eagerness to plan and book personalized tours. Email a request to visit Kanha National Park, for example – Asia's biggest wildlife sanctuary and Kipling's inspiration for The Jungle Book – and they'll arrange everything, including "ethnic dances and souvenirs".

Myths and Mountains

www.mythsandmountains.com

These US specialists pride themselves on "socially responsible" tourism, offering a rich and varied set of tailor-made tours throughout India. One's designed as a family trip in search of wildlife; another focuses on yoga, meditation and Ayurvedic traditions; and there's a very fancy "opulence and decadence" trip to Rajasthan.

Oksana

www.oksana.co.uk

This British operator arranges adventurous expeditions worldwide, with an Indian programme that includes trekking in Ladakh or taking a camel safari in Rajasthan. The reasonable tour prices do not include flights from your home country. Print and mail the onscreen form to book.

123India.com

www.123india.com

This specialist search engine should be able to answer any question about India you care to throw at it. Topics range widely through news, business, and pop culture, but visitors will gravitate to its Travel page, which offers links to destination and practical information of every kind.

S D Enterprises

www.dandpani.dircon.co.uk

S D Enterprises, run from north London by the friendly Dr Dandapani, specialize in putting together complex itineraries for independent travellers wanting to explore India by rail. As well as planning and reserving all the train connections at bargain rates, and selling rail passes where they work out cheaper, they can also book accommodation. The Website has full details and schedules, including prices.

SAMACHAR – The bookmark for the Global Indian

www.samachar.com

This portal makes the best gateway site for news of the subcontinent, with extensive links to Indian newspapers as well as international newsgatherers such as the BBC.

Welcome to India

www.tourindia.com

This Website, maintained by the Government of India Tourist Office in the US, is considerably easier to use, and more reliable, than the garish and very skimpy India-based equivalent. As well as providing masses of its own general information about destinations and activities throughout the subcontinent, it also links to state and regional sites countrywide. However, it's not so hot on the practical side of things, with only rather rudimentary links to hotels, tour operators and the like.

Worldwide Adventures

www.worldwidequest.com

This US company specializes in adventurous trips to remote places the world over. Much of their India programme is devoted to expensive tours of cultural and historical highlights such as the Taj Mahal and the palaces of Rajasthan, though they do offer a 15-day "affordable India" tour for under $1000, as well as more active pursuits such as month-long Himalayan treks and wildlife-watching trips to the national parks further south.

Indonesia

Bali Indonesia Travel Portal

www.indo.com

Although the Indonesia Travel Portal proclaims itself a resource for the entire archipelago (or "necklace of equatorial emeralds"), for the most part it concentrates on Bali, and on the upper end of the tourism market at that. The main emphasis is online hotel booking, with gorgeous photos of luxury resorts, but there's also a useful section on "Budget Bali", with a backpackers' forum. Hotel listings for several other islands can be found, plus a reasonable guide to Jakarta; the Top 10 hotels each week offer discounts of up to sixty percent.

The Bali Travel Forum

www.balitravelforum.com

This very busy forum draws on the experiences of residents and visitors to provide information and advice for travellers to the "Ultimate Island". Polls reveal the best and the worst of Bali (in the latter category, 3.44 percent of respondents voted for "stray dogs", as opposed to 9.92 percent for "greedy or rude tourists"). If you can't find what you want in the archives, you can always just ask a direct question, like "White Water Rafting – which river?" or just "is it raining?". The site is maintained by two associated Hong-Kong-based sites, the Bali Hotel Bargain Finder and **http://balivillas.com**, which claim to offer the best available prices in a limited range of accommodation.

Footprint Adventures

www.footprint-adventures.co.uk

Specialist wildlife and trekking company, based in the UK, whose wide range of Indonesian trips include safaris devoted to orang-utans and komodo dragons, and five-day hikes up Mount Rinjani. Follow the site's simple hierarchy to get full details on any tour; you can then book, and pay a deposit, by emailing a form or using the secure online server. Tour prices are ground-only, so travellers from anywhere, including those already in Indonesia, are welcome to use the service. You can also buy a range of Footprint travel guides from here (though the two companies aren't officially linked).

Indonesia and Bali Tourism

www.indonesia-tourism.com

Indonesia's official tourism Website does a pretty good job of covering the whole archipelago, as opposed to just Bali. Clicking on the interactive map on the home page will take you to any island that catches your fancy, each of which holds plenty of further links exploring local history and culture. There's not all that much useful practical information, however, and what there is is pretty hard to find. Whether you're looking for hotels, restaurants or travel agents in any one region, you have to go via the "Accommodation" page, and you won't find links to individual hotels, just an overall booking agency.

The Web-site of Indonesia and Bali Tourism

your genuine experience!

Komodo Tours

www.komodotours.com

Straightforward, easy-to-use Website maintained by an Indonesian-owned travel and tour agency, based in Denpasar on Bali, which specializes in arranging three- to nine-day guided wildlife expeditions to the three tiny islands that constitute Komodo National Park, in pursuit of the legendary ten-foot Komodo dragon and even giant crocodiles. They also offer visits, including day-trips as well as longer stays, to several other islands. Prices are quoted in US dollars to suit international customers; reservations are made by submitting an email form.

Symbiosis Expedition Planning

www.symbiosis-travel.com

London-based operator that arranges all-inclusive adventure and/or special-interest expeditions to Indonesia (and other Asian destinations) from the UK. The Website is very attractive, but can be a bit clumsy to use; the "Where We Go" section, detailing destinations, doesn't automatically link up with the "What We Do" pages, which describes the actual trips. With a consistent emphasis on eco-tourism, they cover several islands, including cycling trips on Sumatra and West Java and courses in batik painting or scuba diving on Bali. Download a questionnaire and email it in to make a booking.

Tourism Indonesia

www.tourismindonesia.com

The most comprehensive directory to all matters Indonesian, bursting with cultural, historical, and practical links. It can tell you the going rate for a block of Danish Lurpak butter in Jakarta (it's 3000 rupiah), or connect you to 28 sites about the orang-utan, including one that shows a streaming video of an orang-utan playing the piano. The "Tourism" page can put you in touch with any number of operators, agencies and general destination guides.

Worldwalks

www.worldwalks.com

British tour company Worldwalks use their Website to advertise their small programme of guided walking tours on the island of Java, which take in active volcanoes as well as the magnificent temple of Borobodur. Ground-only rates quoted, so customers from all over the world are welcome; booking is via email.

Ireland

Dublin Tourism

www.visitdublin.com

The official visitor information Website for Dublin carries full what's-on listings for the city, along with links to places to stay or rent a car, and a huge programme of special offers ranging from musical pub crawls to speedboat rides. Detailed enquiries tend to connect you to the Irish Tourist Board's national databases, but if you're only visiting the capital you should find everything you need right here.

Hill-walking in Ireland

www.simonstewart.ie

Simon Stewart's enthusiastic personal site is devoted to all aspects of hill-walking in Ireland, and complements his own fully illustrated step-by-step trail guides with lots of links to commercial tour operators and other information sites.

Simon Stewart's

Hill-Walking in Ireland

Photographs of Mountain Landscapes
Descriptions and Routes
of Long Walks
Links, Maps, Utilities.

Ireland's Blue Book

www.irelands-blue-book.ie

Choose "Members" from the home page of this accommodation site to find full listings of characterful (and, as they put it, "gracious") independent B&Bs, hotels and restaurants throughout Ireland. Search by key words, or simply point and click on the map. All are in scenic rural locations, and most are housed in historic buildings. Each has its own page here, with links to its own site for online reservations.

Irelandhotels.com

www.irelandhotels.com

This large database of hotels and guesthouses, searchable either by clicking on a map of the entire island or using pull-down regional and town menus, comes up with accommodation options for virtually every destination in the country, with an emphasis on fishing and golfing holidays. For most, you're given links to their own Websites, or just the phone numbers, but you can specifically request those that offer instant availability checks and online booking via Irelandhotels.

Irelandyes

www.irelandyes.com

In addition to promoting her Best Little Guide to Ireland guidebook, self-styled "Ireland expert" Michele Erdvig, who lives in Atlanta, uses her Website to sell her itinerary-planning service to prospective US visitors to the Emerald Isle. However, there's enough useful free information here, in the form of her archive of FAQs and copious links to other sites, to make it worth a few minutes of anyone's time.

Irish Farm House Holidays

www.irishfarmholidays.com

An association of farmhouses all over Ireland that offer officially approved lodging for both short- and long-stay guests, and offer genuine country cooking into the bargain. There are 22 properties in Galway alone, for example; almost all have their own Websites, or at least an email address, and you can also email booking requests to the Website itself.

Irish Tourist Board

www.ireland.travel.ie

The official site of the Irish Tourist Board (Bord Fáilte) is exemplary, with masses of advice on what to see and do in every part of Ireland, complete with links to operators, photos and a great route finder, plus very full accommodation listings – there's a selection of hotels and B&Bs in every town, including 18 hostels in central Dublin alone – and detailed background information on history, music and culture. Further links connect to the Board's top-notch subsidiary sites, including those devoted to pursuits such as golf, cycling or walking, and others geared towards visitors from specific other countries, all of which can be accessed independently via **www.tourismireland.com**. The one for the US is especially good, with lengthy listings of specialist operators all over North America.

Ryanair

www.ryanair.com

For anyone planning a trip to Ireland from the mainland UK, the Website of budget airline Ryanair (see p.38) makes an essential first stop. Quoted one-way fares between six airports in Ireland and fifteen in the UK start as low as an amazing £1, with nothing higher than £20. True, you have to add in airport taxes, and put up with drawbacks like the lack of inflight food, but Ryanair has engineered a boom in Irish tourism, even if it has yet to offer all-inclusive packages itself.

Time Out Tours

www.timeoutireland.com

Donegal-based operator that provides a huge assortment of Irish holidays. They'll schedule a detailed sightseeing or pub-crawling itinerary for you, arranging accommodation to suit your needs, or fix up an activity-based package such as a multi-day cycling trip or a tour of Ireland's narrow-gauge railways. There's an email form to request a firm booking, or you can simply ask for further advice.

Israel

AMI Travel

www.amitravel.com

North American/Israeli company specializing in inter-denominational pilgrimages to the Holy Land. Also, as the US representatives of the SPNI (Society for the Protection of Nature in Israel), they offer some great adventure trips, including desert hiking, camel trekking and snorkelling, lasting between one day and a fortnight. You can email them direct to make a provisional booking, or reserve a place using their downloadable enquiry form.

Israel Kibbutz Hotels Chain

www.kibbutz.co.il

The kibbutz has come a long way since 1909, when Israel's first cooperative agricultural community was established in a wave of idealism. Today many of the country's 270 kibbutzim offer accommodation for tourists for up to a few days at a time. The Kibbutz group has some fifty hotels, holiday villages and "country lodgings", most of them in lovely surroundings and many of them with up-market resort facilities. You can click on a map to read details of each, with room photos and rate charts (look out for the special Internet-only deals), and make secure online bookings for both accommodation and car rentals.

Israel Ministry of Tourism

www.goisrael.com

With its tag line "No one belongs here more than you", Israel's North American tourist Website, keen to emphasize the safety of travel to Israel, makes trip planning a dream. Features include links to airlines, cruise operators and hotel groups, while various search mechanisms allow you to hunt for an Israel travel specialist near you or for adventure tours, family holidays, inter-denominational tours and such like for a range of budgets.

Kibbutzim Site

www.kba.org.il/eng/welcome.htm

Links to various kibbutzim and related organizations, with details of volunteer opportunities for overseas visitors.

Longwood Holidays

www.longwoodholidays.co.uk

UK operator with a choice of holidays to Israeli resorts, including Eilat, plus Jerusalem and Galilee. There's too much distracting movement on the site, but it does cover the resorts and the hotels, along with ground tours and special packages, including PADI diving courses and kibbutz fly-drive deals. To actually make your travel arrangements, however, you need to call their hotline.

Maven Search

www.maven.co.il

Far-reaching portal with some 5000 reviewed links arranged by subject. Though it's a portal to the "Jewish World", which of course extends far beyond Israel, its "Travel and Tourism" channel pulls up local tour operators, scores of hotel groups and guesthouses, museums and galleries. To keep abreast of political matters you can click on "Israel", or sift through a variety of sources in "News and Information".

Italy

Alternative Travel Group

www.atg-oxford.co.uk

This excellent Website, run by a British operator, advertises and sells escorted walking tours, and self-guided walking and cycling tours, in several distinct Italian regions, such as Unknown Tuscany, Unknown Umbria, and Sicily. More specialist trips include one to the Palio horse race in Siena, a truffle hunt in Umbria, and the Path to Rome. Each tour is described in impressive detail, complete with maps, terrain guides, climate charts and instant availability checks, and priced in both pounds and US dollars for international travellers. Assuming you pass the Fitness Quiz to assess whether you're up to the challenges, you can book by completing and mailing the onscreen form.

Best of Sicily

www.bestofsicily.com

This comprehensive destination guide to the island of Sicily, written and maintained by Sicilians, makes a perfect introduction for prospective visitors. Arranged by themes as well as by region, it combines practical advice and recommendations with a wealth of information on local culture and history. While it won't help you book your holiday, its objective reviews of hotels, restaurants and rival guidebooks will certainly help you plan it.

Citalia

www.citalia.co.uk

UK company specializing in Italian holidays of all lengths and degrees of luxury, ranging from bus tours to apartment stays, and from city breaks in Rome to villa rentals in Tuscany. Contact by phone, mail or email to make a reservation; significant savings are offered on late bookings.

Cook Italy

www.cookitaly.com

UK operator that, as the name suggests, offers cookery holidays in several parts of Italy, as well as add-on gourmet eating tours in Florence, Bologna and Venice. Email the on-site form to make a reservation.

Florence Tourism

www.fionline.it/turismo/wel_eng.html

Offered by one of Florence's leading ISPs, this English-language site combines general city information with links to useful resources for potential travellers, including travel agencies, hotels, apartments for rent, restaurants, and discos. Following the sightseeing links soon leads you into Italian-only areas, however.

From Cottages to Castles

www.cottagestocastles.com

UK operator with a wide array of exclusive rural villas for rent, from the top to the bottom of Italy, with a gorgeous selection in the hill country of Tuscany and plenty near the sea in Sicily. You have to order a printed brochure to get a full list of their properties, and you can't make firm bookings online, but a substantial number can still be inspected on screen.

Il Chiostro

www.ilchiostro.com

Named after the Italian for "cloister", this US-based company organizes cooking, painting, photography and writing retreats in Tuscany, Puglia, and Rome. The Website lists workshops both by date and by theme; call or email to reserve, or print and mail the onscreen form.

In Italy Online

www.initaly.com

This vast US-based compendium of virtually anything to do with Italy includes a staggering amount of background material, from detailed and well-illustrated historical accounts to tips for travellers and feature articles by its own team of specialists. There's also a region-by-region bibliography, complete with online ordering, and links to tour companies of all kinds, including hiking and biking operators. Its main raison d'être, however, is to sell a wide range of accommodation, both in hotels and self-catering apartments and villas. All are fully detailed, with availability and a database of candid appraisals from previous visitors, and online bookings can be made from anywhere in the world.

Italian Breaks

www.italianbreaks.com

UK agency representing a long list of hand-picked rental properties throughout Italy. The greatest concentration is in Rome, but they can also offer the other major cities as well as rural locations, with photos and full descriptions. The (high-ish) prices are quoted exclusive of flights, which they can also arrange; phone or email to book.

Italian Connection

www.italian-connection.com

This US company specializes in both cooking and walking holidays throughout Italy, often but not always combining the two in perfect harmony. Highlights include a week exploring Sicily's "Couscous Coast", or searching for wildflowers in the Dolomites. Email or phone to book.

The Italian Parks Portal

www.parks.it/Eindex.html

The English-language section of Italy's official natural parks site suffers somewhat from poor translations, but its images of both national and regional parks are mouthwatering. It also suggests itineraries, provides details of public transport access and guided walks once you're there, and lists hotels and campsites in the vicinity of each one, with links wherever possible.

Italian State Tourist Board

www.enit.it

Italy's official tourism site is designed as more of a portal than as an information source in its own right, although it does hold general overviews of topics such as food and drink, nature, and art (finding time to boast that "more than half the world's historical and artistic heritage is found in Italy"). Clicking on its multi-coloured maps, however, soon brings you to long sets of reviewless links, offering connections to tourism offices, tour companies, museums, monuments and individual hotels all over the country.

Stay and Visit Italy

www.stayandvisit.com

US tour company, with offices in Naples and Washington DC, that offers a programme of 13 different upscale small-group vacations in north, south and central Italy. Each covers a wide area while basing itself in a succession of hotels for several nights apiece, rather than moving on every day. As well as full itineraries, the site quotes "one soup to nuts price" for each trip, including all meals but not international airfares; email or phone to reserve.

Summer In Italy

www.summerinitaly.com

The interface may not be all that eye-catching, but the Summer In Italy site is a superbly efficient resource for booking privately owned rental properties in the far south of Italy, whether on the Amalfi and Sorrento coasts or the island of Capri. Search by all sorts of criteria, check out the illustrations and the availability – despite the name, most villas and apartments can be reserved year-round – then complete your booking online.

Tourism Portal of the City of Roma

www.romaturismo.it

The very fancy, Flash-heavy, English-language official site for the "Happening City" of Rome. Once you've got used to the constantly flashing lights, and the way the various colour-coded symbols flit about the screen, it's actually extremely useful, with a huge searchable database of hotels, a "fanzine" and calendar of events, details on sightseeing and transport, and even a complaints form.

Tuscany Net

www.tuscany.net

Run by the Italy-based Charming Escapes group – primarily as a vehicle for its online accommodation booking facility – Tuscany Net covers all aspects of visiting Tuscany, from practical access details to general information. It also provides connections to local tourist offices, public transport, and attractions.

The Uffizi Gallery

www.uffizi.firenze.it

The English-language site of Florence's most famous art gallery provides full details of its opening hours and prices (though you can't buy tickets online) as well as a full catalogue of its contents. Selected paintings come with a text description and a full-screen reproduction. While the scans are no substitute for the real things, the QuickTime 360° tours of individual rooms are mouthwatering.

Visit Venice

www.visitvenice.co.uk

This simple, attractive site is maintained by the English owners of two lovely canal side rental apartments in the Cannaregio district of Venice. As well as enticing illustrations of the accommodation, with a set of FAQS that answer every conceivable query with refreshing honesty, the site holds an excellent links page for further information on the city. Once you've checked availability and price, email to make your booking.

Jamaica

In the UK, most of the major travel agents offer packages to Jamaica; see p.29 for reviews of the best. For honeymoons and weddings in Jamaica, see p.153.

Airtravel

www.airtravel.com

US travel agency specializing in the Caribbean. The site is simplicity itself, with no banners, sponsor pop-ups or Flash effects: select Jamaica to pull up a list of some forty hotels, including the major resorts. Clicking each one pulls up a very lengthy description, with everything you need to know, including room rates, amenities, meal plans and photos, plus sample airfares from the US. Email to check availability and they will contact you to make a reservation.

Beingee's Internet Negril

www.negril.com/beingee2.htm

Enthusiastic, useful site maintained by a couple of locals. Head straight for "Where to Stay", which brings up a very detailed map of Negril, with active links to the hotels lined up along the beach. Special deals are detailed on a separate page, and there's lots of stuff on bars and gigs. "Traveller Information" is a ragbag, with weather forecasts and exchange rates, property to buy and a gallery of photos of boozy tourists – most useful are the "Traveller to Traveller" FAQs, which deal with such issues as drugs, driving and getting a good deal.

The Gleaner

www.jamaicagleaner.com

Online news site from Jamaica's leading daily paper, with all the main stories (and archives), plus weather forecasts, a chatroom, and a Webcam from downtown Kingston. There's little travel information here – "Book a Vacation" is for Jamaican travellers planning a trip abroad – but you can link to the Gleaner-published **www.discoverjamaica.com**, which has useful links to local tourist authority sites, plus a few individual hotels and restaurants.

Jamaicans.com

www.jamaicans.com

Lively portal with links to news, community projects, language sites, culture, music and cookery. Click on the travel channel, updated monthly, for practical information (a rundown of Jamaican public holidays, mileage charts, maps, weather forecasts) and well-written articles on the tourist destinations, with lists of hotels, restaurants and transport options. The (moderated) message boards, on subjects including politics, travel, spirituality and cooking, are superb. Some sections are less well updated than others, and there are rather too many slow-loading jumbo pop-ups, but all in all this is one to bookmark.

Jamaica Tourist Board

www.jamaicatravel.com

Very comprehensive if somewhat blandly uncritical official site, packed with information on resorts and holiday possibilities in each of eight main areas of the island. "Planning Your Trip" enables you to search for packages from anywhere in the world, whether you're open to whatever it suggests or you have a specific hotel in mind, and there's online booking if you like what you see.

Jamaica Travel Net

www.jamaica-tours.com/promo.html

Managed by the hideously named US tour operator Changes in L'Attitudes, this links page is always worth a look if you're planning a resort holiday: a compilation of current last-minute and special deals offered by resorts around the island, it can save you loads of time trawling through the individual Websites. The rest of the directory isn't bad, either, divided into sections including general information, travel, resorts and weddings.

Montego Bay

www.montego-bay-jamaica.com

Bright and breezy, if ramshackle, tourist guide to Jamaica's second city. The content is upbeat without being syrupy, with news of upcoming events, quick-to-load city maps and a jumble of links to local hotels, tour operators, real estate brokers, restaurants and attractions, plus a separate links page with all sorts of Jamaica-related material.

Sandals Resorts

www.sandals.com

The big name in all-inclusive Caribbean resorts, with six luxurious complexes, "created exclusively for couples in love", in Negril, Ocho Rios, Montego Bay and Dunn's River. All offer online availability checks and reservations. Standard rates start at around $200 per person per night (not including airfare), but the special deals detailed on the site can shave quite a bit off. The Sandals offshoot Beaches, at **www.beaches.com**, extends its welcome to families and groups as well as couples, and charges slightly higher rates.

Sumfest

www.reggaesumfest.com

The not very detailed official site for the festival of Jamaican music that's held every summer in Montego Bay holds news on artists, line-ups, travel tips, and links to US operators offering festival packages, but it's of most use for its colossal set of links to every imaginable reggae site, both on and off Jamaica.

TourScan

www.tourscan.com

US-based Caribbean specialist agency whose nicely designed and user-friendly site is a good resource when booking a Jamaican package holiday. They've done the legwork of slogging through all the bumf from thousands of operators, airlines and resorts to come up with the best-value offers, and they guarantee not to be undersold. They have more than 1000 options in Jamaica: the speedy vacation finder allows you to search for a holiday by season rather than exact date, adding your price range (rates are per person plus airfare from NY) and destination, choosing whether you want to be oceanfront, all-inclusive, self-catering and so on. The "further information" on each hotel is scanty, though those with Websites have links; for full details, and to book, you need to email them or call direct.

Villa Jamaica

www.villa-jamaica.com/links

Very useful links directory, categorized by subject, and with short reviews. Well over 200 for hotels alone – from guesthouses through private villas to all-inclusives – with a separate section devoted to travel (local operators, restaurants, car rental and so on).

Japan

DNP Museum Information Japan

www.dnp.co.jp/museum/icc-e.html

Don't be too put off by the dreadfully dull look of the home page, and its endless scroll of tiny print; persevere instead, to find information on hundreds of museums in Japan, organized by area, and with links to home pages where appropriate.

Exodus Travels

www.exodus.co.uk

UK adventure-tour specialists offering an unstrenuous two-week tour of "Japan: Ancient and Modern", covering Kyoto, Nara, Hiroshima, Takayama, Matsumoto, Yudanaka and Tokyo, including four nights in ryokans and some meals, from £1835 land-only, £2285 with flights. Availability can be checked, and bookings made, online.

Geographic Expeditions

www.geoex.com

Californian luxury trekking and adventure-tour operator that offers several itineraries in Japan. By way of example, the two-week "Strangeness of Beauty" tour will set you back from $5890 (land costs only), while a fortnight from Tokyo to Kyoto, staying at ryokans on the old Nakasendo Road and in Nikko National Park goes for around $5650 (again, land costs only). Email them for detailed itineraries. Booking, which they recommend at least four months in advance, is done over the phone.

Grand Sumo Home Page

www.sumo.or.jp/eng/index.php

Background articles, who's-who features on the great rikishi and yokozuna, and blow-by-blow accounts – and Quicktime movies – of major sumo tournaments. Also schedules, news and ticket information (you'll need some grasp of Japanese to make the confirmation call), photos and guides to the arenas, with maps showing transport access. You can also watch a Quicktime clip of Tokyo's Ryogoku Kokugikan arena, just to whet your appetite.

The Imaginative Traveller

www.imaginative-traveller.com/japan

UK operator offering a whistlestop "Empire of the Sun" fifteen-day package, taking in Tokyo, the mountains, Kyoto, Nagasaki, Kyushu hot springs, Miyojima and Mt Fuji. Land costs are quoted from the UK, North America and Australasia. No online booking as such, although travellers from the UK can fill in a form to make reservations, which will be confirmed by email.

Jaltour

www.jaltour.co.uk

Specialist UK operator, part of the Japan Airlines group, which can arrange tours, accommodation, rail passes and flights. Their many tours include Tokyo-Kyoto and Honshu-Okinawa, as well as evocative-sounding ventures "in the footsteps of" the samurai and the shogun. Prices vary, starting at just under £1000 for five nights in Kyoto or Tokyo, but two-week tours hover at around £2000 including international flights, accommodation (often including traditional ryokans), and sightseeing. Special deals are highlighted on the home page, and you can extend your trip to cover Hawaii or Bali. They can also book accommodation, including Buddhist lodges and ryokan, but choice is limited, and no costs are quoted. No online booking; email, phone or fax the downloadable form.

Japan Times

www.japantimes.co.jp

Online arm of the English-language *Japan Times*, with all the major news stories, plus features on arts and crafts, festivals and music, and the rundown on the latest sumo tournaments.

Japanese National Tourist Office

www.jnto.go.jp

Sharp, well-written content replaces the usual glossy photos and puff pieces on this official site. Intelligently designed and very engaging, it covers every aspect of travel, with country and city maps, local weather reports, and an archive of news stories. Illustrated "looks into Japan" cover Japanese gardens, tea ceremonies, sumo, temples and ukiyo-e prints, while you can also search an enormous database of tourist sights, accommodation, festivals and the like, or work your way through the Special Interest Tour Planning Library. Further links connect to sites aimed at travellers from specific countries; both the UK (**www.seejapan.co.uk**) and US (**www.japantravelinfo.com**) versions are exemplary, with extensive listings of tour operators.

Japan Update

www.jandodd.com/japan/index.htm

The co-author of the Rough Guides to Tokyo and Japan maintains this straightforward and very useful home page, which offers her own and other peoples' subjective Top Tens for travellers in Japan, plentiful current updates since the last editions of her books appeared, and, best of all, an excellent links page to Japanese sites of all kinds.

Kabuki for Everyone

www.fix.co.jp/kabuki

Nice little site devoted to the traditional Japanese theatrical art of kabuki, with a history and a bibliography, details of upcoming shows in Japan, and links to other traditional arts including puppetry and mask making. Plus an online theatre, with scene-by-scene accounts of popular kabuki plays, Quicktime clips of onnagatas (male actors taking on female roles), and sound files of kabuki drums and flutes.

Made in Tokyo

www.dnp.co.jp/museum/nmp/madeintokyo_e/mit.html

Beautiful, supercool architecture site focusing on fifty of Tokyo's most distinctive buildings – practical, streamlined places that are really rather strange. Check out the ghost train factory, the graveyard tunnel and the bus station apartments, for example. Click on the buildings for name, address, function and details, and on the red flags for surprising virtual experiences.

Quirky Japan Homepage

www3.tky.3web.ne.jp/~edjacob/index.html

A mixed bag: best when directing you to off-the-beaten-track attractions and weird museums and away from overrated and "don't bother" sites; less interesting when posting music reviews. Well worth a look, though, for all sorts of intriguing snippets about Japan's fringe groups and distinctive tourist attractions, and a page of SAQs – Seldom Asked Questions – which reveal such insights as that "historically, Japanese people considered green to be a shade of blue".

Rei's Anime and Manga Page

www.mit.edu:8001/afs/athena/user/r/e/rei/www/Anime.html

Lively US-based fansite devoted to Japanese comic books and animation, with links to scholarly articles, conference papers and the like.

Tokyo Food Page

www.bento.com/tokyofood.html

With listings and reviews of more than 1000 Tokyo restaurants and bars (searchable by cuisine, area, name or opening days), this wonderful site offers plenty to feed the imagination. Don't miss the "Culinary Explorer", a cornucopia of quirky food-related travel destinations, with photos of market stalls, weird restaurant signs, reviews of noodle museums and the like (check out the completely mad sushi sound files). Then there's the "Speciality Cuisines", with articles on home kitchens, menu poetry, temple cuisine and more, the recipes, the foodie links, the weekly reports on restaurant openings and food events, the food shopping guides, the sake reviews ...

TOKYO FOOD PAGE

The Tokyo Food Page is a complete guide to Japanese cuisine and more. In English and Japanese.

THE CULINARY EXPLORER
Food-related travels and armchair adventures

EATING & DRINKING IN TOKYO
Over 1,000 restaurant listings, and local shopping guides

JAPANESE SPECIALTY CUISINES
Find out what people really eat

JAPANESE RECIPE COLLECTION
The do-it-yourself section

Weekly Post

www.weeklypost.com

Online version of Japan's best-selling news magazine, known for its sharp investigative reporting on current and economic affairs. You can read all the major news stories and editorials here, and browse or search through archives of old stories.

Kenya

For more reviews of safari sites, see the "Wildlife and Nature" section, which starts on p.185.

Africa Tours

www.africasafaris.com

US safari specialist with half a dozen or so good-value Kenya itineraries costing upwards of $1500 (land only; packages with flights cost considerably more). You can join scheduled trips or take a customized tour, including the two-week "Best of Kenya", where you stay at camps in the Amboseli, Aberdares, Samburu and Masai Mara parks, among others. There are further choices under "Specials" – one-offs and seasonal migrations – and "New Programmes". To book, you need to call or email them in New York.

BZ's Kenya Travel Guide

www.bwanazulia.com/kenya

Home page of one Bwana Zulia, devoted entirely to all things Kenyan, with discussion boards, FAQs, useful links, bibliography, travel tips and photos.

The Daily Nation

www.nationaudio.com/News/DailyNation/Today

Online English-language newspaper with strong, opinionated editorials on international and local news, putting a fascinating Kenyan spin on all the major stories.

Exodus

www.exodus.co.uk

Reliable British soft adventure-tour operator (see p.101) with a good choice of hiking, camping and overland safaris in Kenya. The quickest way to find them is to use the search tool: pull up a list of all holidays in Africa, click on the first Kenya trip you see, and from there you can choose to see all the Kenya options. Trips range from seven days (the "classic safari") through longer itineraries taking in Tanzania (including a seventeen-day holiday climbing mounts Kenya and Kilimanjaro) right up to a nine-week "Kenya to the Cape" trail to the southern tip of Africa. There's plenty of information on each trip – though you need to download or email for really detailed notes – and online booking is fast and easy. Prices are quoted according to your country of origin, and most trips can be booked with or without flight.

Guerba

www.guerba.co.uk

UK-based adventure company offering good-value African camping and lodge safaris and a variety of overland trips. The Website is hard to use, though in fairness that's largely because there are so many possibilities to choose from; for example, "accommodation", "comfort camping" and "truck" safaris are all listed separately. Options include four days at a tented camp in the Masai Mara National Reserve and a six-day guided Kilimanjaro trek; anyone with more time can take 23 days in the parks of Kenya and Tanzania, or even a ten-week camping trip gawping at endangered gorillas throughout eastern and southern Africa. Read thumbnail details and itineraries on the site, then click to download full tour dossiers, check dates, prices and availability, and make provisional bookings.

Kenya Tourist Board

www.magicalkenya.com

Highly visual, interactive and informative official tourist board site, which allows you to choose between "so much to see" – wilderness, coast, desert, cities and so on – or "so much to do" – a number of options, assorted "safaris", from wildlife to culture – for general information, destination guides, and practical details on accommodation, restaurants and shopping. There's lots about Kenya's culture and its landscapes, with accounts of all the national parks and reserves and plenty to read about Kenyan music, art and cookery. Also links to safari and tour operators, 360° virtual tours and a selection of real-life travellers' tales.

Kenya Web

www.kenyaweb.com

Informative portal with a variety of channels. The Tourism section has details on all the national parks plus links to ground operators and the like, but there's plenty more of interest elsewhere on the site. The history, in particular, is accessible and well written, and there's a handy page listing the timetables for major international and domestic airlines.

2Afrika.com

www.2afrika.com

US company specializing in South African safaris, with a good range in East Africa, too, and plenty in Kenya. While they offer several flight-inclusive packages from New York – from less than $2000 for nine days – you can also opt for land-only options that include day safaris, short excursions, camping trips and white-water safaris, plus perhaps golf or bird-watching. All details are covered on the site, with itineraries, (reasonable) prices, accommodation details and even visa information. You can email a form to reserve a place, but it's best to call them direct to make a booking.

Laos

Adventure Center

www.adventurecenter.com

The established Californian operator offers a creative choice of adventure holidays, around the world and throughout the year, and at competitive prices. Enter "Our World" for an interactive world map; you're then just two clicks away from the list of Laos trips. Apart from the very shortest, a five-day excursion out from Vientiane, all the rest start and end in Thailand. Though the longest is a 21-day overland loop from Bangkok, to maximize your time in Laos, plump for the seventeen-day Spirit of Laos. Once you've read the trip summary, go to "Trip Summary" for full details and updates, and then check the availability table. Additional downloads offer more complete details, and you can also download a form to request a reservation.

Adventures Abroad

www.adventures-abroad.com

Classy North American operator, specializing in small-group (4–21 people) cultural tours for slightly older travellers. Non-Americans can research and book trips on this site, too, as all costs and details are quoted according to where you are travelling from. Laos itineraries range from eight days out of Bangkok, taking in Vientiane, Luang Prabang, the sacred Pak Ou Caves and That Luang, to trips that combine the country with Myanmar, Vietnam, Cambodia, or Thailand, or a combination of these; the longest is a 45-day trip through them all, with five days in Laos in the middle. You can read full itineraries on screen or download PDF files; simply click "Book It" for secure online reservations.

Journeys International

www.journeys-intl.com

High-quality, small-group eco-tourism and cultural tours from an established US operator. They offer trips all over the world, classifying them from Grade I (relatively active, staying in lodges, with up to three miles walking per day) to demanding Grade IV wilderness travel itineraries. The two scheduled Laos tours, which both last six days, are classified as Grade I: the Laos Odyssey, which includes two days' river travel down the Mekong, and the Laos Highlights loop from Vientiane to Luang Prabang, which takes in temples, palaces, villages and a river trip. Costs and itineraries are covered on the site, along with honest and thoughtful destination reviews. To reserve, click on "Sign Up", where you can either download a form with Acrobat or key in your details online, making sure to follow up with a phone call.

LaoNet's Community Homepage

www.global.lao.net

Useful Lao directory, with articles from the Australian Lao Study Review, a news story archive with links to papers throughout Southeast Asia, a message board ("Announcements"), plus Laotian poems and prose. The formal Links page is often disabled,

so head instead to the "virtual library", where links are arranged into categories such as art and culture, government, human rights, biographies, publications, tourism and travel. Again, too many are disabled, but persistence pays off, and you can glean useful nuggets, particularly on history and human rights issues, plus a number of interesting home pages from expat Laotians.

Steppes

www.steppeseast.co.uk

UK operator Steppes maintains this very fancy, swirling site to promote its worldwide programme of tailor-made itineraries and guided tours. Either design your own trip, or join an escorted one to spend fourteen days' learning about traditional textiles. Prices hover around £2000 for a group of ten, including international and domestic flights, full-board accommodation and tours. Fill in a booking form or email them direct to discuss your plans.

Symbiosis Travel

www.symbiosis-travel.co.uk

Environmentally aware travel operator, based in London, offering tailor-made itineraries and occasional small-group (four to twelve people) scheduled trips throughout Southeast Asia. Group tours to Laos rotate around special events or festivals, such as the boat race in Luang Phabang, while the custom-designed trips can emphasize adventure travel (such as a seven-day kayak itinerary), cultural activities, or wildlife. Amid all that tantalizing copy, there's only minimal price information; you can email any requests, or call them direct.

Vientiane Times

www.vientianetimes.com

This nicely designed online version of the country's one English-language newspaper should be your first stop for Laos information on the Web. As well as tourist information for visitors from specific countries, you'll find Laos-related articles from around the world, along with readers' emails, usually long and impassioned political arguments from expats (proclaiming itself the "Gateway to Democracy", this section is flanked by pictures of Lenin and George Washington), and there is a page devoted to accommodation, with links. The lengthy links page itself is indispensable, directing you to everything from music sites and Hmong bookshops to embassies and travel and tourism groups. Many of the sites are rudimentary, but there's heaps of stuff out there.

Madagascar

Rainbow Tours

www.rainbowtours.co.uk

Nicely designed site from this Africa and Indian Ocean specialist, with lots of articles and background. In addition to preparing individual itineraries (samples of which are described on the site), they organize half a dozen scheduled, small-group trips each year, including birding and wildlife tours. The bird-watching tours are phenomenal, covering rainforests, tropical dry deciduous woodlands, deserts and wetlands, where along with scores of wildlife – lemurs galore, of course – you can see hundreds of rare birds including Madagascar fish eagles and pygmy kingfishers, Chabert's, nuthatch and rufous vangas, greater and lesser vasa parrots ... Tours start at around £2000 for two weeks, all in, including flight from London or Paris. No online booking; email or call.

Malaysia

Borneo Online

www.borneo-online.com.my/tourism.htm

The tourism pages of this links directory can usefully direct you to online articles, tourist offices, travel operators, hotels and domestic airlines, among other things. Most sites are specific to Borneo (with lots on Sabah and Sarawak), but many relate to the whole of Malaysia.

Exodus

www.exodus.co.uk

UK adventure-travel company with a handful of Malaysia tours, usually including the country as part of a longer overland itinerary. The one trip that stays within Malaysia, the 16-day Borneo Explorer, is a real adventure, involving remote jungle treks, mountain climbing and some very basic accommodation. You can read a daily itinerary on the site – downloading or emailing for really detailed notes if you need them – while checking availability and prices. These are quoted according to where you're flying from, though most trips can be booked without flight in any case. Online booking is simple and fast.

Malaysia Homepage

www.geographia.com/malaysia

Produced by the Malaysia Tourism Promotion Board in New York, this is an impressive, extensive online guide, with lots of meaty stuff on destinations (including the national parks), lively pieces on cultures, arts, people, myths and traditions, detailed accounts of various activities – from visiting a longhouse to spelunking – and a graphic and informative timeline. "Essentials" concerns itself mainly with North American travellers: how to get there, where to stay (a non-interactive accommodation list, organized by region), and which operator to use (another list, with full contact details, of operators on the east coast).

Malaysia My Destination.com

www.malaysiamydestination.com

The official portal of Malaysia's tourism ministry is a gruelling read (sample: "Almost anywhere you go you'll be reminded of food (as opposed to pure sustenance) in its many splendours and variation of enticements"), but efficient and useful enough, with good general destination information, a rundown on how to get there from the UK, North America, Australasia and elsewhere in Asia, guides to special-interest holidays, including diving and bird-watching, with lists of hotels, homestays and other practical information. You can book accommodation, though the cumbersome logging in process will deter anyone but the most determined.

Malaysia Net

www.malaysianet.net

This hotel-booking site is primarily geared towards business travellers, but still holds plenty of inexpensive three-star options. The best deals are highlighted for each region, but you can also choose a city and price range to pull up a list of matches, arranged in descending order of cost and with star ratings. Online booking is swift, but while the quoted discounts are certainly impressive – many of them around 75 percent off standard rates – there is no guarantee rooms will be available at that rate on the nights you actually want. It's worth double-checking with a couple of the accommodation sites reviewed on pp.62–67 to see what they quote for the same hotel on the same nights.

Malta

For diving holidays on Gozo, see **www.regal-diving.co.uk**, reviewed on p.114.

Holidays Malta

www.holidays-malta.com

This clearing house comes in handy when planning an independent Maltese holiday, with databases of hotels and guesthouses, along with self-catering apartments, villas, and farmhouses, featuring contact details and Websites for online booking. You can also book car rental and local taxi service, as well as check out the local diving schools, restaurants and clubs. Plus links to Amazon for Malta and Gozo travel guides.

Visit Malta

www.visitmalta.com

Nicely designed, varied site from the Malta Tourism Authority, with general information about Malta and the archipelago, plenty on the islands of Gozo and Comino, and a section devoted to diving, linking to courses, sites and diving holiday operators from around the world.

Mexico

For language schools in Mexico, see p.173. For cookery schools, see p.169.
For art and painting vacations, see p.1790.

Eco-travels in Mexico

www.planeta.com/mexico.html

An easy-to-read, visually appealing information clearing house with a cornucopia of articles revolving around adventure travel and responsible tourism in Mexico, many of them from published writers. Hosted by Ron Mader, a Mexico-based travel writer and environmental journalist, it's updated regularly, and the range of content is vast, with lots of links to tour operators throughout Mexico. Also book reviews and ordering (through Amazon), details of community projects and environmental reports, and an online Yahoo club for discussion and real-time chats.

Exodus Travels

www.exodus.co.uk

UK adventure-holiday operator (see p.101) with a reasonable assortment of Mexico itineraries, ranging from a fourteen-day Maya and Aztec route or a challenging cycling trip through the Sierra Madre up to a few weeks as part of a six-month trip on the Pan-American Highway from Alaska to Cape Horn. You can choose to pay with or without flight.

Frida Kahlo

www.fridakahlo.it

Stylish site dedicated to the extraordinary artist Frida Kahlo, with critical essays, a bibliography, reviews of temporary and permanent exhibitions of her work around the world, and features relating Kahlo to contemporary culture. There's even stuff on "Frida and comics". It's produced by an Italian fan, so some of the translation is clunky, but the content is sound.

Guide2mexico

www.guide2mexico.com

Nicely put together one-stop shop, travel guide, and directory from the US. With links to fare-beaters, hotel-finders, package deals and tours, the home page can also direct you to destination information, feature articles, shopping sites, forums and a whole kitbag of travel tools. Click on a city name to pull up a new page, and you'll get a host of great links, which are soundly reviewed – they include more tours, rental cars, flights and cruises, plus images, maps, hotel groups, Web guides, travellers' tales, travel guides, and so on. You're also directed towards an intelligent range of relevant historical and cultural studies that you can order from Amazon.

Hotelguide – Cancun

http://cancun.hotelguide.net

Online directory of selected Cancun hotels, divided between Cancun island, the mainland and the nearby islands of Cozumel and Isla Mujeres. Click on the area you're interested in and up comes a list of options with address and number of rooms; click again for contact details, rates, a brief rundown of facilities, and ways to pay. Some entries allow you to check availability and prices for the days you wish to travel, and most offer online booking.

Journey Latin America

www.journeylatinamerica.co.uk

Quality UK specialist operator with a clean and user-friendly site. Click Mexico on the interactive map to pull up an introduction, from where you can access a table of best-buy flight deals to eight Mexican cities from the UK (usefully, this details return, inbound and one-way tickets); email them direct for the latest quotes or to order a Mexi-pass (also valid on flights into the USA, Central and South America). JLA suggests around twenty specimen independent itineraries for Mexico: many allow you to choose between "tourist-class" hotels or more up-market places, and some include flights. Two people sharing a tourist-class room on a tour that takes in Mexico City, Oaxaca, Merida, and Chichen Itza pay around £1850 each (including flight), while a four-night train journey through the Copper Canyon (hotel accommodation but not flights included) goes for £950 for two sharing. There's no online ordering; email them direct to make a booking.

Mexicanwave

www.mexicanwave.com

An online travel and lifestyle site based in the UK, this good-looking venture is strong on content. The home page features the main stories of the day, with well-written travelogues as well as articles on food and drink, culture (wrestling, Day of the Dead, ceramics, etc), music, art and movies. While it's particularly good on books, with reviews, author interviews (and links to Amazon), it doesn't skimp on the practicalities, with city guides – some adapted or taken from the major travel guides, others written especially for the site – plus links to recommended hotels, a map, currency converter and visa information.

Mexico City Guide

www.mexicocity.com.mx/mexcity.html

Useful, if scattily organized, guide to Mexico City, divided into Overview (with FAQs, maps, geographical and historical information), Activities (museums, folkloric celebrations, shows, restaurants), Attractions (by area), Facilities (restaurants, hotels) and Assistance (general orientation, communications). Before leaving, browse the archive of articles on current affairs and culture, and check the separate (Spanish-only) links page for more hotel reservations, the subway map, weather forecasts and such like.

Mexico Connect Magazine

www.mexconnect.com

Extremely good monthly online magazine, produced in the US, offering major news stories, practical travel services, and an above-average "general" forum (one of thirteen on the site). What makes the site stand out is its quality content – between fifteen and thirty new articles and columns per month, on art, cookery, destinations, history, books, travel, architecture and the like. These, plus photographs, essays, reports and all sorts of useful information are available on the vast database, arranged into subject categories. Do a quick search or browse the indices to get quickly to where you want. Under "Services", you can search for a hotel, find out about local events, browse a classifieds section and access around 1500 links.

Museo Mural Diego Rivera

www.arts-history.mx/museos/mu/index2.html

A must for anyone interested in Mexican art, this Website is produced by the Mexico City museum that houses Diego Rivera's huge, extraordinary mural Dream of a Sunday afternoon in the Alameda. Painted in 1948, it is a classic example of Rivera's work, and one of Mexico's greatest murals. Crammed with figures from history and from Rivera's past, it originally bore the slogan "God Does Not Exist", and was kept from the public until 1956, when the artist changed it to something utterly innocuous. The site has a history of the mural, images from it, and a fascinating section called "recognize the characters" where you can click on an individual to find out who he or she is, and why they were included at all.

S&S Tours

www.ss-tours.com

The Arizona-based company S&S Tours offers culturally and ecologically sensitive small-group trips through Mexico's Copper Canyon, including journeys on the Chihuahua Pacifico

Railroad, but can also take you whale-watching in Baja, to the colonial cities, on a special Day of the Dead trip to the northern city of Alamos or birding and butterfly-watching in the Sierra Madre. Those that include flights usually depart from Tucson, Arizona. You can also read travelogues from past clients; peppered with anxieties about how to use the toilets, these are no budding Paul Therouxs, but they do give a taste of the pace and structure of the trips.

Suntrek

www.suntrek.com

Californian operator offering an inventive choice of overland adventure tours in customized vans (see p.125). Prices are good, depending upon whether you camp or stay in hotels: Mexican itineraries include La Ruta Maya – two weeks through the Yucatan out of Cancun from $839, three weeks from Mexico City to Cancun (or vice versa), or three weeks from LA to Mexico City from $1077, and six weeks from LA to Cancun (or vice versa) from $2099.

Teotihuacan Home Page

http://archaeology.la.asu.edu/teo

Arizona State University maintains this accessible repository for information about Teotihuacan, the extraordinary pre-Columbian settlement just north of Mexico City, with lots of colour photos, maps, chronology charts, excavation reports, QuickTime movies, archeology and anthropology articles – some in Spanish – and a bibliography, plus links to their own similar site covering the Aztec Templo Mayor in Mexico City.

Mongolia

Mongolian Tourism Board

www.mongoliatourism.gov.mn

An impressive interactive venture from Mongolia's tourist board. Head for the "fact pack" for practical information on everything from the current visa situation to how to avoid drunks (whom the site assures us "are easily recognized by a stumbling walk"); from there you can follow links to directories of restaurants, bars and discos, all with photos and short reviews. "No fences" ranks high among its top ten reasons to visit Mongolia, while if you're after cultural snippets, goodies include sections on history, music, textiles, the Mongolian calendar, domestic life and so on. There are lots of photos and links, too – a genuine pleasure to read.

Mongolian Butterfly

www.mongolianbutterfly.com

Beautifully illustrated, very intricate and elegant site that promotes a programme of eco-tours in Mongolia. Although they're especially devoted to travellers interested in Mongolian butterflies and insects – which it has to be said is quite a specialist market – you'll also find camel treks and palaeontological expeditions into the Gobi Desert.

Morocco

For walking holidays in Morocco, see **www.sherpaexpeditions.com** (p.132), for bird-watching see **www.eagle-eye.com** (p.188), and if you fancy learning a language in Marrakech, check out **www.languagesabroad.com** (p.174).

Best of Morocco

www.morocco-travel.com

Clunky-looking site from this UK-based Moroccan specialist. Ignore the typos, bad writing and poor design and concentrate on the very good custom-designed holidays – they can fix up anything, from beach holidays to city breaks, hiking in the High Atlas, camel trekking in the Sahara, golfing holidays, bird-watching … You can create your own holiday by moving a mouse over a map, adding nights in hotels as you go (they have a great choice, from riads in Marrakech to simple desert inns). Email for a quote, then call direct to discuss the finer details.

Encounter

www.encounter-overland.com

Though we could do without the yoof posturing ("r u 1 of us?"), the youth-oriented division of UK overland operator Dragoman organizes interesting overland trips. Morocco, as well as being included on longer African itineraries, has its own fortnight-long tour – a Casablanca loop via Fes, the Atlas Mountains and Marrakech – that encounters "oceans, deserts, mountains and markets"; prices are low as can be, as entry fees, permits and adventure activities are paid from a group kitty while on the road. It's worth knowing, though, that your tour leaders "are NOT tour guides, because you are not a tourist." Phone, fax or complete an email form to book a trip.

Exodus

www.exodus.co.uk

Soft adventure-travel company (see p.101) with more than a dozen holidays in Morocco – including ski/mountaineering trips, off-road bike journeys through the Atlas Mountains, and day-hikes around Marrakech based in a lovely old gîte – lasting from 8 to 22 days.

Though initially ugly and off-putting, with underlined text throughout, the site does provide the salient details of each trip (use the advanced search to find them). If you're happy to forego the detailed trip notes, which you need to download or email for separately, you can book online immediately.

Guerba

www.guerba.co.uk

British soft adventure company offering good-value tours of Morocco, including treks, accommodated safaris, and escorted cultural tours, some of which are exclusive to the Website. A fourteen-day trip covering Fes, Marrakech, Rabat, the holy town of Moulay Idriss, the Roman ruins at Volubilis and the walled town of Essaouira, costs less than £400, while a twelve-day trek in the High Atlas, including accommodation in a Berber village, goes for little over £300, not including flights. Read thumbnail details and itineraries on the site, then click to download full tour dossiers, check dates, prices and availability, and make provisional bookings.

The House of Morocco

www.maroc.net

Many sections of this information site are in French, though you can read English-language news and subscribe to receive email news bulletins. In addition to the links to a variety of cultural sites including magazines and ezines, the site has hundreds of music files from Radio Casablanca, which also beams out a live daily news broadcast.

Naturally Morocco

www.naturallymorocco.co.uk

Small independent company offering "eco-holidays" based in a lovely old house in the elegant walled city of Taroudant. As well as holding the offices of two environmental organizations, the house sleeps up to 30 guests in twin, double or family rooms, with a couple of self-catering apartments. One-week packages, which include the assistance of on-site staff, who cook, lead excursions to the mountains, oases and the ocean, and generally look after you, cost around £400 per person including flights. There are discounts on longer stays, for children and for groups, and they can make provision for budget travellers. Email to check availability.

Tourism in Morocco

www.tourism-in-morocco.com

Moroccan travel portal that offers a busy message board, plus links to everything from airlines and car rental to accommodation, restaurants, museums and online travel operators, some of them in French.

Nepal

Footprint Adventures

www.footprint-adventures.co.uk

While this popular UK tour company runs small-group adventure and wildlife tours in most regions of the world, their Nepal programme is especially appetizing. Besides high-altitude treks in all the major destinations – priced according to whether you stay in basic local lodges (which work out cheaper) or carry camping equipment – they also offer bird-watching expeditions. All itineraries are fully described and priced, and there's secure online booking for US and UK customers.

Green Lotus Trekking

www.green-lotus-trekking.com

Exemplary site from a small, high-quality Kathmandu operator. They can arrange as much or as little as you need, from trekking, rafting and jungle safaris, to city tours, domestic flights and hotel rooms. The site is packed with background information on each trip, with maps, itineraries, altitude graphs, photos and costs (quoted in US$), as well as on the whole country, and also full details on their nice selection of hotels, from one- to five-star, with links to sites where available. Online reservations – but not bookings – are simple; submit the form to receive an email invoice, then fax them with credit card details to secure a non-refundable deposit. The balance is paid on your arrival in Kathmandu. The message board is a good place to find trekking partners.

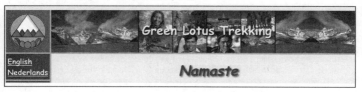

Himalayan Explorers Club

www.hec.org

Join the HEC online (it's based in Boulder, Colorado, and charges $30 a year) to get such perks as use of clubhouses in Kathmandu and Pakistan (free luggage storage, email/Web access, phone and fax, use of trip reports, etc), a downloadable version of the Nepal Volunteer Handbook, access to HEC homestay programmes, hard copy and online newsletters (also available to non-members), and discounts in Kathmandu hotels and shops. There's plenty on the site for non-members, too, with links to discussion groups, trek operators and so on, an online catalogue of books and maps (no secure server yet, and they only ship international orders to members), plus a good list of FAQs, answered by David Reed, author of the *Rough Guide to Nepal*. The HEC also leads treks around Everest and the Annapurna circuit (from $2200 for 24 days from the US); email to book direct.

Malla Treks

www.mallatreks.com

Very good Nepali trekking operator partnered with US adventure-travel specialists Mountain Travel Sobek. The site is good, too, with itineraries and costs for a nice variety of treks, from a tea-house trek with guide, porter, meals and lodge accommodation to a 23-day pilgrimage to Tibet's holy Mount Kailas for around $4000. Online ordering is secure, and US bank account holders can use the failsafe Internet-cheque system.

Muir's Tours

www.nkf-mt.org.uk

Owned by the Nepal Kingdom Foundation, Muir's Tours is a UK-based, Buddhist-run operator promising eco-friendly small-group travel with all profits going to good causes in the places they visit. Their tailor-made and fixed options combine outdoor travel with immersion in local conservation efforts and time spent with locals. Sadly, the site is a mess, however laudable the organization. But it does provide enough detail to be going on with, describing such trips as a fourteen-day jaunt rafting trip on the Karnali River and a month-long trek into the Makalu-Barun region southeast of Everest. The last-minute deals are well worth a look, and you may want to check out their volunteer programme.

Nepal Home Page

www.nepalhomepage.com

Extremely useful resource site, a cornucopia of discussion forums, directories of trekking agencies, domestic flight schedules, and a detailed festival calendar. Plus general country information, trip reports, feature articles, news stories, weather reports, a bibliography, travel FAQs and a travel bulletin board – everything, in fact that you could ask for.

Nepal Tourism Board

www.welcomenepal.com

This official site has been progressively improving, and now covers a vast range of activities and possibilities in Nepal, combining a general overview of the country with details on everything from bungy jumping and ballooning to trekking and rafting. However, the overall accommodation listings remain scanty and hard to use; as the hotels and resorts are not divided regionally, it takes a while to find one in the right location.

Roama Treks and Tours Nepal

www.roama.com

This UK company provides a highly recommended programme of customized trips to Nepal. They insist these aren't packages; a single all-inclusive price covers the entire itinerary, but it's nonetheless individually tailored and remains flexible. The Website spends more of its energy on outlining their philosophy than on nitty-gritty details, but you can read about anything from mountain treks to elephant safaris, and then call them to discuss it all in more depth.

Snow Lion Expeditions

www.snowlion.com

Flexible small-group tours from this reputable Utah-based US operator, which specializes in adventure travel throughout Asia. Look under "Himalayas" or "Everest" for details of their many trekking and cultural tours (which coincide with pilgrimages or local festivals), and be sure to browse the extra articles, features and bibliographies. They have three Everest itineraries (with a choice of moderate trekking or challenging mountaineering), several Annapurna expeditions (check the trekking/rafting/jungle safari combination), and a gem of a trek through the little-known Dolpo region. To book, download the application form, print it and fax it direct.

Tiger Mountain

www.tigermountain.com

Slick site from one of the more up-market local operators (clients, they claim, include Jimmy Carter and Diana Ross), who also bring you the famed Tiger Tops jungle lodges and tented camps in Chitwan and Bardia national parks, Pokhara, and elsewhere. Finding anything via the bemusing hierarchy of menus can be hard going, but persevere and you'll realize they deal with everything, from trekking, river-running trips and safaris to booking cars, buses and accommodation in hotels, lodges and tented camps. Email Tiger Mountain direct if you want a tailor-made trip.

Trekking In the Nepal Himalaya

www.trekinfo.com

The first stop for anyone considering trekking in Nepal, this invaluable site provides all you need to prepare yourself: sensible country information, health advice, up-to-date news on permit requirements and fees, and a downloadable visa application form. Bonuses include Nepali news stories and feature articles, and, best of all, a really good bunch of links to trekking companies, bookstores and trekking gear outfitters. There's also a handy message board for anyone seeking a trekking partner.

Visitnepal.com

www.visitnepal.com

This very comprehensive site was set up by a computer entrepreneur in Kathmandu to pre-empt the government's own "Visit Nepal" campaign, but has since grown to be a worthy resource in its own right. As well as lots of its own information, arranged under such categories as "legalese in Nepalese" and "Do's and don'ts", it serves as an invaluable directory, its links to hotels and agencies including around fifty trekking operators.

The Netherlands

Bookings NL

www.bookings.nl

Hotel-booking site, developed in and dedicated to the Netherlands, that centres on a gazetteer of over a hundred Dutch cities, from Aalsmeer to Zwolle. For each destination, it produces a lengthy list of accommodation options of all standards, the majority of which offer both availability checks and real-time booking online. If you're wary about security, you can choose to fax your details instead.

Coffeehouse Culture

http://coffeehouseculture.com

With its garish swirling colours, huge screaming type, obsessive paranoia and general incoherence, this Website, brought "direct to you from the Nether Regions", doesn't make a great advert for the mind-enhancing properties of cannabis, but if you're interested in Amsterdam's enduring counter-culture of "dope-smoking coffee houses", this is the place to get the details – and also to find out what lies behind each of the three doors of its mysterious Inner Sanctum.

Hindriks European Bicycling Tours

www.hindrikstours.com

Hindriks European Bicycle Tours 2004

tours
about
tour snapshot
reservations
inquire

Californian company that has expanded from its original speciality of well-priced cycling tours of Holland – which it loquaciously calls "ideally suited to this mode of transportation" – to cover 12 other European countries. Both the main Dutch itineraries – the (Spring-only) Tulip Tour and the Southern Holland Tour – start and finish in Amsterdam and over the course of ten days take in several lesser-known destinations. Air travel is not included, and add-ons are easy to arrange. To complete a booking, either mail or email the onscreen form together with a deposit.

The Official Holland Website

www.visitholland.com

The excellent official Website for the Netherlands holds tell-it-like-it-is details on all the towns and cities – in the virtual tour of Amsterdam, it tells you to avoid the alleyways "riddled with miserable-looking junkies" – as well as good links to buy package tours, or make hotel or activity reservations wherever you choose to go. You can even buy Dutch cheese online.

Radio Netherlands

www.rnw.nl

The best single online source of information on what's going on in contemporary Holland, with well-written English-language reporting on news and current affairs, together with reviews, previews and feature articles on cultural events and activities, all peppered with audio clips.

Van Gogh Tours

www.vangoghtours.com

Based in Vermont, USA, Van Gogh Tours concentrates most of its operations in Holland, offering three small-group cycling tours (including one timed to coincide with July's North Sea Jazz Festival), several more self-guided cycling itineraries you can take at any point in the summer, and half a dozen trips that combine cycling with canal barging. There's no online booking; just call or email the owner.

New Zealand

100% Pure New Zealand

www.purenz.com

With a clean interface and easy navigation, New Zealand's official tourism site offers far more than the usual glossy illustrations and puff pieces. Beyond its own detailed content, which includes thorough destination guides accessible via simple maps, it makes a great portal to reach activity operators throughout the islands, listing 213 boat cruise operators alone. It also plays the *Lord of the Rings* card for all it's worth, with video clips about the movie's production and several driving and walking itineraries of Middle-Earth locations.

AA New Zealand Accommodation Guide

www.nz-accommodation.co.nz

Good all-round site, quick to load and easy to use. To find somewhere to stay, search by destination and by accommodation type, then refine your search by tapping in any special needs. You'll get a review, rates, and reservation details, with links where applicable. The same site also holds links to leading museums, wildlife tours, cruises, adventure operators, shops, tour groups and transport companies. You can do a simple search by activity or region, perhaps adding details of your budget and your interests. There's also useful general destination information.

A J Hackett Bungy

www.ajhackett.com

A J Hackett, the original bungy jump operator, now has six NZ sites, including Kawarau, Queenstown (the first bungy bridge in the world); a "wilderness jump" 71m above the Shotover River in Skippers Canyon; and the awesome 134m Nevis canyon. You can read breathless accounts, view scary photos and book any of the jumps online, and then you can buy rugged and sensible fleeces and sweats from the online store.

part three: destinations

Best of NZ Pass

www.bestpass.co.nz

Easy-to-use travel pass, which combines trains, ferries and buses and lets you travel for up to six months with unlimited stopovers. You typically save a little under 25 percent on standard adult fares for every journey you make, and can also gain discounts on accommodation and sightseeing. There are three versions, depending on how much travel you plan to be doing, priced at $499, $646 and $783 – don't overestimate, as unused portions are not refundable. Email direct to buy.

Budget Backpacker Hostels

www.backpack.co.nz

Low on design, and high on information, this online version of New Zealand's BBHs directory is really useful. Two easily downloadable "Quick Reference" guides, one for the North Island and one for the South, give prices for each hostel (there are over three hundred of them) plus their BPPs, or "Backpacker Perception Percentages", awarded by hostellers themselves. If you prefer to browse online, use the clickable map or a pull-down menu to find more detailed hostel reviews with rates, BPPs and enlargable thumbnail pictures. You can also email to order their BBH card, which gives good discounts on buses and flights.

The Flying Fox

www.theflyingfox.co.nz

The kind of thing that New Zealand does so well. Reached by jet boat or the eponymous aerial tramway, this remote little "eco-resort", set by the Whanganui River on the North Island, is remarkably good value. The site features lots of sun-dappled photos of sparkling streams, freshly brewing coffee and simple, cosy cabins (just two of them), and tempts with accounts of delicious organic food, total peace and quiet, and possible bushwalks, horsetreks, and canoe trips. Email them to book.

Franz Josef Glacier Guides

www.franzjosefglacier.com

Named for the focal point of the Westland National Park on the South Island – the world's steepest and fastest-flowing glacier open to tours – this outfit can take you to places normally only accessible to experienced mountaineers. Options range from half-day treks to challenging overnight trips, with safety equipment and professional guides included. Online bookings are not secure, but you can supply credit card details by fax or phone; your card is not debited until you take your trip, and cancellations can be made up to 24 hours in advance.

Guest in New Zealand

www.ginz.com

Christchurch-based travel shop specializing in tailor-made itineraries throughout Australasia. Their accommodation-booking service is simple: view lodges, hotels, B&Bs and farmstays in each region – choose a location, get a list, select a name, get a photo and full details – or simply browse through full listings. A secure server allows safe online booking; written confirmation and vouchers are mailed, faxed or emailed to you. They can also fix you up with rental cars (plus motorbikes and camper vans), domestic flights, train and ferry tickets and guided tours (divided into categories such as walking, nature, special interest and adventure).

Holiday Accommodation Parks of New Zealand

www.holidayparks.co.nz

Formerly known as the Camp and Cabin Association, New Zealand's Holiday Parks offer more than 280 camps, ranging from simple tented sites to comfortable complexes with motels and backpacker lodges. The rather joyless-looking site, an online version of their directory, is divided into geographical zones, with a map showing the parks on each island. Clicking the map will bring up a brief description of that area, with a list of all the parks in that zone: click again for maps, descriptions, facilities, average costs, contact details and home pages.

Māori Resources Online

www.aotearoalive.com/culture

Busy Maori site, updated daily, packed with high-quality content. The recipe section, for example, details the history and spiritual significance of traditional dishes, while message boards accessible from the umbrella home page include cultural discussion and politics, with links to newsgroups. Te Karere Ipurangi, a full listing of Maori news, is worth a look, and you'll want to browse through the reviews, biographies, and weighty research articles. Links are well chosen and intelligently placed.

New Zealand Bed and Breakfast Book Online

www.bnb.co.nz

The online version of Moonshine Press's handbook is a handy and user-friendly list of more than 1500 B&Bs all over New Zealand. Either pinpoint your destination on the map, or search by criteria (homestay, farmstay, cost, preferred bathroom details, etc), and you'll get a list of options with rates; click again for pictures, reviews, and online (invariably effusive) guestbooks. Bookings are made direct with the hosts, by email or through their own Websites. The site is updated daily and new B&Bs are inspected to ensure they meet required standards.

New Zealand Lodge Association

www.lodgesofnz.co.nz

Simple, pared-down site run by an umbrella organization of around thirty of the country's rather fabulous full-board boutique hotels, which are invariably set in stunning locations. Just click on a map to find reviews and contact details for every lodge in New Zealand; from there you'll be sent to individual home pages (though these do not always have online booking). Also some general information about outdoor activities throughout the islands.

New Zealand Sites

www.newzealandsites.com

Super fast, very well organized directory of NZ Websites, with more than 7000 reviewed links for travel alone. Divided into subsections including accommodation, attractions, destinations, information, maps, tour operators, transportation and travel agents, categories are further subdivided as necessary, with a running tally of links for each one. The design and interface is soothing, despite its huge volume, which is a boon on a directory like this.

New Zealand Wine

www.nzwine.com

Official site of New Zealand's wine industry, with background details, history, a directory of vineyards and relevant links. You'll probably want to skip the news section – it's geared towards the business side of things – but if you're thirsty for knowledge about cabernet and merlot, including what to eat with them and which wineries produce the best, this is the place to come. You can also search for contact details of every winery on the islands.

NZCity

http://home.nzcity.co.nz

Customizable, varied portal with daily links to New Zealand's news, weather, travel and sports stories. The site takes a while to load, partly because of their database of news links, but it's worth the wait, and they don't overdo the images.

Pedallers' Paradise

www.paradise-press.co.nz/ppguides.html

Bearing all the clunky design hallmarks of a lovingly put-together amateur site, this is the online companion of *Pedallers' Paradise*, the best cycling guides to New Zealand. The guides, which look almost as rudimentary as the site, are useful and lively, updated annually, with route descriptions and profiles, distances between main centres, and information on local attractions and services (including places to stay, eat and mend your bike). The site includes full details – including online updates – and contact details for international stockists. They've also come up with a good introduction to the perils and pleasures of cycling in New Zealand, and handy backpackers' links.

Wellington NZ

www.wellingtonnz.com

The official tourism site of New Zealand's capital takes a while to load, but digs deeper than the gushing home page suggests, featuring searchable databases of accommodation in all budgets (with secure online booking) and restaurants, along with lots of bumf on restaurants and bars, shops, events and festivals, and even a couple of suggested itineraries. You can buy ferry tickets and make travel plans at their online travel centre. The links, related to Wellington and New Zealand, are well chosen.

Whale Watch Kaikoura

www.whalewatch.co.nz

The waters around the Maori village of Kaikoura, on the South Island, attract more than a dozen species of whales, which come closer to shore here than anywhere else in the world. Whale Watch organizes boat trips out to see the colossal Sperm Whale along with (in summer) migratory species including Humpbacks and Orca. New Zealand Fur Seals and the Royal Albatross also make an appearance, and you can even arrange to swim with dolphins. Book your tour online (at least a few days in advance) – they'll refund up to eighty percent of your fare if you don't spot a cetacean. You can also book local accommodation on the site, and read about local restaurants and attractions.

YHA New Zealand

www.yha.org.nz

Although the cartoonish interface, all clashing colours and jazzy fonts, is off-putting, the official New Zealand YHA site is handy enough and simple to use. It provides full details on membership, and of all the hostels (fewer than sixty in NZ); you can apply to join and book a bed up to 48 hours in advance. Read here about discounts available to card holders, and of YHA's various packages and travel passes.

Zorb Online

www.zorb.com

It's wacky! It's crazy! And that's just the Website! New Zealand (Rorotura, to be precise) is the home of Zorbing (that's where grown-ups climb into big inflated bouncing balls and hurl themselves down hills), and on this site its inventors tell you everything you need to know about this adrenalin-pumping hobby of madmen. In Rorotura, by the way, you can hydro-Zorb: they add a bucket of water to the ball so you can slide about and get drenched, with the Zorb rotating wildly and the water churning like rapids around you.

Norway

Borton Overseas

www.bortonoverseas.com

Based in North America's Nordic heartland, Minneapolis, Borton sell their Scandinavian tour packages to US residents only. As well as all-inclusive trips, they can also arrange hotel passes or simply book accommodation for specific nights. Booking requests are handled via email.

Nordique Tours

www.nordiquetours.com

Californian operator whose Norwegian tours range from short independent itineraries like the two- and three-day "Mystic Fjords" trips, up to the fully guided twelve-day Nordique Adventure, which takes in Denmark and Sweden as part of the bargain. Email the onscreen form to register your interest.

Norway.com

www.norway.com

Massive portal whose concern with Norway extends to offering links to businesses, tour companies, and even newspapers, all over Scandinavia. The best feature for prospective visitors, however, is the ability to create personalized guides to major Norwegian cities; **www.my-guide-oslo.com**, for example, invites you to specify your interests, travel dates, and practical needs, takes you on a "virtual walk" if you so desire, and returns your own detailed, printable document.

Norwegian Coastal Voyage

www.norwegiancoastalvoyage.com

Cruises to view Norway's legendary fjords are such big business that this operator utilizes twelve vessels, and has at least one cruise underway every day of the year. This Website is designed to sell packages including flights to visitors from the UK, and sells itineraries from four to twelve nights long. The actual cruises start from Bergen but there are optional add-on visits to Oslo. Email the booking form to make a reservation.

Norwegian Tourist Board

www.visitnorway.com

This official tourism site – itself a subsection of the all-encompassing Norwegian government site **www.norway.org** – lists and links to information offices all over the world, holds a zoomable map of the country, and provides both a general introduction and detailed advice for travellers. It makes an excellent first port of call, linking to tour operators based in your home country and suggesting possible itineraries, though once you get as far as working your way through to a specific hotel, you may find the English text gives way to Norwegian.

Peru

Andean Trails

www.andeantrails.co.uk

British adventure specialists, based in Edinburgh, whose amazing programme of Peru trips takes in guided adventures in relatively obscure regions of the country, such as the Huayhuash mountains in the north, and the Tambopata rainforest reserve in the southeast, as well as trekking and mountain-bike expeditions along the Inca Trail, and self-guided itineraries. Details and prices are given on screen; email any further questions, or email the booking form with your payment information.

Andean Travel Web

www.andeantravelweb.com/peru

Albeit visually cluttered and unimaginative, the Andean Travel Web gathers a compendium of links to companies that offer tours to and within Peru, from the US and UK, with listings for all the major cities and destinations.

The Inca Trail

www.ex.ac.uk/~RDavies/inca/

If your interest in Peru stems from its pre-Columbian heritage, and the "lost city" of Machu Picchu in particular, this exuberant fan site, run by British traveller Ron Davies, will certainly whet your appetite. In addition to his own journals and photos, it features a massive set of links to other sites, covering all aspects of South American history, travel, and archeology, and also includes lists of tour operators both Peruvian and international.

Lost World Adventures

www.lostworldadventures.com

US company, based outside Atlanta, whose extensive range of South American tours includes a truly mouthwatering array of Peruvian expeditions. Most centre on archeological wonders, but potential add-ons include staying in jungle lodges and rafting down mountain rivers; all trips can be customized to meet your needs. Discuss your plans via email, then mail your details to make a reservation.

Peru.com

www.peru.com/index_english.asp

Although run by a Lima-based travel agency primarily in order to sell its customized tours and adventure trips, the Peru.com portal features a great deal of useful information, news, an English-language message board, and statistics about the country. Either negotiate its hotel-booking facility, or simply email the company and they'll make all arrangements for you.

Rumbos Online

www.rumbosperu.com

The comprehensive Rubos Webzine covers all aspects of travel to Peru in enthusiastic and unbiased details, featuring an archive of articles on themes such as archeology, culture and ecology, and practical recommendations for visitors. Although it holds very few links to specific operators, for general planning it's invaluable.

Poland

Poland Home Page

http://poland.pl

Links directory divided into useful categories – environment, sports, information and so on. The vast majority of sites are in Polish, but there are enough English-language options to make it worth a look. Check out "Geography" as well as "Tourism and Travel", and you'll find sections on hotels, "most interesting regions", "holidays in Poland for foreigners", and even "holidays on a horseback". You can't say fairer than that.

Sophisticated Traveler

www.affordablepoland.com

Californian travel agency and tour operator specializing in good-value trips to Central and Eastern Europe from a variety of US cities. Independent packages start at $575 for a week

– if you book a flight with them they can fix up hotels, guided tours, car rental and train travel. They also arrange half a dozen escorted tours, which start at around $1700 for an eight-day "The Scenic Poland" trip, and also take in the nicely conceived ten-day "Folklore and Leisure" and the fifteen-day "Grand Heritage". No online booking; email them for more.

Travel to Poland

www.visit.pl

Poland-based online travel service with a database of hotels, castles and guesthouses in a variety of major destinations; click to read reviews, see photos and check availability. Prices are quoted in US dollars. Package details – Jewish culture in Krakow, say, or weekend breaks in Warsaw – are laid out in the same way: click on a destination, then the accommodation name, to read all about the excursions and activities included in the price of a stay. There's also the option to fill in a form detailing your interests so they can tailor an itinerary for you.

Portugal

Algarve Home Page

www.algarvenet.com

Algarve portal, with regional information, practical details, links to hotels and guesthouses, a villa rental section (and lots more in the classified ads) and a bibliography. You can use the searchable database to find anything from accountants to watersports.

Association of Tour Operators to Portugal

www.atop.org

ATOP is an organization of twenty or so major US tour operators with established Portugal programmes. Each listing comes with a brief review and contact details, including email addresses, and you can also click on a list of specific packages.

Magellan Tours

www.magellantours.com

US operator specializing in custom-designed travel to Portugal, with a wide range of options including the Azores and Madeira, Douro river cruises, golf holidays, weekend breaks in Lisbon, wine-tasting trips, fly-drives and accommodation-only deals. There are few indications of costs on the site; submit a form, stating all requirements including your budget, to receive a quote.

Portugal Hotel Guide

www.maisturismo.pt

Searchable database of hotels; hunt by name, star rating, type of accommodation, or area to pull up a list of names and addresses. It's all rather patchy, but there are enough links to Websites to make it worthwhile.

Portugal inSite

www.portugal-insite.pt

The Website of the Portuguese tourist board is bursting with detail, including a searchable database of hotels and restaurants, with lists of ground operators, travel agents and car rental companies. You can also read some suggested short itineraries and in-depth destination notes about all the regions.

Portugal Post

www.portugalpost.com

The opening page here is devoted to news from all over the world, but dig deeper and you'll find plenty on Portugal itself, with main news stories from a variety of press and online sources, along with links to all the country's key newspapers, including *The News*, the largest English-language weekly. There are also links to travel guides, portals, and general country information.

Portugal Travel and Tourism

www.portugal.org/tourism

Another official government site, geared around business and investment, with a tourism channel that's of most use to North American travellers. The lodging section needs some beefing up, but click on "Before You Go" for all sorts of practical information, including flight schedules from the US, and, best of all, a table of operators leading tours to Portugal, organized by theme (adventure, nature, golf, religious, river cruises and so on).

Pousadas de Portugal

www.pousadas.pt

Though occasionally slow, this fabulous site, which entreats you to "Discover Pousadas Land", is worth a bit of patience for its wealth of detail on the country's forty or so distinctive hotels, many of them in historic buildings. Search for regional or historical pousadas, by facilities or environment, or simply click icons on a map. There's lots of background stuff, plus reviews of each, with photos and virtual tours, prices, details of facilities and sample menus, and accounts of local festivals and sights. Anyone on a touring holiday will find the themed itineraries useful, and there are discounts for honeymooners, young people, over-60s and so on. To book, either contact the pousada direct, call the reservation centre in Lisbon, email the site, or submit a booking form. They also provide contact details for pousada agents around the world.

Bem-vindo ao País das Pousadas
Welcome to Pousadas Land
"ボウザーダスの国へようこそ"

Edição Portuguesa
English Edition
Japanese Page

Pousadas de Portugal - Reservations / Reservas
Avenida Santa Joana Princesa nº 10 | 1749-090 LISBOA
Tel.: +351 218 442 001 | Fax: +351 218 442 085 | e-mail:
guest@pousadas.pt

Simply Portugal

www.simplyportugal.co.uk

Recommended British Portugal specialists with a great range of places to stay throughout the country. Click on a map to search by destination, or choose by property type (from rustic cottages and beachside apartments to luxurious pousadas), checking the local weather as you go. Many holidays include car rental, and they also offer self-drive "wandering holidays", where you can book a couple of nights each in a string of places. There are enough details here for you to confidently make a booking: fill in the online enquiry form and they'll call you direct.

Virtual Portugal

www.portugalvirtual.pt

Admirably clear and no-nonsense, this portal displays all its contents on the home page, where you click into channels such as transport, food, leisure and tourism, to find a mixture of links and original content. The links directories are laid out in user-friendly tables, with lots of good stuff on food and drink and a handy directory of restaurants (the overwhelming majority of them in Lisbon) grouped by cuisine.

Russia

Beetroot Backpackers

www.beetroot.org

"It's Russia at proletariat prices" winks this Website knowingly, offering backpacker tours around Russia on (non-Russian) minibuses in summer, or by "Beet Train" – sadly, just a normal train – in winter, with weekly departures from Moscow or St Petersburg. They'll pick you up before the tour, fix your visa (for a fee) and organize budget accommodation (in hotels, camps or lodges) along the way. Prices start at around £350 for ten days, though you can add on all sorts of extras, like trips to White Sea islands or even roller-blading itineraries, and they'll also book accommodation before or after the trip. To book, download a form and fax or email it to the specialist UK operator, The Russia Experience, in conjunction with whom they also run Trans-Siberian expeditions (see opposite).

Regent Holidays

www.regent-holidays.co.uk

Specializing in Russia, Eastern Europe and the former Soviet bloc states, this worthy operator – "holidays for thinking people" – offers a number of suggested itineraries and customized tours, including city breaks in Moscow and St Petersburg. A six-day tour of the Golden Ring, a string of ancient towns northeast of Moscow, costs around £575, excluding flight. Download the brochures with Acrobat, and then contact them via email or phone.

The Russia Experience

www.trans-siberian.co.uk

Excellent British company providing exciting itineraries for independent travellers, predominantly in Russia but also covering points east, including Mongolia, Tibet and China. Most trips involve at least some time in the company of a "buddy" – a local who will show you the ropes and lead you to little-known sights – and they'll fix you up with as many experiences as you choose: trekking in Siberia, horse riding in Kyrgyzstan, rafting in the Altai Mountains, jeep trekking in the Mongolian Gobi ... Along with backpacker-oriented train and bus tours (see **www.beetroot.org**, above), overland trips, language schools in Moscow and city breaks, Russia Experience specializes in Trans-Siberian train journeys. Costs are extremely reasonable, starting from just over £1000 for the "Big Trans-Sib", for example, a fifteen-day trip from Moscow to Beijing via Lake Baikal and Ulan Bator, including Siberian saunas, and time with the nomads of Mongolia. There's also a message board full of advice and questions, and a set of lively links. Download the brochure to read full trip details and background information; then email, fax or post the booking form with a deposit.

Russia Tourism

www.russia.com

The most general links on this directory site tend to stray away from matters Russian, but click lower down the hierarchy, on topics like "Russian travel" or "Russian history", and you'll be connected with hosts of independent sites covering anything from links museums and eco-tourism, to weather, women and money.

Russian National Tourist Office

www.russia-travel.com

Idiosyncratic site where you can fill in a visa application form, use the tracking system to check how much longer you're going to have to wait for it to be processed, read about a handful of hotels, check out the river cruises and tours (great if you yearn to hunt wood birds or attend an aviation show), or even book a berth on the Trans-Siberian railway from Moscow to Vladivostok.

Singapore

Asia Cyber Holidays

www.asiacyberholidays.com/singapore/singapore_hotels.htm

Though the background information provided by this online travel marketing company – based in Switzerland and Bangkok – isn't bad, with thumbnail sketches of all Singapore's most interesting neighbourhoods, the site is most useful for anyone wanting to book accommodation online. They've got a choice of around fifty hotels in the city, ranging from $50 per night to over $300 for the likes of the Four Seasons and the Raffles Hotel. Click on the name to see photos and brochure blurb, and submit an online availability form – then double-check with the general accommodation booking sites listed on pp.62–67 to compare rates at your chosen hotels. It's also possible to reserve day tours online, from walking tours of Chinatown to junk cruises around the harbour.

Makan Time – Singapore Unofficial Food Page

www.makantime.com

Lively dining guide to one of the world's great foodie cities, with a huge database of restaurant reviews and restaurant home pages, readers' reviews (with a no-holds-barred "hall of shame" for complaints), lots of background information, a host of intriguing articles and plenty of links (look under "Magazine" and "Directory").

South Africa

For a handful of good safari sites, see "Wildlife and Nature", which starts on p.185.

Africa Tours

www.africasafaris.com

US Africa specialist with scheduled and customized safaris and tours of South Africa, including three- or four-day packages to Kruger National Park, Cape Town and so on, with options to travel on the luxurious *Blue Train*. There are further choices under "Specials" – one-offs and seasonal migrations – and "New Programs". To book, you need to call or email them in New York.

Africa Travel Centre

www.africatravel.co.uk

An impressive list of tours – some scheduled, others customized – is offered by this culturally sensitive British Africa specialist. Choose from cricket and rugby holidays (combining

Email Us now **Welcome to the Africa Travel Centre.**

matches with tours of key areas such as Kruger Park, the Mpumalanga region and the Cape vineyards); a "South Africa in Depth" fly-drive itinerary; luxury tours – including a trip on the Blue Railway; short city breaks from Johannesburg, and a host of other options. Costs, typically upwards of £1500, include international flights. Email to book.

African Adrenalin

www.africanadrenalin.co.za

Nicely organized clearing house for a variety of South Africa-based companies offering accommodation, safaris, train journeys and adventure holidays both at home and throughout the continent. Speedy links take you to the company concerned, many of which offer online booking.

African Odyssey

www.africanodyssey.co.uk

British operator specializing in southern Africa and Arabia. Although you can request a quote for any of their accommodation options (they have a good choice throughout the country, from guesthouses through safari lodges to luxury towers), and book any of the specials (usually themed holidays – family adventures, sun and sand, wine-tasting, yoga and so on) through the site, you'll need to contact them for a brochure to get details of their escorted tours and tailor-made itineraries.

Ananzi South Africa Search Engine

www.ananzi.co.za

Useful South African links directory with a speedy search engine. The "Travel" section covers subjects as varied as backpacking, hunting and fishing, time shares, travel operators and vineyards, and it's also worth taking a look at "Entertainment" (cybercafes, bars, music sites, restaurants) and "Reference" (newspapers, city guides, magazines).

Ecoafrica.com

www.ecoafrica.com

Ecoafrica acts as an agent for a South Africa-based operator specializing in scheduled and customized cultural and nature tours throughout southern Africa. From the home page you can link to overland expeditions, game lodges, safaris, adventure tours and national parks, along with a selection of special deals and promotions. There's lots of choice, from back-packers' safaris to cultural history tours and dinosaur tracking, canoe trips and long-term overlanding, with plenty of detail on each. Email them to check availability and make a provisional booking.

Global Exchange

www.globalexchange.org

San Francisco-based non-profit organization offering political and cultural "reality tours" around the world, examining how US economic and foreign policies impact on other countries. Trips are one-offs, so it varies what's on offer, but there are always a handful of

South Africa itineraries, focusing on women's history, maybe, or giving an overview of the work of the Truth and Reconciliation Commission. Tours include meetings with grass-roots workers and community leaders, as well as sightseeing and nights out. They cost around $2500 for two weeks, with everything included but flights. To book, fill in the online form and fax or send by snail mail.

InnerAfrica

www.innerafrica.co.za

"Holistic holidays", incorporating massage and bodywork plus African dance and spirituality, and costing around £650, excluding flights, for a ten-day package. Organized by the authors of several Rough Guide books on Southern Africa, the trips are centred on Cape Town but include excursions out to shanty towns and Bushmen rock-art sites. They also arrange customized itineraries for groups or individuals.

Spain

Anyone intending to walk the Camino de Santiago pilgrimage trail should turn to the review of the Confraternity of St James Website on p.174.

Abreu Tours

www.abreu-tours.com

Large US agency, whose densely packed Website holds reams of details on its varied programme of Spanish vacations, which include city breaks, tours, villa rentals, and hotel stays. Visits to mainland Spain can be combined with add-ons in Portugal or the Canary Islands. You can cost your itinerary for yourself, or simply email the form and they'll do it for you.

Andalucia Com

www.andalucia.com

Privately run Web portal, based in Andalucia and designed to promote regional businesses in general, and tourism in particular. As well as its own introductory overviews, including excellent details and illustrations of local natural parks, it holds masses of links to rental properties, hotels, adventure-tour operators and the like.

Andalucian Adventures

www.andalucian-adventures.co.uk

Full details of idyllic walking and painting holidays in the hills of southern Spain, such as the Alpujarra range in the Sierra Nevada National Park. Guides include best-selling author and Rough Guide stalwart Chris Stewart. There's no online booking, but at least the "Useful Links" really are useful.

Barcelona On Line

www.barcelona-on-line.es/eng/

A handy web directory for Barcelona, centring on up-to-the-minute accommodation listings, but also providing a massive array of links to other Barcelona and Spain-related sites. Searching for hotels or rental apartments, by area, price, or other criteria, enables you both to access properties' Websites, or to submit an email request to Barcelona On Line's own discount booking service.

Magical Spain

www.magicalspain.com

Small-scale operation, run by American expatriates in Seville, that offers walking tours of that city as well as nearby Cordoba and Granada, day-trips in the Andalucian countryside, and multi-day tours in the region that focus on themes such as the Moorish heritage or local cuisine. Call or email to create your own personalized itinerary.

On Foot in Spain

www.onfootinspain.com

Small company, run by two Lonely Planet authors, that specializes in small-group walks and hikes across northern Spain and Portugal, especially along the pilgrim route of the Camino de Santiago (see p.174), in the Picos de Europa, and in the Basque country. The emphasis is less on clocking up the miles than in appreciating your surroundings. As well as introducing the flora and fauna, guides attempt to bring to life regional culture, folklore and history. Accommodation is in rural inns, monasteries, and small hotels. Email to book.

Paradores

www.parador.es

The concept of Spain's parador hotels, set in beautifully converted historic buildings, has been copied worldwide, but the originals remain as irresistible as ever. Once you've followed directions to "find your parador", you'll see photos, rates and other details of each one, and can email direct for reservations. The home page also lists special offers and multi-night discounts.

Rustic Blue

www.rusticblue.com

Appealing, nicely illustrated site, filled with testimonials from happy clients, promoting a small Granada-based company that arranges both guided walking and horse-riding holidays, and also villa and apartment rentals, in rural Andalucia; they can even put you up in a furnished cave. They don't sell flights, but have good deals on rental cars. Full details are available on screen, but you have to call Spain to book.

Si Spain

www.sispain.org

Created and maintained by the Spanish embassy in Ottawa, this excellent English-language directory site has mushroomed to become perhaps the best overall online Spanish resource, featuring links to cultural, political, linguistic and historical sites of all kinds. Though its focus is not primarily on tourism, the "Travelling to Spain" section makes a useful introduction for visitors, and lists assorted Canadian operators.

Spanish Harbour Holidays

www.spanish-harbour.co.uk

This UK operator concentrates on the quieter, family-oriented areas of Catalunya, offering hotels and self-catering accommodation both along the Costa Blanca and in one or two more remote mountain villages. All prices and details are provided on screen, but bookings can only be made by direct phone or email contact.

Spanish Steps

www.spanishsteps.com

North American operator that leads small-group walking and photography tours of varying lengths, including inn-to-inn pilgrimages along northern Spain's Camino de Santiago, and multi-day adventures in Andalucia's Cabo de Gato National Park. They can also create customized bike tours on request; call or email to book.

Tourist Office of Spain

www.spaintour.com/indexe.html

Although lumbering English translations make this huge official site less user-friendly than it could have been, it's still a great resource for anyone planning a trip to Spain. A searchable database provides listings – though not availability or booking – for accommodation of all kinds, and you can also find operators for a wide range of adventurous activities, plus calendars of upcoming events, suggested itineraries, useful contacts, and much more.

Try Mallorca

www.tryholidays.com

Independent British company, formerly known as "Alternative Mallorca" which offers roughly seventy rental properties and thirty hotels in the obscurer, less frenetic regions of the Balearic island of Mallorca. Search for your ideal villa using such criteria as sea view, degree of peacefulness, pool, or nearby restaurants. They can also arrange walking holidays in the Soller valley. Call or email for reservations.

typicallyspanish.com

www.typicallyspanish.com

This Spanish-run directory site boasts as dull an interface as you could imagine, but it's worth persevering to reach its many thousands of links to all matters Hispanic, from bullfighting to history to property for sale.

Sweden

Stay on a Farm

www.bopalantgard.org

Umbrella organization that arranges self-catering or B&B accommodation – supposedly, suitable even for business travellers – on hundreds of farms throughout Sweden. You can either search by various criteria to find full descriptions of general regions and specific farms, then contact your choice directly by email, or list your requirements and let the Website management choose something suitable.

Sweden Information Smorgasbord

www.sverigeturism.se/smorgasbord

Huge English-language information site with well-written articles on every aspect of the culture, and loads of links (many of them to Swedish sites) so you can pursue your interest in anything from youth hostels to typical moose size in Gotland. The tourism section includes links to all the regional tourist boards.

Sweden Tourist Information

www.visit-sweden.com

Glossy site from the Swedish Travel and Tourism Council, with destination guides and articles, pretty pictures, and intelligently organized links for each section. Other than an entertaining audio section of typical Swedish non-committal sounds, there's little chance for interactive activity, but it's a good start as an information source.

Swedish Touring Club

www.meravsverige.nu/STF_INT/bo.asp

A voluntary organization promoting hearty holidays in the great outdoors, the Swedish Touring Club has 315 IYHF-affiliated youth hostels, 9 mountain stations, and 40 or so mountain huts, all set in gorgeous countryside. You can search the site for any accommodation that takes your fancy, using the "special selection" menu to refine your search if you want such things as disabled access or good fishing nearby. Matches come with photos (except in the case of the mountain huts), a rundown of facilities and daily rates. You can't book in advance for the mountain huts or stations, but there are online reservation forms for the hostels.

THE SWEDISH TOURING CLUB
Accommodation

Accommodation
Search Youth hostel
Search Mountain

Travelling with STF and staying under an STF roof opens up a whole world of new travel discoveries. Stop for a night at a youth hostel, mountain station or mountain hut, or stay for several nights before continuing your journey. You'll find STF almost wherever you want to - and always it's a gateway to new adventures.

Switzerland

Camping.ch

www.camping.ch

Searchable database of Swiss campsites with three search criteria (type of site, site facilities, facilities within 2km) and an incredibly detailed set of refinements - no trees, numerous trees, drain connections, washing facilities... Unfortunately you can only pick one category from each pull-down menu, which leads to a few difficult choices (footsink or hot shower?

children's play area or children's swimming pool?). When the results appear on the screen, click to read full details of each site, with tempting photos. Many have their own Web pages, to which you are directed for online booking.

Ski Switzerland

www.skiswitzerland.com

Dull to look at but does the job: at the very least, when you click on a resort on the extensive master list you'll be able to read an overview of conditions and facilities, see photos, and peruse skiing and summer maps. You can also search for hotels in a number of resorts, find relevant online maps, and print hotel and resort brochures. In most instances, you can also connect to the resort's own Website.

Switzerland Tourism

www.myswitzerland.com

If you can get past the purple prose (though it's always good to know that "mountains, lakes and valleys will put forward their best foot"), Switzerland's official tourism site is a sophisticated operation, with lots of interactive city and resort information, and online booking for hotels, holidays, excursions and special events. Choose from a pull-down menu of categories such as art and culture, city breaks or scenic tours to read about special offers, or use the search facility to hunt down attractions and holidays geared towards special interests (cycling, skiing, gastronomy, "water fun"), refining the search if you want a family holiday, or to go at a particular time of year, or if you have a certain region in mind. With a database of more than 2500 hotels, this is also a good place to search for accommodation.

Tanzania

For safari sites, see "Wildlife and Nature", on p.185.

Another Land

www.anotherland.com

US-based operator specializing in small-group cultural holidays to Tanzania, Zanzibar and Uganda. Scheduled trips change regularly, but typical Tanzania trips have you staying in luxury lodges and tented camps while experiencing the traditions, crafts and culture of the Chagga people. Their customized "family and friends" expeditions include a "Tanzania for Two" itinerary which gets you to off-the-beaten-track destinations inaccessible to larger

Thanks so much for a wonderful expedition... I feel I had the chance to see an East Africa so few tourists see.'

- Michelle P., Madison, WI

ANOTHER LAND
EAST AFRICAN CULTURAL AND WILDLIFE SAFARIS
Tanzania • Uganda • Kenya

groups. They also custom-design trips, and provide a form with a list as long as your arm. So whether you're into banana fibre craft or tinga tinga, initiation rites or scuba diving, they can fix something up. There's lots of interesting background material, and plenty to tempt you – but you'll need serious money (from around $4000 for a fortnight) if you succumb. Submit an online form to make a reservation.

Simply Tanzania

www.simplytanzania.co.uk

Headed by an ex-VSO programme director and study tour leader for the Britain-Tanzania Society, this company organizes quality customized tours. You can choose from a selection of tried and trusted two-week itineraries – including Serengeti safaris, beach stays in Zanzibar, sojourns with the Chagga people of Kilimanjaro, and game-viewing in the Selous wilderness – or get them to design one for you. Accommodation varies from tourist lodges, tented camps and farms to simple guesthouses. No online booking; email for full details.

Tanzania Tourist Board

www.tanzania-web.com/home2.htm

This official Website is sleek and impressive, with destination guides, reviews of the national parks, and links to lodges and recommended operators in Tanzania and the UK. The message boards are useful for making contacts.

Zanzibar Travel Network

www.zanzibar.net

Very thorough online guide, boasting destination overviews (including links to hotels, restaurants and dive centres), along with a detailed history, getting there information, and a list of links to some seriously obscure sites (as well as an A–Z of Zanzibar-born Freddie Mercury).

Thailand

See p.167 for more companies that offer cooking holidays in Thailand.
All Thailand Experiences

www.all-thailand-exp.com

Reputable, eco-conscious US tour company, based in Oregon but with offices in Chiang Mai and an especial focus on northern Thailand. Via the Website, you can custom-design Thai holidays of all kinds, incorporating such components as hill-tribe treks, dive courses, white-water rafting, and bird-watching – or just sitting on the beach. Once you've agreed an itinerary by email, you can confirm your booking and pay online.

Chiang Mai Thai Cookery School

www.thaicookeryschool.com

Highly recommended cookery school offering a range of one- to five-day courses, some of which involve extras such as vegetable carving, market visits, and curry-paste making. You can choose either to be taught at the chef's restaurant or at his family home just outside Chiang Mai, and places can be reserved online.

Chiva Som

www.chivasom.net

The luxurious Chiva Som, south of Hua Hin, has space for just 57 guest suites in a seven-acre beachfront setting dotted with lagoons and waterfalls. The twenty treatment rooms offer such delights as sound healing, chakra balancing, floatation therapy and no-knife face lifts. Packages start at around $1000 for a three-night retreat, rising to well over $10,000 for two weeks in the palatial "Golden Bo" suite. Email a reservation form to check availability, and they'll contact you direct.

Dreaded Ned

www.dreadedned.com

The site that claims, like namesake Ned Kelly, to have "a bucket on its head" is in fact a gay guide to Thailand, with good general information about what it means to be gay in Thailand, and what the country is like for gay visitors, with contact details for gay groups, a bibliography, legal details, etiquette tips and a good set of links to related sites. The gay venue guide makes up the core of the site, covering hotels, bars, clubs, restaurants, businesses and commercial sex venues, with reviews, full contact details and links. It's strongest on Bangkok, but has good stuff for other areas including Chiang Mai, Phuket and Pattaya, and even the more remote regions. Most pages are regularly updated; for current local gossip, click on "Scene and Heard" under "What's New".

Exodus

www.exodus.co.uk

Reliable UK adventure travel company (see p.101) offering four tours that concentrate exclusively on Thailand – the most comprehensive involves eighteen days' trekking, bussing, train-riding, rafting, elephant-riding and island-hopping starting at £630 (excluding flight), and eleven others that include the country as part of a longer Southeast Asia itinerary, climaxing with the 28-week trans-Asia overland marathon, which will set you back almost £5000 (again, not including flight).

Footprint Adventures

www.footprint-adventures.co.uk

Eco-friendly UK company offering a really nice range of small-group adventure, birding and wildlife tours around the world. The Thailand adventure holidays – including jungle safaris, trekking and a diving/canoeing/caving combo – start at £115/$172 for six days' jungle trekking, not including flight. The priciest, at £315/$505, gets you twelve days exploring northern Thailand and the Golden Triangle, and includes a three-night trek, an overnight in a hill-tribe village, elephant rides and a rafting trip. Bird-watching holidays range from four days with the rare Gurney's Pitta near Krabi to a trip that takes in Khao Yai, Kaeng Krachan, Doi Inthanon and Doi Suthep national parks. You can email a reservation form or use the secure online booking system, and you can also buy a range of Footprint travel guides (though the two companies aren't officially linked).

Gecko Travel

www.geckotravel.co.uk

Enthusiastic British company that organizes a good range of group adventures and chill-out holidays in Thailand. Three-week tours of the whole country start at around £1000 excluding flights, with ten-day regional sojourns costing perhaps half that for an eight-day hill-tribe trek. Email full details to make a booking.

Infothai.com

www.infothai.com

Wide-ranging directory of Thai Websites plus on-site Bangkok magazine (with lots of tourist information and articles). You can also access **welcome-to.chiangmai-chiangrai.com** and its useful Travel Help facility. The links ("Show me the list of available Sites") are arranged alphabetically rather than by subject, which can mean a bit of a trawl, but throws up a few unexpected gems among the restaurants, guesthouses, shops and NGOs, including Chiang Mai's International Training Institute of Thai Massage, reviewed on p.175. Check out, too, the site devoted "to a very talented man who happens to be King", HM Norodom Sihanouk of Cambodia, who has directed, produced and scored music for 28 films.

Elephant Riding in North Thailand

Journeys International

www.journeys-intl.com

High-quality, small-group eco-tourism and cultural tours from an established US operator. They offer trips all over the world, classifying them from Grade I (relatively active, staying in lodges) to demanding Grade IV wilderness travel itineraries. The three scheduled Thailand tours – including a hill-tribe trek and a rainforest safari – go up to Grade II, with land-only costs starting at $1195 for eight days. Call or email to reserve.

Magic of the Orient

www.magic-of-the-orient.com

Up-market UK operator specializing in scheduled and custom-made packages to Asia. Choose Thailand in the Destination Information section, then use the search facility to find the Tour Modules (private tours). There's a good choice here, from a simple car plus driver to cruises aboard a converted rice barge and a five-day Northern hill tribes/Golden Triangle combination. Searching for Hotel Information brings up a list of accommodation – all rather swanky, even the quirky beach-hut style places – complete with reviews and photos, and there's also a full set of packages from cooking courses to beach holidays. Add anything that catches your eye to the travel planner, a kind of as-you-go shopping basket. To book, email the details from your travel planner, and they'll send you a quote within 24 hours.

Myths and Mountains

www.mythsandmountains.com

Nevada-based operator specializing in cultural, educational and eco-tours of Asia and South America (for US travellers only). Trips concentrate on cultures and crafts, holy sites, traditional healing, or wildlife and the environment. Their fixed Thailand itineraries, which take only four to six people, include sea canoeing (3–7 days from $500 without airfare), and a visit to the hill-tribe villages of the north (8 days for $1500). The site holds brief details, but to see a comprehensive itinerary, or to request a custom-designed tour, you'll need to submit an enquiry form. And when it comes to booking a scheduled trip you'll need to fill in yet more forms, either online or downloaded, and send them hard copy, along with a deposit.

Thaifocus

www.thaifocus.com

This large, comprehensive Thai portal is run by a Chiang Mai travel agency that also operates an elephant park, and is better regarded as a source of useful general information and advice on visiting the country than as offering any especially good bargains of its own. It's still worth checking out the detailed accommodation listings and reservations service, however, and you can always drop in on its "Online Elephant and Map store".

Tourist Authority of Thailand

www.tat.or.th

Thailand's official tourism authority bids you "warmest greetings from the land of smiles", with a site chock-full of sensible, useful content. There's masses on each region and all sorts of odds and ends including audio files of basic phrases, weather reports, and Thai horoscopes. Look at Special Interests under "Adventures and Activities" for good stuff on where to seek tuition in Buddhism, the martial art of Muay Thai, and Thai cooking.

Welcome to Chiang Mai and Chiang Rai

http://welcome-to.chiangmai-chiangrai.com

Online magazine full of information about north Thailand, with lists of recommended accommodation, restaurants and activities, plus articles on everything from elephants, festivals and hill tribes to fortune-telling and carrot-carving. The site design leaves a lot to be desired, but the content can't be bettered: their Travel Help (also accessible at **www.infothai.com** – see p.312) is particularly useful. Simply fill in an email form outlining your interests, and you'll get an automatic response full of detail about relevant accommodation, operators and activities. They're happy to give even more detailed advice if you email them direct.

Trinidad and Tobago

Welcome to Trinidad and Tobago

www.visittnt.com

Produced by TIDCO, the islands' tourism authority, this official site isn't flashy, but it's gratifyingly easy to use, and genuinely useful, with a searchable accommodation database featuring guesthouses, host homes and hotels, many of which offer online booking; you can search on each island. The background information on carnival is superb, with histories, food reviews, mas camp listings, audio tapes and more, and there's a lively section on the islands' other main festivals, with a good account of Divali, the Hindu "festival of lights".

You can even check flights to and between the islands, using Travelocity (see p.32) to book online, and there are links to charter and ferry companies too.

Turkey

For relaxation weeks at a mountain retreat in southwest Turkey, see **www.huzurvadisi.com** on p.175.

Aka Kurdistan

www.akakurdistan.com

An offshoot of the book *Kurdistan, in the Shadow of History*, by Susan Meiselas, this stunning, emotive site calls itself a "borderless space .. to build a collective memory with a people that have no national archive". The ongoing timeline uses old photographs and testimony from Kurds and colonial administrators, anthropologists, missionaries and journalists to create a personal impression of Kurdistan's history and culture; you can also check the bibliography and follow links to relevant sites.

Bodrum Super Guide

www.bodrum4u.com

Local guide with information on Bodrum's history, cuisine, local customs and the like, and some links to local tour operators. There's a lot to read about the extensive nightlife, though more for a general impression than anything particular.

Bora Özkök Tours

www.boraozkok.com

California agency specializing in cultural tours of Turkey and the "Stans", stressing history, folklore, and archeology, with a few adventure trips and explorations of remote regions. Bora himself leads eight or so 15–30-day tours per year, providing flute and dance accompaniment along the way (you can buy his CDs on the site), and there are plenty more options besides, including shorter "Tastes of Turkey" covering Istanbul and the western and central regions. Accommodation is in luxury hotels – or as close as possible – and prices, at around $1500 for a fortnight (land costs only), aren't bad. Call or email for full details.

Cagaloglu Hammam

www.cagagloglluhamami.com.tr

A guide to Istanbul's glorious three-hundred-year-old marble hammam (Turkish baths) with lots of pictures, a history, opening hours and directions.

Explore Turkey

www.exploreturkey.com

Information portal that is especially strong on Turkey's history. Although there are brief destination guides and patchy links to hotels, it's of most use for its thorough, well-written cultural information, covering subjects such as historical figures, architecture, archeological sites and folk traditions.

HiTiT

www.hitit.co.uk

For once the term "alternative guide" just about hits the mark: this site tells it like it is about Turkey's most popular destinations, giving a balanced overview and spicing it all up with travellers' tales. There are also plenty of photos, links to local news sources, feature articles and details on outdoor activities and shopping. You can search by region, destination or subject.

Kalkan Region

www.kalkan.org.tr

Useful guide to the southwestern resort town of Kalkan and its surroundings, with lots of photos, links to hotels and restaurants, and a limited amount of practical information, including addresses of local health providers.

Pacha Tours

www.pachatours.com

New York-based Turkey specialists offering a wide range of holiday options. Their escorted tours, which have a cultural emphasis, range in length from 8 to 32 days and come suited to a variety of budgets. The popular seventeen-day Cultural Heritage, which includes in-depth museum trips, folkloric performances, and lectures throughout the west and central regions, starts at $3000 (land costs only), staying in luxury hotels; the Super Value Western Turkey, which emphasizes art and archeology, also lasts seventeen days, but goes at a faster pace, uses simpler hotels and starts at $900. You could also choose to follow the footsteps of St Paul, trace the country's Jewish heritage, or explore the remote east, among other options. The drawbacks are that groups aren't small, and there is no online booking; download a form or call them direct.

Tapestry Holidays

www.tapestryholidays.com

At pains to distance themselves from the "package holiday" concept, promising an exclusive entrée into the "real Turkey", this classy UK operator provides a nice range of holidays

– including special-interest breaks – to the less commercial Turquoise coast resorts around Dalaman, along with short jaunts to Istanbul and Cappadocia. You can read full, refreshingly honest reviews of the accommodation options, which range from boutique hotels to cave houses and rustic cottages, along with dates, costs, flight details and tempting photos. Prices are good, and there is usually a happy selection of late availabilities. To make a provisional booking you can either call them, submit an online form, or get them to call you, when, unusually, you can discuss the finer details of every room available, and choose the one you prefer. They can also provide childcare facilities.

Turkey.com

www.turkey.com

Sophisticated portal with reviewed links grouped into channels for business, news, travel, culture, community, sport and shopping. Plus a wide range of forums (you need to register to post) on history, politics, cuisine, human rights, music, literature, travel – many of which, even those that might seem to be totally innocent, are aflame with political debate.

Turkey Central

www.turkeycentral.com

The largest and most useful Turkey portal offers links to everything prospective travellers might need, with very comprehensive destination listings, translation software, and an extensive section devoted specifically to budget travel that's bursting with small-scale independent operators.

UK

UK tourist boards

The official tourist board sites for England, Scotland, Wales and Northern Ireland are reviewed under the relevant country headings.

Travel Britain

www.travelbritain.org

This tourist board site, designed specifically for visitors from North America, bears a strong resemblance to **www.visitbritain.com** (see p.318), with the added bonus of lots of travel details. Here you'll find agents who specialize in British vacations, along with special deals from airlines, hotels, and tour operators, and a variety of discounts on passes and admission fees. There are also extensive sections on "specialty travel" – mature, family, student and gay.

Visit Britain

www.visitbritain.com

One of the best tourist board sites on the Web – efficient, intelligently laid out, and very nicely designed. Among its many useful features, the travel information pages do a great job of picking their way through Britain's confusing tangle of bus, train and ferry lines, highlighting various money-saving passes and linking to the major travel-planning sites. The comprehensive accommodation database runs the gamut from castles to hostels, more of which are featured in "Britain for Less", where you're directed to good-value hotels and restaurants, free events and attractions. "Before You Go" includes a searchable database of all Britain's tourist offices with contact details and opening hours.

Tour operators

British Travel International

www.britishtravel.com

This garish one-stop US travel agent might look like a nightmare, but it can offer all sorts of help with independent arrangements. Come here for deals on apartments, cottages and hotels, plus national rail and bus passes, admission tickets and cellphone rental; but you shouldn't expect a lot of detail – the hotels they deal with, for example, are simply listed with name, address and price. They provide more information for self-catering; London apartments and country cottages, organized by region, come with photos and reviews as well as a price chart. Only a selection of self-catering options are on view here; for the full list, you need to send off, and pay, for their catalogues. It's possible to book online, but the server isn't secure, so you may prefer to call the toll-free number.

CIE Tours

www.cietours.com

This US operator has been organizing escorted bus tours around the UK and Ireland for more than seventy years. All you need to know about the many tours – which have soggily evasive names like "Scottish Dream", "British Elegance", "Irish Charm" and so on – including daily itineraries, price (with or without flight) and hotel information is detailed on the site. They can also arrange self-drive itineraries (including "London at Leisure"). To book, you need to fill in a detailed online form and, if paying by card, download a printable payment form.

The English Experience

www.english-experience.com

Somewhat misleadingly named, this specialist US operator arranges small-group and independent tours all over the UK, including Scotland, Ireland and – unusually – Guernsey, as well as Sussex, the Yorkshire Dales, the Cotswolds and the Lake District. You can choose from escorted, fixed-departure tours, tours with driver/guides, or custom-designed trips. They also offer day-trips – including from London to Paris – and door-to-door airport pick-up service. Call to make reservations.

Historic Homes of Britain

www.specialtytraveluk.com

If your vision of the UK is all turrets, moats and Old Masters, this is the site for you. Offering customized tours of castles, country houses, stately homes and gardens, they can also design trips around special interests – as long as they're of the antiques, architecture, cathedrals, gardens or literary kind. You stay in manor houses and country estates, and in many cases eat lunch and dinner with the owners. The site also details a couple of scheduled tours per year, often timed to coincide with the Chelsea Flower Show, which are geared towards American travellers and go for around $2700 for ten days, excluding flight. Email them for more details.

Home At First

www.homeatfirst.com

Specializing in independent self-catering holidays throughout the UK and Ireland, US company Home At First can book your entire trip, arrange accommodation only, or organize all ground arrangements – lodging, transportation, guide services and so on. While the accommodation is undeniably top-notch, featuring the kinds of places that send anglophiles weak at the knees – an abbey cottage in Shropshire, riverside flats in London, apartments on a country estate in the Lake District – you should bear in mind that only the best are shown on the site. Each place can be booked for a week minimum, and you can combine as many as you wish.

Lord Addison Travel

www.lordaddison.com

A city gent with a cane and bowler – presumably his lordship himself – welcomes you to this US site, which offers a wide range of small-group escorted tours around the UK. You can search for trips for every month up to a year ahead: tours may revolve around stately homes and gardens, castles and cathedrals, battlefields, the English Reformation or maritime history. "His Lordship" may be alarmingly fond of clichés, including the old chestnut about being "a traveler and not a tourist", but to be fair he seems to have put considerable thought into coming up with interesting themes. Clicking on the tour name brings a detailed itinerary plus costs from all the major US airports. There are separate forms should you wish for further information or to make a booking request.

UK accommodation

For more on lodgings in the UK, look also at the tourist board Websites reviewed for each country and the general accommodation sites starting on p62.

Camp-sites.co.uk

www.camp-sites.co.uk

Searchable directory of campsites and caravan parks around the UK. Choose your country – England, Scotland or Wales – to pull up a list of matches with contact details and links to Websites. Links highlighted on the home page also allow you to choose hotels, cottages and self-catering apartments around the country.

Country Holidays

www.country-holidays.co.uk

More than three thousand self-catering options throughout the UK, from farmhouses through urban studios to barn conversions. You have the reassurance of knowing that the properties are all vetted and regularly inspected, and many offer a "short break" two- or three-night option, which saves having to book for a full week. Use the search mechanism to specify your needs, and then browse the list of results, clicking the photo for more details and to book.

Farm Stay UK

www.farmstayuk.co.uk

A co-operative of over a thousand inspected and vetted working farms throughout the UK that provide guest accommodation – some even offer camping pitches. Searching by region brings up sophisticated zoomable maps showing the precise location of each farm,

and at this point you can choose between self-catering or B&B. Each review comes with photos, star ratings, a rundown of facilities and contact details. To book, you need to call or email the farm direct.

Great Inns of Britain

www.greatinns.co.uk

Neat little Website representing seventeen classy, independently owned inns. In pretty villages in England and Scotland, all are chosen for their friendly, local atmosphere, their good food and drink, and their welcoming hosts. There's plenty of information on the site, including tariffs, with photos and vaguely irreverent reviews, but bookings must be made with the owners direct.

The Landmark Trust

www.landmarktrust.co.uk

The Landmark Trust snaps up intriguing properties – follies, forts, manor houses, mills, cottages, castles, gatehouses, towers – on the point of falling down, restores them and rents them out. Today they have almost 200 "Landmarks" across Britain, all of them available for rent by the week, providing peaceful retreats with no TV, radio, phone, or microwave. To see the full range, and to make a reservation, you need to order the handbook, which you can do online (they refund the cost if you book a stay). To whet your appetite, the site also features price and availability charts, gushing guest book testimonials, and photos of projects currently in the pipeline.

The National Trust

www.nationaltrust.org.uk/cottages/nt.asp

A charity established in 1895 to buy and protect threatened buildings, coastal stretches and areas of countryside, the National Trust now offers more than 300 holiday properties in England, Wales and Northern Ireland. Many of them stand in the grounds of historic homes, and would originally have housed estate workers. You can search by location and party size, or browse a full list organized by geographic region: each cottage is described in full with photos, a rate tariff and availability check. You can also read visitors' comments on individual properties before filling in an email form, or calling, to book. The National Trust in Scotland (**www.nts.org.uk**) has about thirty properties.

The Vivat Trust

www.vivat.org.uk

Like the Landmark Trust (see above), Vivat rescues important listed buildings, spruces them up, and rents them out as luxurious holiday lets. Though it has fewer properties than Landmark – and many of them are smaller – the site is more immediately satisfying in that you can see everything, check availability, and book online. It's also possible to arrange mini-breaks of three to five nights rather than stay a whole week. Prices aren't low, but these places, from medieval chantries to follies, are special, and ideally suited to romantic breaks.

UK public transport

National Express

www.nationalexpress.com

The site of the British intercity bus network, National Express, features information on all its passes and ticket options and an online booking service. You can also buy Student, Young Persons and 50-plus passes. Tickets are mailed out if you book more than four days in advance, otherwise you have to collect them. If you do a lot of travelling by bus you might want to register: it speeds up the booking process by storing your contact information, gives you priority when it comes to special offers, and each journey you make adds points to a loyalty card.

Public Transport Information (UK)

www.pti.org.uk

A great example of intelligent, user-friendly Web design, this site offers links to every public transport service – rail, air, coach, bus, ferry, metro and tram – in the UK, and between the UK and Ireland. You can also look up all rail, ferry and coach routes between the UK and mainland Europe. It's beautifully organized, and whatever you're looking for, it gives clear and concise tips on how to find it.

The Trainline

www.thetrainline.com

This site allows you to book any train journey within the UK – though not a sleeper. You need to register, and to have a specific journey in mind, and can then search according to whether you want to get to your destination quickly, or pay as little as possible.

Traintaxi

www.traintaxi.co.uk

It couldn't be simpler: click on the name of any rail station or underground stop in Britain to find out if and when there will be taxis waiting to take you "those last few miles", and whether advance booking is necessary. If there is no rank they list at least three local minicab numbers and/or suggest alternative stations.

UK Railways on the Net

www.rail.co.uk

UK portal with links to Railtrack timetables, National Rail's daily train information, and all the Websites of British train networks. The "Travel Bureau" sets its sights higher, with links to international train companies, along with British regional tourist information, travel operators and accommodation sites.

UK information

@UK

www.atuk.co.uk

You'll find everything relating to travel and tourism in the UK in this directory, arranged by region: operators offering all-in holidays or day tours; restaurants, pubs, accommodation; public transport sites; local events listings, and so on. Bear in mind, though, that businesses can add their entry to any section, so looking up "shops in Shropshire", for example, rather than highlighting cute craft stores in Gobowen, is liable to bring up the same lot of e-commerce sites found in every other shopping section.

Curry House

www.curryhouse.co.uk

Online guide to Britain's most popular cuisine with links, arranged by geographic region, to the hundreds of curry restaurant guides out there on the Web. Plus curry recipes from around the world, cooking tips, news on the UK curry scene, and links to crazy curry fan sites.

Good Beach Guide

www.goodbeachguide.co.uk

Check out Britain's best and worst beaches with information from the Marine Conservation Society, who grade water quality according to EC guidelines (which are available to peruse on the site). Search by region to read about recommended beaches, with a general overview including details on water quality, litter, facilities, tourist information and such like – or click "Beach Results" to discover which ones have proved to be dismal, filthy failures.

Holidays in the UK

www.holidayuk.co.uk

Links to ground operators offering activity breaks throughout the UK, including walking, cycling, boating and so on, with a special section devoted to several thousand self-catering cottages in England and Wales and another for specialist activities (from classic car rental to sea kayaking). For each category you can choose operators by picking them from a map or browsing a full list with short reviews – clicking the company name brings up details. To make an enquiry or provisional booking, you need to fill in their email form.

The Knowhere Guide

www.knowhere.co.uk

This utterly addictive Website started out as a list of places to skateboard in the UK, but has mushroomed to include anything and everything its many contributors have felt the urge to write about their local area, including famous and not-so-famous residents, architectural eyesores, restaurant recommendations and reviews of street entertainers. Often the information is contradictory – there's usually more than one contributor for any one locality – it's generally poorly written, and it may well be out of date. In effect it reads like a big newsgroup, a free-for-all which will appeal most to anyone under 25. Anyone over 35, however, should enter with caution.

UK The Guide

www.uktheguide.com

"Your survival guide to Britain", they call it – a links directory for travellers on a budget, organized into areas including countryside, food and drink, gay, sport, history, accommodation and bands. The site consistently comes up with interesting selections, and there's a separate

Hundreds of links to the very best British web sites in our bite-size list of easy-to-use categories

section for practicalities such as itineraries, offers (anything from clubbing breaks in Leeds to hostel discounts) and getting to Britain, with links to relevant operators depending upon your country of departure.

England

English tourist boards

VisitEngland

www.visitengland.com

The organization on this official site is not immediately obvious to grasp, with its main categories being "discover", "explore", "experience" or "relax", so it takes a while to find anything you're looking for. However, you're likely to stumble on other interesting snippets along the way, like "holiday horoscope" that suggests an itinerary to suit your star sign, and in the end everything is in here somewhere, including searchable databases for accommodation, attractions and events, and thorough regional guides with links to local tourist offices.

East of England www.eastofenglandtouristboard.com

Heart of England www.visitheartofengland.com

Isle of Wight www.islandbreaks.co.uk

The Lake District www.cumbria-the-lake-district.co.uk

London www.londontouristboard.com

Northumbria www.ntb.org.uk

The Northwest www.visitnorthwest.com

Southeast England www.visitsouthernengland.com and www.southeastengland.uk.com

West Country www.westcountrynow.com

Yorkshire www.ytb.org.uk

London

Smooth Hound Systems

www.s-h-systems.co.uk/tourism/london

The Smooth Hound Website serves primarily as an accommodation search and booking facility for the whole UK, but its London section has been amplified to provide a detailed guide for the whole city, with pages on all the major sights, plus markets, churches, museums, shopping and the like, and a postcode-by-postcode breakdown of all the city's neighbourhoods.

Top London attractions

British Museum www.thebritishmuseum.ac.uk

Buckingham Palace www.royal.gov.uk

Cabinet War Rooms www.iwm.org.uk

Chessington World of Adventure www.chessington.co.uk

Hampton Court Palace www.hrp.org.uk

HMS Belfast www.iwm.org.uk

Houses of Parliament www.parliament.uk

Imperial War Museum www.iwm.org.uk

Kensington Palace www.hrp.org.uk

London Aquarium www.londonaquarium.co.uk

London Eye www.ba-londoneye.com

London Zoo www.londonzoo.co.uk

Madame Tussaud's www.madame-tussauds.co.uk

National Gallery www.nationalgallery.org.uk

National Maritime Museum www.nmm.ac.uk

National Portrait Gallery www.npg.org.uk

Natural History Museum www.nhm.ac.uk

Royal Academy www.royalacademy.org.uk

St Paul's Cathedral www.stpauls.co.uk

Science Museum www.sciencemuseum.org.uk

Tate Gallery www.tate.org.uk

Tower of London www.hrp.org.uk

Victoria and Albert Museum www.vam.ac.uk

Wallace Collection www.wallacecollection.org

Westminster Abbey www.westminster-abbey.org

Windsor Castle www.royal.gov.uk

Londontown.com

www.londontown.com

This all-embracing London guide is aimed primarily at visitors from the US, and offers a hotel-booking facility that's strong on discounted reservations for chains such as Radisson, Thistle and Millennium – either in central London or near an airport – but it's sufficiently comprehensive to be useful for locals too. The home page highlights special deals on everything from souvenirs and theatre tickets to airport transfers, while an events calendar gives background on all the major events and festivals – with links where available – and seasonal articles highlight the best upcoming exhibitions, concerts and happenings. The directory is divided into areas including travel (tour operators, ground operators and so on) and "going out" (shopping, bars, clubs), and enables users for example to find a lengthy list of restaurants close to a specified tube station, but it's disappointingly short of critical reviews rather than straightforward lists.

English attractions

The Eden Project

www.edenproject.com

Colourful and informative site from the wildly successful Cornish ecology centre – "a living theatre of plants and people". With all the practical information you need for a visit, and lots of luscious photos and videos, the site also affords glimpses into the project's huge conservatories – or biomes – and their recreated habitats, where they grow plants from places as diverse as the Brazilian rainforests, Oceania, West Africa, and California.

English Heritage

www.english-heritage.org.uk

Responsible for protecting England's historic buildings, natural features and archeological sites, EH has some 400 properties open to the public. The site allows you to search for them by name, region and type, from Prehistoric or Roman to Industrial Archeology or Defence of the Realm; there's a particularly good section on Stonehenge. Each entry comes with a brief review, access information, opening hours and rundown of facilities, along with news of special events. UK residents can join the organization online to get free admission to all sites, while overseas visitors can order a money-saving pass, valid for a week, by fax or phone.

Longleat House and Safari Park

www.longleat.co.uk

This magnificent Elizabethan house, with its landscaped grounds designed by Capability Brown, was the first stately home in the UK to establish a safari park on site. Since the

1960s Longleat has become synonymous with "seeing the lions", while its owner, the Marquess of Bath – not your typical aristocrat (songwriter, creator of erotic murals, liberal democrat, old hippie) – is a constant source of fascination. The house itself comes with a host of tourist experiences – a menu as long as your arm lets you read about them all, from the library of medieval documents through the Dr Who museum to the longest hedge maze in the world, along with photos and brief overviews of the major rooms in the house.

National Museum of Photography, Film and Television

www.nmpft.org.uk

Bradford's hugely successful media museum has an efficient, stimulating Website, with all relevant visitor details, special events listings, and an interactive floor plan detailing the permanent galleries and temporary exhibitions. You can read about the museum's star artefacts, including the world's first negative, first television footage and first moving picture – an 1888 film of Leeds Bridge – and read film schedules for the towering IMAX cinema and the only Cinerama cinema in the world that's permanently open to the public.

The Shakespeare Birthplace Trust

www.shakespeare.org.uk

Visitor information on the five Shakespeare houses in or near Stratford-upon-Avon, a calendar of Shakespeare-related events, and general information about the Bard. For RSC performances in Stratford, check **www.albemarle-london.com/rsc-stratford.html.**

Stonehenge and Avebury Stone Circles

www.stonehenge-avebury.net

Clumsy-looking but informative site, which covers Stonehenge, probably the most famous Megalithic monument in the world, and the nearby Avebury, where the standing stones are even bigger. A simple chart runs through opening times, costs, history, new discoveries, theories, and research news for each, and you can click a link for QuickTime movies of the sites, including one from Stonehenge's interior, which is normally closed to visitors. The Website is brought to you by the Megalithic Society, who also lead tours to ancient sites around Britain – email them for details.

Treasurehouses

www.treasurehouses.co.uk

Umbrella organization for nine of England's most important palaces, stately homes and castles, including Blenheim Palace, Castle Howard, Chatsworth, Leeds Castle and Woburn Abbey. Click on the thumbnail photos for overviews, practical details, and links to Websites.

English city sites

For each major city listed below we've chosen two sources of Web information: an official site, produced by the local tourist board, city council or other such civic body, and an unofficial site – perhaps an online guide, home page, local listings magazine or newspaper site. These, while they may not necessarily be particularly "alternative", all have something to offer visitors over and above the official sources.

Bath

official www.visitbath.co.uk

unofficial www.thisisbath.com

Blackpool

official www.blackpooltourism.com

unofficial website.lineone.net/~johnfinlay/blacpool/blakpool.htm

Brighton

official www.visiting-brighton.co.uk

unofficial www.theinsight.co.uk

Cambridge

official www.cambridge.gov.uk/leisure/TICWEB/tourism.htm

unofficial www.gwydir.demon.co.uk/cambridgeuk/index.htm

Durham

official www.discovercountydurham.com

unofficial www.virtualdurham.co.uk

Liverpool

official www.visitliverpool.com

unofficial www.pool-of-life.co.uk

Manchester

official www.manchester.gov.uk/visitorcentre

unofficial www.manchester.com

Newcastle-upon-Tyne

official www.newcastle.gov.uk

unofficial www.tyne-online.com

Norwich

official www.norwich.gov.uk

unofficial www.ubooty.co.uk

Oxford

official www.visitoxford.org

unofficial www.oxfordcity.co.uk

York

official www.york-tourism.co.uk

unofficial www.thisisyork.co.uk

Scotland

Scottish tourist boards

Scottish Tourist Board

www.visitscotland.com

Scotland's official tourism site is a fine example of the genre, attractively designed, packed with information and easy to navigate by means of the interactive map and menus. The searchable accommodation database, with almost ten thousand places to stay, provides all the information you need to research your hotel, B&B, hostel, campsite or self-catering apartment, and in many cases you can book online. They've also gathered contact details for a range of travel operators from mainland Europe and the USA, and, along with a database of thousands of activities, compiled events calendars with listings for music, art and festivals. The itinerary ideas (including a "castles, coves and kittiwakes" combo) are a nice touch, too, and there are scores of good links.

Aberdeen and Grampian Highlands www.agtb.org

Angus and City of Dundee www.angusanddundee.co.uk

Argyll, the Isles, Loch Lomond, Stirling and the Trossachs www.scottish.heartlands.org

Aviemore and the Cairngorms http://aviemore.org

Ayrshire and Arran www.ayrshire-arran.com

Dumfries and Galloway www.galloway.co.uk

Edinburgh and the Lothians www.edinburgh.org

Kingdom of Fife www.standrews.co.uk

Greater Glasgow and Clyde Valley http://seeglasgow.com

Hebrides www.visithebrides.com

Highlands of Scotland www.visithighlands.com

Orkney www.visitorkney.com

Perthshire www.perthshire.co.uk

Scottish Borders www.scot-borders.co.uk

Shetland Islands www.visitshetland.com

Scottish information and attractions

About Scotland

www.aboutscotland.co.uk

Lively, nicely illustrated guide with a changing roster of articles on major features or landmarks, and historical essays, by local writers.. The accommodation listings are superb – each place has been approved and reviewed by the About Scotland team – with lots of photos and details for each hotel, B&B or self-catering cottage.

Caledonian Castles

www.caledoniancastles.co.uk

One of the best of many such sites on the Web – labours of love, all of them, produced by misty-eyed castle fans from around the world. This one has pictures and information on more than a hundred Scottish castles, including lesser-known places not found on other sites. It's easy to navigate, searching by region or castle name, with lovely photos, location maps and ground plans, and plenty of historic background on each place. Those that are open to the public have links to their official site.

Caledonian MacBrayne

www.calmac.co.uk

Caledonian MacBrayne is the main ferry operator serving such Scottish islands as Arran, Bute, Harris, Iona, Lewis, Mull and Skye. You can check out their schedules on the site, or download the full timetable in PDF format, but actual online booking is available for travellers with cars only, and for straightforward single or return journeys only. It is also possible, however, to buy Island Rover tickets, which offer unlimited travel for eight or fifteen days, and in any case availability for foot passengers is not a problem.

Edinburgh Festivals

www.edinburghfestivals.com

Really useful venture, pulling together information on all Edinburgh's major festivals, including the Edinburgh festival, the fringe, the film festival, the military tattoo, the jazz and blues festival, and Hogmanay, with contact details and programme information for each, along with highlights of all current and forthcoming festivals, schedules of related events, and links to the official Websites.

Edinburgh Galleries Association

www.edinburgh-galleries.co.uk

Don't expect any bells and whistles on this worthy site, just monthly updates on exhibitions at the major private and public galleries, with photos, locator maps, admission fees, opening hours, contact details and links to Websites.

Extreme Sports Scotland

www.wannabethere.com

Once the excitement of the Flash 4 interface has worn off, and you retreat perhaps to the stolid safety of the HTML site, you may feel that there's a little less to this all-action off-shoot of the main Scottish Tourist Board site than meets the eye – its accommodation and travel sections just direct you to **www.visitscotland.com** (see p.330). However, if you're into action sports, its main pages are bursting with possibilities, divided into Ice (not just skiing, but also snow-holing, dog-sledding and other activities), Water (such as kayaking and yakking), Earth (scrambling, street luge), Air (windsurfing, blokarting, freefall) and Fire (drag racing, quad bikes, etc), with links to Scottish operators.

Home At First

www.homeatfirst.com

US tour operator that offers self-drive packages to all regions of Scotland, with a network of self-catering cottages throughout the country, an extensive programme of activities including golf, and introductory group activities for first-time visitors. Having mapped out and priced your itinerary online, email the details to complete your booking.

Rampant Scotland

www.rampantscotland.com

This is the kind of links directory that makes you want to kiss the screen – huge, functioning, searchable and genuinely useful, linking you to anything and everything from hotels, haunted castles, folklore sites, city guides, poetry sites, magazines and newspapers – even a whole page of jokes about bagpipes – what more could you ask for?

Scotland's Malt Whisky Trail

www.maltwhiskytrail.com

The Highland region of Speyside has seven malt whisky distilleries – more than half of Scotland's total – and a tourist industry geared up to appeal to anyone partial to a wee dram. The site's interactive map allows you to click on distillery icons to discover more details about each, and pop-up windows advertise recommended local accommodation.

Walk Scotland

www.walkscotland.com

Whether you're into munro bagging or simply fancy a day's hiking somewhere pretty, this impressive site – which extends its scope to all sorts of activity holidays, including canoeing and kayaking – is a gem. As well as the database of routes (anything from two miles up), which is updated weekly, come here for walking news and mountain reports, gear reviews, weather forecasts and live Webcam images for Ben Nevis, Aonach Mor and the Cairngorms. The online bookshop sells used outdoor and travel books, which are also offered on the message board (a good place to find walking companions). The links page is a volume in itself.

Wales

Welsh tourist boards

Visit Wales

www.visitwales.com

Wales' official tourism site features seasonal news and offers on the home page, plus a searchable directory of more than 600 Welsh links, an accommodation database and an events calendar. Separate sections deal with activity holidays, cycling, walking and golf, with links to accommodation, operators and routes relevant to each. North American travellers who specify their country of origin on the home page are whisked to a dedicated section holding details of operators that offer escorted and independent tours or adventure holidays, complete with contact details and Websites, and accommodation deals from the bigger, more up-market hotels.

Isle of Anglesey www.anglesey.gov.uk

Cardiff www.cardiff.gov.uk

Mid- and west coast Wales www.mid-wales-tourism.org.uk

North Wales www.nwt.co.uk

South Wales www.southernwales.com

South Wales valleys www.valleyswelcome.org.uk

Southwest Wales www.pembrokeshire-holidays.com

Swansea www1.swansea.gov.uk/tourism/

Welsh information and attractions

Castles of Wales

www.castlewales.com

Labour of love from American castle enthusiast Jeff Thomas, with information and photographs on more than four hundred medieval castles. It's a good read, with learned accounts of Welsh medieval history, biographies of all the great castle builders, locator maps and a bibliography, plus a small section on Welsh abbeys and religious sites. You can also follow links to castles offering accommodation.

Centre for Alternative Technology

www.cat.org.uk

This self-sufficient 40-acre eco-community was established in Powys during the oil crisis of 1974. Six families now live on the site, which has become one of Wales' major tourist attractions. Using wind, water and solar power, self-built environmentally sound buildings, organic farming and alternative sewage systems, the centre has seven acres open to the public; entrance is via a water-powered cliff railway. Along with displays on conservation, recycling and organic farming, a smallholding and loads of kids' activities, CAT offers courses on anything from blacksmithing to the art of composting. There's an email form if you want to book online, plus all the practical details for anyone hoping to visit and stay nearby.

Data Wales

www.data-wales.co.uk

Labour-of-love private site focusing on Wales and its history; the spotlight is cast on all sorts of fascinating information about the country. Certain pages set out to meet the needs of prospective visitors, so there's some practical travel information to be gleaned, but really the fun of it is just to pique your curiosity.

Portmeirion

www.portmeirion-village.com

Most famous for being the other-worldly village in the cult 1960s TV series *The Prisoner*, the surreal coastal settlement of Portmeirion is one of Wales' major attractions. The site offers an informative guide to the whole village, with snippets on the writers and actors who've spent time here, the local pottery and Prisoner connections, and the very particular look of the place, dreamed up by maverick architect Clough Williams-Ellis. You can also check out the accommodation in the swanky Hotel Portmeirion, along with a number of quirky self-catering cottages, and fill out an availability request form online.

Welsh Rarebits Hotels of Distinction

www.welsh.rarebits.co.uk

More than forty hand-selected quality hotels – country houses, inns, spas – with maps, reviews, photos, tariffs and links to Websites. Though prices in the main aren't low – these are luxurious, award-winning places – most properties offer special short-break deals. Bookings are made direct with the hotel.

WELSH RAREBITS
Hotels of Distinction 2004

Northern Ireland

Northern Irish tourist boards

Northern Ireland Tourist Board

www.discovernorthernireland.com

This fully searchable site has lots of good features, including a database of local information centres. Many tourist offices, including those for Down and Belfast, have their own pages here. Pull-down menus allow you to view lists of attractions, activities, hotels (bookable online) and restaurants by region. Once you've selected something from any of these you can go on to search for nearby features in all sorts of categories.

Derry www.derryvisitor.com

Fermanagh www.fermanagh-online.com

Lisburn www.lisburncity.gov.uk

North Antrim (Giants Causeway) www.northantrim.com

Northern Irish tours and attractions

Belfast City Black Taxi Tours

www.belfasttours.com

Lively taxi tours of Belfast, taking in all the historical and political sights – including the murals on the Shankill and Falls roads, and "plenty of craic" – as well as longer excursions to the north Antrim Coast. The site features contact details, photos and testimonials; you can book by email or phone.

Federation of Retail Licensed Trade

www.ulsterpubs.com

Searchable database of Northern Irish pubs, with opening hours, a rundown of facilities, contact details and photos for each. You can hunt for your tavern of choice by clicking on a region, refining your search by specifying places that welcome kids, or places that offer food and music.

The Channel Islands

Guernsey Tourist Board

www.guernseytouristboard.com

Attractive and user-friendly site linking to all carriers with flights to the island, along with operators from the UK and mainland Europe. The searchable accommodation database features photos, reviews and contact details (including Websites) for every place it lists, and there's a rundown of sites and attractions organized by subject area.

Jersey Tourism

www.jersey.com

Jersey's official tourist site links to all the other main Jersey sites on the Web, making it pretty comprehensive. You can hook up with a variety of accommodation sites, most of them with online booking, along with ferry companies and airlines, and there's a searchable database of specialist operators for holidays and short breaks. Travellers from North America have their own separate sections.

Sark Tourism

www.sark-tourism.com

The smallest of the Channel Islands – just three miles by one and a half – has a rather sophisticated site, with an events schedule and a directory listing all the accommodation, including self-catering and campsites. You can even book flights and ferries. The front-page news story, updated weekly, gives the site a homely, local feel.

Isle of Man

Isle of Man Government

www.gov.im/tourism

Good information about this fiercely independent island enclave, just sixty miles off the northwest coast of England. The official site provides details on how to get there, where to stay (with a searchable accommodation database) and a special offers page covering deals offered by airlines, ferry companies and hotels.

USA

This section is primarily intended to point readers towards the official tourism Websites for all US states and major cities, as well as selected high-profile attractions and national transportation operators.

Bear in mind that other sites of use to anyone hoping to travel within the USA are scattered throughout this book. See, for example, the online travel agents, airlines and accommodation sites detailed in Part One, and the many operators specializing in specific activities and interests who are included in Part Two.

State tourism sites

Every US state runs its own Website to promote local tourism. As all follow very much the same formula, there's no point reviewing each one in detail here. Suffice it to say that all offer descriptions and photographs of regional attractions, listings and links for accommodation, and provide email addresses and toll-free numbers for specific enquiries. You'll also find details of free maps and brochures, mailed out on request.

Alabama www.touralabama.org

Alaska www.dced.state.ak.us/tourism

Arizona www.arizonaguide.com

Arkansas www.arkansas.com

California www.gocalif.com

Colorado www.colorado.com

Connecticut www.ctbound.org

Delaware www.visitdelaware.net

Florida www.flausa.com

Georgia www.georgia.org

Hawaii www.gohawaii.com

Idaho www.visitid.org

Illinois www.enjoyillinois.com

Indiana www.enjoyindiana.com

Iowa www.traveliowa.com

Kansas www.travelKS.com

Kentucky www.kentuckytourism.com

Louisiana www.louisianatravel.com

Maine www.visitmaine.com

Maryland www.mdisfun.org

Massachusetts www.massvacation.com

Michigan www.michigan.org

Minnesota www.exploreminnesota.com

Mississippi www.visitmississippi.org

Missouri www.missouritourism.org

Montana www.visitmt.org

Nebraska www.visitnebraska.org

Nevada www.travelnevada.com

New Hampshire www.visitnh.gov

New Jersey www.state.nj.us/travel

New Mexico www.newmexico.org

New York State www.iloveny.com

North Carolina www.visitnc.com

North Dakota www.ndtourism.com

Ohio www.ohiotourism.com

Oklahoma www.travelok.com

Oregon www.traveloregon.com

Pennsylvania www.state.pa.us

Rhode Island www.visitrhodeisland.com

South Carolina www.discoversouthcarolina.com

South Dakota www.travelsd.com

Tennessee www.tnvacation.com

Texas www.traveltex.com

Utah www.utah.com

Vermont www.vermontvacation.com

Virginia www.virginia.org

Washington www.tourism.wa.gov

West Virginia www.callwva.com

Wisconsin www.travelwisconsin.com

Wyoming www.wyomingtourism.org

City sites

Many of the Websites listed in our "Finding What You Need" section (see p.3) provide detailed online guides to specific US destinations. Full listings for all major US cities, for example, can be found both on guidebook sites such as **Rough Guides** and **Frommers**, and via the online-only services of **about.com** and **away.com**. Similarly, accommodation throughout the United States can be booked using the general lodging sites reviewed on p.62 onwards. In addition, however, every city and destination has its own official site, usually run by the local Convention and Visitors Bureau. All the official sites listed below facilitate online accommodation reservations, and most also hold thorough guides to dining, sightseeing, activities and forthcoming events. Many regional newspapers and magazines also offer good online destination guides, which tend to concentrate on restaurant and entertainment listings rather than accommodation. For each city below we've listed the most useful local media Website for prospective visitors.

	Official city site	Local media
Atlanta	www.atlanta.com	www.creativeloafing.com
Baltimore	www.baltconvstr.com	www.sunspot.net
Boston	www.bostonusa.com	www.bostonphoenix.com
Charleston	www.charlestoncvb.com	www.charleston.net
Chicago	www.choosechicago.com	www.chicagotribune.com
Cincinnati	www.cincyusa.com	www.citybeat.com
Dallas	www.dallascvb.com	www.dallasobserver.com
Denver	www.denver.org	www.denverpost.com
Houston	www.houston-guide.com	www.houston-press.com
Las Vegas	www.lasvegas24hours.com	www.lvrj.com
Los Angeles	www.lacvb.com	www.laweekly.com
Memphis	www.memphistravel.com	www.commercialappeal.com
Miami	www.miamiandbeaches.com	www.miaminewtimes.com
Minneapolis	www.minneapolis.org	www.startribune.com
New Orleans	www.neworleanscvb.com	www.bestofneworleans.com
New York	www.nycvisit.com	www.villagevoice.com
Orlando	www.orlandoinfo.com	www.orlandoweekly.com
Philadelphia	www.pcvb.org	www.philadelphiaweekly.com
Phoenix	www.phoenixcvb.com	www.phoenixnewtimes.com
Salt Lake City	www.visitsaltlake.com	www.slweekly.com
San Antonio	www.sanantoniocvb.com	www.mysanantonio.com
San Diego	www.sandiego.org	www.sdreader.com
San Francisco	www.sfvisitor.org	www.bestofthebay.com
Santa Fe	www.santafe.org	www.santafenewmexican.com
Savannah	www.savannahvisit.com	www.savannahnow.com
Seattle	www.seeseattle.org	http://seattlep-i.nwsource.com
St Louis	www.explorestlouis.com	www.stltoday.com
Washington DC	www.washington.org	www.washingtoncitypaper.com

part three: destinations

Major attractions

Crazy Horse Memorial

www.crazyhorse.org

An extraordinary monument to one man's obsession, the Crazy Horse Memorial is an equestrian figure of the Sioux leader that has been whittled from a mountainside in the Black Hills of South Dakota ever since 1948. On completion it will, at 563ft high and 641ft long, be the largest statue in the world, larger even than the Great Pyramid. Use the Website to find out about visiting, follow the work in progress, make a donation, or even apply for a job.

Disney Vacations Online

www.disney.com

As you may already know if you have kids, it's possible to spend hours exploring every nook and cranny of the Disney Website. In essence, however, its Vacation Planner facility is quite straightforward, and especially if you choose the simpler HTML version, it's surprisingly concise, providing a basic rundown of the various "lands" and "towns" in both Walt Disney World and Disneyland, plus overviews of the resort hotels plus some general travel information (weather charts, driving distances, park hours, etc). When you're ready to book, simply choose the most popular package (hotel of your choice, park passes and various perks) or piece together one of your own (adding car rental, maybe). A quick availability check will come up with an alternative if your preferred hotel is full. Links facilitate booking at Disney parks elsewhere in the world, but flights to or from the US are not available online. Stern warnings admonish users not to suggest or encourage illegal activity, or even post recipes. If it's all too overwhelming you can simply order printed brochures.

Graceland

www.elvis.com

Over twenty-five years since Elvis left the building, his official Website is still largely dedicated to encouraging visits to his former Memphis home of Graceland. Assuming that a virtual tour of the mansion persuades you to buy a ticket for the real thing, you can also book a room at the nearby Heartbreak Hotel, as well, of course, as shopping for souvenirs and ingesting reams of online trivia.

Mardi Gras, New Orleans

www.mardigrasneworleans.com

America's greatest street party is celebrated in all its mind-boggling detail by this privately run fan site. As well as tips on how to get the most out of Carnival, and fascinating historical links, it enables users to buy costumes, accessories, and grandstand seats online – or simply to watch the parades on streaming video.

Rock and Roll Hall of Fame

www.rockhall.com

Cleveland's premier tourist attraction maintains an entertaining online presence with a Website that's devoted as much to the many legendary inductees into the hall as to practical advice for visitors. Highlights include the daily "Today In Rock History" feature (holding such gems as "Billy J. Kramer appears on the Ed Sullivan Show"), or you can work your way through an interactive "timeline" to explore different genres and artists.

"I'm the originator, the emancipator, and the architect of rock and roll."

Smithsonian Institution

www.si.edu

The Smithsonian Website celebrates fourteen US national museums and its National Zoo, most but not quite of all of which are in Washington DC. The collection of the National Air and Space Museum, in particular, lends itself to being displayed online, but all the museums are covered well, with full practical details for visitors plus news of current and forthcoming temporary exhibitions. To get the best of the "Virtual Smithsonian" section you'll need a high bandwidth connection.

Universal Studios

www.universalstudios.com

Universal Studios make a bit more effort than Disney to provide lively interactive guides to their Florida and California theme parks, though all that Flash animation can be a strain on an ordinary modem. If you feel the urge to turn your virtual visit into an actual one, it's easy to make the necessary arrangements online, from simply buying park tickets to reserving a fully inclusive package.

Transportation sites

Alaska Railroad

www.akrr.com

The Alaska Railroad, the last full-service railroad in the US, offers short train tours through Alaska's amazing scenery. Options range from a two-day excursion from Anchorage to Kenai Fjords National Park, including overnight hotel accommodation, for $464, to an ten-night tour of the state, including a night in Anchorage, for around $2100 (excluding flight to Alaska). Email the reservation form, or print it and fax it direct; they will confirm by phone, fax, or mail.

Amtrak

www.amtrak.com

The wordy Website of the US national rail network allows users to browse schedules, route maps, timetables and fares, then buy tickets for straightforward or multi-city itineraries online. However, foreign travellers cannot buy any of their good-value train passes through the Website; it simply lists mailing addresses and telephone numbers for international sales representatives.

Green Tortoise Adventure Travel

www.greentortoise.com

This much-loved, vaguely counter-cultural, long-distance bus company, based in San Francisco, has been running transcontinental "adventure trips" in buses kitted out with bunks, fridges and music systems for over thirty years. The site is clumsy to look at but assured in tone, featuring full schedules – destinations include the national parks, New Orleans, and Alaska, with special trips to festivals such as Burning Man and Mardi Gras – and last-minute discounts, with a downloadable booking form. There's also a chat room and bulletin board, plus news of the "frequent crawler" scheme, which earns users points towards a free trip.

Greyhound

www.greyhound.com

The quick, slick site of the US intercity bus network features a route map and pull-down menus for travel planning and buying tickets (check "Discounts" for special fares, and "Terminals" for contact details for every bus terminal in the USA). You can also pick up details of Greyhound's Discovery pass (for North American travellers), and the Ameripass and regional passes (for non-US travellers), which offer unlimited stopovers from anything from four to sixty days. To search for individual fares or check schedules simply key in dates, departure point and destination. US citizens can buy tickets online up to three months in advance (the exact figure varies according to your destination), but international travellers have to buy their passes via the relevant agents in their own countries.

Train Hoppers Space

http://catalog.com/hop

The lovingly prepared Train Hoppers Space isn't exactly high-tech, but it's got everything the twenty-first century hobo – or armchair hobo – could desire. Perhaps the history of train brake systems isn't for you, but the train-hoppers' slang is a treat: so now you know that a Reefer is a refrigerated box car and that a Bull is a railroad security person, "usually driving white American trucks around the yard". Links connect to the National Hobo Association and The Hobo Times as well as lots of rail fan sites and train-related newsgroups.

The great outdoors

Americansouthwest.net

www.americansouthwest.net

A privately run fan site devoted to the national parks and wilderness areas of the desert Southwest, featuring some great photos, masses of links, and an especially copious section on the region's little-known, but stunningly beautiful, slot canyons.

GORP

www.gorp.com

As detailed on p.103, the GORP (Great Outdoors Recreation Pages) Website makes an invaluable tool for adventurous travellers the world over, but it's strongest of all on its home territory of the USA. It offers step-by-step practical guides to all the major national parks and wilderness areas, and also sells its own programme of adventurous tours. All trips are bookable online, though prices are seldom cheap.

National Park Service

www.nps.gov

This invaluable Website covers every component of the wonderful national park system, with full practical details for the whole gamut of National Monuments, National Historic Sites, National Seashores and so on, as well as for the parks themselves. For big names, such as the Grand Canyon, Yellowstone and Yosemite, the range of information is breathtaking, covering camping, hiking, wildlife and lodging, with full links to private accommodation options and activity operators in the vicinity.

National Scenic Byways Online

www.byways.org

Sponsored by the Federal Highway Administration, this luscious site honours America's most beautiful driving routes, detailing highly illustrated itineraries across the length and breadth of the country.

Roadside America

www.roadsideamerica.com

An online version of the book of the same name, this entertaining compendium of wayside oddities includes such highlights as the world's only life-size Chocolate Moose, and the rival towns that boast populations of all-white and all-black squirrels.

Sierra Club

www.sierraclub.org

The veteran environmental organization uses its Website to promote awareness of issues and events throughout the US, with links to "chapters" in each individual state for coverage of local activities. For travellers, however, its most useful feature is the "Outings" section, accessed under "Get Outdoors", which as described on p.105 details the club's lengthy list of adventure-travel expeditions, all of which can be booked online.

UK tour operators

AmeriCan Adventures

www.americanadventures.com

UK company operating budget-oriented small-group tours in all regions of the US, including coast-to-coast trips, and with an emphasis on outdoor adventures. Accommodation is in hotels and camp sites as well as in independent Roadrunner youth hostels. Complete the email form to check availability and request a reservation.

Complete North America

www.completenorthamerica.com

Helpful and informative Website run by UK operator that offers tailor-made itineraries throughout the US, including fly-drives, bus trips, and city breaks. Flights and car or RV rental can also be arranged separately. Prices are not the cheapest; the focus instead is on guaranteeing a problem-free holiday, with accommodation in high-standard hotels. They claim to have so many special offers that they can't even show any on screen; email for the latest deals or with specific enquiries.

Just America

www.justamerica.co.uk

This thorough and comprehensive site outlines the full US programme offered by a British agency that specializes in both self-guided trips (travelling either in a rental car or by rail) and escorted coach tours, and also features ranch holidays, cruises and weekend breaks. Use the interactive map to get full details, then email them your provisional thoughts and they'll talk to you directly.

part three: destinations

Titan Travel

www.titantravel.co.uk

UK operator Titan's extensive list of guided bus and rail tours of the US are intended primarily for older and more sedate travellers, but they provide comprehensive coverage of the country's natural splendours as well as its most historic cities, and enjoy a reputation for efficiency. Availability can be checked via email. If you're more interested in a fly-drive, follow the home-page link to Connections Worldwide instead.

Vietnam

Exodus

www.exodus.co.uk

This stalwart UK adventure-travel company (see p.101) organizes a nice choice of Vietnam holidays. To find them, type Asia into the holiday search, then click on the first Vietnam trip you see. From there you can choose to view all the Vietnam itineraries, including a hill-tribe tour and a nineteen-day Saigon to Hanoi trip travelling by bike, boat and train. Vietnam also features on a combined overland and train trip with Laos, Cambodia and Thailand, and on an unusual south Indochina trip with Cambodia and Thailand. The site provides itineraries for each – though you need to download or email for really detailed notes – and online booking is straightforward. Prices are quoted according to where you're flying from, though most trips can be booked without flight.

Journeys International

www.journeys-intl.com

This US operator organizes small-group eco and cultural tours, classified from Grade I (relatively active, staying in lodges) to Grade IV (demanding wilderness travel). They currently offer seven Vietnam itineraries, varying from straightforward country tours (grade I–II) to a week-long kayak adventure (Grade II) and more challenging three-week cycle tour (Grade II–III). You can read daily itineraries on the site, along with trip reviews from past clients. To reserve, click on "Sign Up", where there's a downloadable application form and an online booking facility.

Myths and Mountains

www.journeystovietnam.com

Nevada-based operator offering an unusual selection of cultural tours. The ten or so Vietnam trips they run each year are varied and creative: a typical example would be "Ancient Medicines in Modern Vietnam", which includes lakeside Tai Chi, a visit to a traditional hospital, medicinal herb and tree walks, while a twelve-day folk art tour combines gallery trips with the chance to watch craftspeople at work, travelling from the hill communities of the north, through Hanoi, and down to Hue, Hoi An and Danang. They can also arrange biking holidays, sea canoeing, and tours of Vietnam War battlegrounds. Each is described tantalizingly on the site, but to see a detailed itinerary, or to request a custom-designed tour, you'll need to submit a form. And when it comes to booking a scheduled trip you have to fill in yet more forms, either online or downloaded, and send them with your deposit.

Vietnam Adventures

www.vietnamadventures.com

With its combination of travelogue, articles and practical detail, this US-produced site can save you a lot of time trawling around the Web. The "adventures" themselves are short travel features, most of them written by sitemaster Martin Wilson. And they're not all adventures, exactly – among the obligatory travellers' tales you'll also find plenty about local delicacies and cultural phenomena. More useful, however, is the hotel booking facility – click the name of a city on a map to read about a selection of hotels, with photos and readers' reviews. Vietnam Adventures offers discounted rates on most of them, and you can book a room online. The site also details up-to-date flight deals from North America, with an online enquiry form.

Visit Vietnam

www.visitvietnam.co.uk

Indochina specialists, based in London, with a nice selection of tailor-made holidays, independent itineraries and escorted tours. If you're going it alone, you're looking at around £660 for ten days, flight included, with a few days in a posh hotel; small-group tours, including flight, accommodation and all sightseeing, cost £400 more. They also do a fifteen-day train journey which includes stops at Hue and a Tay village, a boat trip on the Perfume River, and a couple of days in Hanoi and Halong Bay. Active types should check out the "eco-tour", a relatively gentle affair involving short forest treks, cycling and wildlife spotting, or the cycling holiday – with some car pick-ups and train journeys – which stops at Hanoi, Hue, Hoi An, Danang and Saigon. Submit an email form to check availability.

Zimbabwe

For safari sites, see "Wildlife and Nature", which starts on p.185.

Africa Tours

www.africasafaris.com

Though it specializes in custom-designing independent itineraries, this US-based Africa specialist has a handful of scheduled safaris and tours of Zimbabwe, including short packages to Victoria Falls, Matopos, the Eastern Highlands and the Great Zimbabwe Ruins, which leave any day of the week and can be taken in any combination. The longer tours cost upwards of $4000 with international flight, though you can book without airfare too – there's no online booking, so you should call or email them in New York.

Africa Travel Centre

www.africatravel.co.uk

Culturally sensitive Africa specialist offering a really good range of scheduled and customized tours. Click "Itineraries" to see the full rundown: Zimbabwe trips include the ten-day "Zimbabwe Special", visiting Hwange National Park, Victoria Falls and the Matobos Hills, or the shorter "Snapshot of Zimbabwe", which covers all the major sites in just one week. If you want to get off the beaten track, go for "Eastern Delights", which combines a trip to Victoria Falls with the more remote areas of the east. You can also choose a two-centre holiday, with Zanzibar, Mauritius or South Africa. Costs, upwards of £1300, include international flights. Email them to book.

African Adrenalin

www.africanadrenalin.co.za

Clearing house for a variety of travel operators in southern Africa, offering anything from accommodation, train journeys and adventure holidays to elephant, horseback and overland safaris. Click Zimbabwe on the list of countries and then choose a theme from the menu; up pops a list of relevant companies with links. Many of them offer online booking.

THE African safari experts, at your service.

This Week's Adventure Article:

Lynette Oxley takes us - *on foot* - through the astonishing but unpredictable Kruger National Park in "Hooves and Dust" courtesy of Rhino Walking Safaris.

Click here

For previous Adventure Articles, click here

Rough Guides travel...

Rough Guides are available from good bookstores worldwide. New titles are published every month. Check www.roughguides.com for the latest news.

...music & reference

Africa & Middle East
Cape Town
Egypt
The Gambia
Jerusalem
Jordan
Kenya
Morocco
South Africa, Lesotho & Swaziland
Syria
Tanzania
Tunisia
West Africa
Zanzibar
Zimbabwe

Travel Theme guides
First-Time Around the World
First-Time Asia
First-Time Europe
First-Time Latin America
Gay & Lesbian Australia
Skiing & Snowboarding in North America
Travel Online
Travel Health
Walks in London & SE England
Women Travel

Restaurant guides
French Hotels & Restaurants
London
New York
San Francisco

Maps
Algarve
Amsterdam
Andalucia & Costa del Sol
Argentina
Athens

Australia
Baja California
Barcelona
Boston
Brittany
Brussels
Chicago
Crete
Croatia
Cuba
Cyprus
Czech Republic
Dominican Republic
Dublin
Egypt
Florence & Siena
Frankfurt
Greece
Guatemala & Belize
Iceland
Ireland
Lisbon
London
Los Angeles
Mexico
Miami & Key West
Morocco
New York City
New Zealand
Northern Spain
Paris
Portugal
Prague
Rome
San Francisco
Sicily
South Africa
Sri Lanka
Tenerife
Thailand
Toronto
Trinidad & Tobago
Tuscany
Venice
Washington DC
Yucatán Peninsula

Dictionary Phrasebooks
Czech
Dutch
Egyptian Arabic
European
French
German
Greek
Hindi & Urdu
Hungarian
Indonesian
Italian
Japanese
Mandarin Chinese
Mexican Spanish
Polish
Portuguese
Russian
Spanish
Swahili
Thai
Turkish
Vietnamese

Music Guides
The Beatles
Cult Pop
Classical Music
Country Music
Cuban Music
Drum'n'bass
Elvis
House
Irish Music
Jazz
Music USA
Opera
Reggae
Rock
Techno
World Music (2 vols)

100 Essential CDs series
Country

Latin
Opera
Rock
Soul
World Music

History Guides
China
Egypt
England
France
Greece
India
Ireland
Islam
Italy
Spain
USA

Reference Guides
Books for Teenagers
Children's Books, 0–5
Children's Books, 5–11
Cult Football
Cult Movies
Cult TV
Digital Stuff
Formula 1
The Internet
Internet Radio
James Bond
Lord of the Rings
Man Utd
Personal Computers
Pregnancy & Birth
Shopping Online
Travel Health
Travel Online
Unexplained Phenomena
The Universe
Videogaming
Weather
Website Directory

Also! More than 120 Rough Guide music CDs are available from all good book and record stores. Listen in at www.worldmusic.net

Visit us online
roughguides.com

Information on over 25,000 destinations around the world

- **Read** Rough Guides' trusted travel info
- **Share** journals, photos and travel advice with other readers
- Get exclusive Rough Guide **discounts** and travel **deals**
- Earn membership points every time you contribute to the
  Rough Guide **community** and get **free** books, flights and trips
- Browse thousands of CD reviews and artists in our **music** area

INDEX